novum pro

AF114364

Anthony R. Johnson

THERE'S ALWAYS A
Tomorrow

novum pro

www.novum-publishing.co.uk

All rights of distribution, including via film, radio, and television, photomechanical reproduction, audio storage media, electronic data storage media, and the reprinting of portions of text, are reserved.

Printed in the European Union on environmentally friendly, chlorine- and acid-free paper.

© 2022 novum publishing

ISBN 978-3-99131-557-5
Editing: Hugo Chandler, BA
Cover photos: Sven Hansche, Christos Georghiou, Yuri Snow, Carafoto | Dreamstime.com
Cover design, layout & typesetting: novum publishing

www.novum-publishing.co.uk

CONTENTS

NOVEL CHARACTERS	9
NOVEL ORGANISATIONS, PLACES AND ABBREVIATIONS	13
QUOTATIONS MODIFIED TO USE IN PRESIDENT VALENTINE'S SPEECH	16
QUOTATIONS MODIFIED TO USE IN VICE-PRESIDENT SYKES' SPEECH	18

Chapter 1.
YESTERDAY, TODAY AND TOMORROW 19

Chapter 2.
THIRTY MINUTES TO BETRAY GRANDAD 21

Chapter 3.
SAINT JUDE'S 32

Chapter 4.
THE BIRTHDAY PARTY 43

Chapter 5.
NEW JUSTICE 47

Chapter 6.
ON THE RUN 56

Chapter 7.
REVELATIONS 65

Chapter 8.
BETRAYAL AT J.J. MACDONALD'S 73

Chapter 9.
SUSPICION AND CONFESSION 82

Chapter 10.
THE DAILY PARTY NEWS 89

Chapter 11.
BROOKSLADE AIRFIELD 96

Chapter 12.
CHARLEY, MADDY AND THE SEARCH FOR JENNY ... 102

Chapter 13.
NICK LEARNS MORE 110

Chapter 14.
OPERATION ARMAGEDDON 115

Chapter 15.
OPERATION TAKEAWAY 126

Chapter 16.
GEORGE HAS A WOBBLE 134

Chapter 17.
**THE END OF THE BEGINNING
OR THE BEGINNING OF THE END?** 143

Chapter 18.
GERMINATION 152

Chapter 19.
A VOICE FROM THE PAST 158

Chapter 20.
DEMONSTRATION AND REVOLUTION 169

Chapter 21.
DRONE ATTACK 175

Chapter 22.
SPECIAL RELATIONSHIP 182

Chapter 23.
AN OLD FLAME 192

Chapter 24.
ASSAULT ON THATCHER SQUARE 198

Chapter 25.
PROMISE TO THE NATION 206

Chapter 26.
DALLAS DONALDSON'S DEMANDS 209

Chapter 27.
RETURN FROM SAINT KILDA 217

Chapter 28.
TRIAL AND RETRIBUTION 238

Chapter 29.
A FAMILY DESTROYED 254

Chapter 30.
FAMILIES REBUILT 258

Chapter 31.
THE DAY AFTER TOMORROW 267

All the girls and boys would sing
Come tomorrow we get everything.
So as long as we survive today,
Come tomorrow we're gonna find a way.
Yeah, as far as I can see
We gotta let the children lead the way.

Come Tomorrow
Song by Dave Matthews Band

NOVEL CHARACTERS

Joshua Kerley, member of the PYM, (Party Youth Movement).
Tom Chadwick, Joshua Kerley's grandfather.
Edward Kerley, father of Joshua Kerley and son-in-law of Tom Chadwick.
Adam Mollison, Chief Officer (CO) of the Party Enforcement Office (PEO).
Powell, Officer of the PEO.
Willford, Officer of the PEO.
Norma Weedall, dead victim of a heart attack.
Frank Weedall, husband of Norma Weedall.
Sister Mary-Beth, an old nun now helping out at Saint Jude's.
Nick Kaydon, doctor at Saint Jude's, member of People's Democratic Movement (PDM).
Jenny Oakwood, nurse at Saint Jude's and Nick Kaydon's girlfriend.
Glyn Quinlan, Chief Commanding Officer (CCO) of the Anti-Terrorist Squad (ATS), who later became Commander-In-Chief (CIC) of Security Forces.
Tim Beardmore, 90-year-old.
Elsie Beardmore, 86-year-old wife of Tim.
Edward Beardmore, Tim and Elsie Beardmore's grandson.
Janet Beardmore, Edward Beardmore's wife.
James Beardmore, Edward and Janet Beardmore's son, Tim and Elsie's great grandson.
George Grisedale, Justice of The Party.
Peter Denning, Clerk of the Court.
Gerard Tizard, Chief Officer (CO) of the Party Enforcement Office (PEO).
David Andrew Broadbent, a vagrant.

Dan Bridgewood, member of PDM and an old friend of Nick Kaydon.

Ken Townsend, member of PDM and psychic medium.

Jack Kingsbury, double agent. Chief Officer of the DDPU and member of the PDM.

Jonathan Patterson, boy running from ATS.

Phillip Patterson, Jonathan Patterson's father, previously called Dilip Patel.

Idris (Taffy) Llewellyn, member of PDM and ex-sergeant in Welsh Guards.

Derek (Del) McCarthy, member of PDM.

Graham Tucker, member of PDM, former police officer.

Dominic (Dom) Welland, PDM investigator.

Jim Donlon, PDM investigator.

Charlotte (Charley) McCarthy, Del McCarthy's wife.

Madison (Maddy) McCarthy, Del and Charley McCarthy's daughter.

Mr. Rhodes, maths teacher at Hoddington Brook School.

Stuart Woodleigh, friend of Joshua Kerley and pupil at Hoddington Brook School.

Nigel Valentine, President of the United Kingdom, Leader of The Party.

President Grosvenor, former President of the United Kingdom

Edwina Sykes, Vice-President of the United Kingdom, Deputy Leader of The Party

Commander George Richmond, Leader of the P.D.M. Later became President of the U.K.

Deputy Commander Mark Grigson, Deputy Leader of the P.D.M.

Alex (Jock) Munroe, P.D.M. agent.

Sam Jarvis, owner of Brookslade Wood Farm.

Jacob Jarvis, son of Sam Jarvis and brother of Michael Jarvis.

Michael Jarvis, son of Sam Jarvis and brother of Jacob Jarvis.

Agnes Llewellyn, Idris Llewellyn's estranged wife.

Aled Llewellyn, Idris Llewellyn's son.

Dennis Wheatington, P.D.M. agent, explosives expert.

Pete Trattley, P.D.M. agent, engineer.

Fred Whitlow, P.D.M. agent.

Jordan Lorder, P.D.M. agent.
Tim Collinson, P.D.M. agent.
Joe Snark, delivery driver of body truck.
Jason Gibling, delivery co-driver of body truck.
Dewi Griffice, P.D.M. agent.
Ted, security guard for Williamson Meat Corporation.
Harry, security guard for Williamson Meat Corporation.
Declan (Dec) Dunleavy, P.D.M. agent and former Royal Air Force (RAF) Squadron Leader.
Max Nedwell, P.D.M. agent and former RAF Flying Officer.
Tim Sharnwood, commercial pilot.
Dante Pigden, leader of The Collectors, a gang on Hirta.
Bartholemew Grainger, second in command of The Collectors, a gang on Hirta.
Phillip (Pip) Holgrave, P.D.M. boffin. Electronics expert.
Mike Riches, P.D.M. Electronics expert.
Shane Whiteliff, a school friend of Joshua Kerley and Stuart Woodleigh and pupil at Hoddington Brook School.
Hugo Woodwill, Chief Commanding Officer (CCO) in the A.T.S. Newly promoted replacement for Glyn Quinlan.
Lorna Duncan, Joshua Kerley's girlfriend and pupil at Hoddington Brook School.
Dave Bridlane, pupil at Hoddington Brook School.
Paul Bridlane, brother of Dave and Ryan Bridlane. Pupil at Saint Erasmus High School.
Ryan Bridlane, brother of Dave and Paul Bridlane. Pupil at Saint Erasmus High School.
Hadrian Lubeck, Commander-in-Chief (CIC) of the Party Enforcement Officers (PEO).
Ed Gilfedder, Deputy Commander-In-Chief of the PEO.
Freddie Carlysle, volunteer civilian doctor with the United Revolutionary Army (URA).
Dallas Donaldson, President of the United States.
Henry (Hank) Sigmeyer, Executive Secretary to Dallas Donaldson.
Naomi Donaldson, wife of the President of the U.S.A.
Joyce Gilfedder, mother of Ed Gilfedder.

Elizabeth Valentine, wife of President Valentine.
Oliver Valentine, son of Nigel and Elizabeth Valentine.
Esme Valentine, daughter of Nigel and Elizabeth Valentine.
Harry Harefield, Vice-President of U.K. replacing Edwina Sykes.
Sandra Harefield, wife of Harry Harefield.
Jacob Harefield, baby son of Harry and Sandra Harefield.
Arthur Forswick, civilian member of the cabinet in the new U.K. government.
James Radburn, civilian member of the cabinet in the new U.K. government.
Ethan Summervale, Vice-President of the U.S.A.
John Flitnell, Secretary of State for the U.S.A.
Sally Pallette, a nurse at Oban Hospital.
Bill Kempson, a doctor at Oban Hospital.
Ernest Oakdean, Justice presiding over the trials of Dante Pigden and Bartholomew Grainger.
John Trenchard, a survivor from Hirta.
Selwyn Tyneward, Justice presiding over the trials of Glyn Quinlan and Nigel Valentine.
Je Dong Woo, President of North Korea.
Clive Carter, partner of Agnes Llewellyn after she left Idris.
Megan Llewellyn, Aled Llewellyn's wife and Idris Llewellyn's daughter-in-law.
Bryn Llewellyn, Aled Llewellyn's son and Idris Llewellyn's grandson.

NOVEL ORGANISATIONS, PLACES AND ABBREVIATIONS

U.C.N.P. United Conservative and Nationalist Party or The Party, The government.
P.Y.M. The Party Youth Movement. Teenage police cadets.
S.H.S. State Health Service.
P.E.O. Party Enforcement Officers. Police. "Brownshirts".
D.D.P.U. Dissident Discovery and Pursuit Unit. Undercover police.
A.T.S. Anti-Terrorist Squad. Paramilitary police. "Blackshirts".
P.D.M. People's Democratic Movement. Illegal opposition to the government.
N.C.A. National Climate Agency.
C.C.O. Chief Commanding Officer. Senior ranked officer in the Anti-Terrorist Squad.
C.P.E.O. Chief Party Enforcement Officer. Senior ranked officer in the P.E.O.
K.O.S. Legend Kill or Stun 12 millimeter. Commonly used hand gun.
Saint Jude's Hospital. Charity hospital at which Nick Kaydon and Jenny Oakwood worked.
Williamson Meat Corporation. Manufacturers of Human Carcass Reconstruction.
J.J.Macdonald's. Wholesale pharmaceutical warehouse.
D.I.R.C. Deleted Identity Radio Communicator. Type of radiotelephone used by the People's Democratic Movement.
Circuit Repeater SB2. Gadget to cause repeated playback on CCTV.
H.C.R. Human Carcass Reconstitution - Food made from human bodies.
GDN93. Carcinogenic, hepatotoxic preservative used in Human Carcass Reconstruction.
The Collectors. A gang on Hirta.

M.U.B.2. Mobile Untraceable Broadcasting 2. Transmitter used by People's Democratic Movement for TV broadcasts.

Covid-29RS. Coronavirus Disease 2029 Respiratory Syndrome.

Hoddington Brook School. School attended by Joshua Kerley, Stuart Woodleigh, Shane Whiteliff, Lorna Duncan and Dave Bridlane.

Saint Erasmus High School. School near to Hoddington Brook School, attended by Paul Bridlane and Ryan Bridlane.

Saint Erasmus Primary School. Primary school next to Saint Erasmus High School.

U.R.A. United Revolutionary Army.

D.A.F. Drone Air Force.

Grescott Air Base. Home of Number Two Squadron of D.A.F.

Kings Langton Air Base, Home of Number One Squadron of D.A.F.

U.A.C.P. Unmanned Air Combat Plane, Cougar FX.

U.R.P. Unmanned Reconnaissance Plane, Vulture OX.

M.P.A.D.S. Man-Portable Air Defence System. Shoulder launched Surface to Air Missile.

S.A.M. Surface-to-Air Missile, Hornet.

P.O.T.U.S. President of the United States.

I.C.B.M. Intercontinental Ballistic Missile.

Golden Arrows. Short range nuclear missiles.

Knappers End Missile Base. Nuclear missile base housing the Golden Arrows.

Hop Bridge United States Intercontinental Ballistic Missile base. Nuclear missile base housing I.C.B.M.s belonging to the United States of America.

Thatcher Square. Home of the government buildings.

Britannic Empire Building. Headquarters of leading business and financial organizations based in Thatcher Square.

Judge Jeffreys Citadel and Law Courts. Headquarters of the security forces, the law courts and cells based in Thatcher Square.

The House of the Nation. Parliament building and home to the President of the United Kingdom based in Thatcher Square.

G.M.T. Greenwich mean time. Standard time in the United Kingdom.

The Liberty Party. The main political party after the revolution, formed by the United Revolutionary Army.

The Reform Party. The main opposition party after the revolution.

QUOTATIONS MODIFIED TO USE IN PRESIDENT VALENTINE'S SPEECH

We shall judge what British interests are and
we shall be resolute in defending them.
MARGARET THATCHER

This is the road I am resolved to follow.
This is the path I must go. I ask all who have the spirit …
the bold, the steadfast and the young in heart …
to stand and join with me as we go forward.
MARGARET THATCHER

The wind of change is blowing through this continent.
HAROLD MACMILLAN

This didn't come about because of consensus.
It happened because we said;
this we believe, this we will do.
It's called leadership.
MARGARET THATCHER

Where there is discord may we bring harmony.
Where there is error may we bring truth.
Where there is doubt may we bring faith.
And where there is despair may we bring hope.
MARGARET THATCHER

Strong and stable government
THERESA MAY

Most of our people have never had it so good.
HAROLD MACMILLAN

I was the future once.
DAVID CAMERON

I would rather be dead in a ditch
(than ask the EU to delay Brexit).
BORIS JOHNSON

The rule of law must prevail over the rule of the mob.
MARGARET THATCHER

We will strive to make Britain
a country that works for everyone.
THERESA MAY

QUOTATIONS MODIFIED TO USE IN VICE-PRESIDENT SYKES' SPEECH

The root cause of the threat we face is
the extremist ideology itself.
DAVID CAMERON

The extremist world view is the gateway
and violence is the ultimate destination.
DAVID CAMERON

Chapter 1.
YESTERDAY, TODAY AND TOMORROW

Yesterday the United Kingdom was a democracy with a reasonably fair and competent government and a judicial system as good as almost any in the world. People went about their daily lives taking freedom, justice and safety for granted. I use the word "yesterday" metaphorically as changes had actually taken place very gradually over the last thirty years. Thirty years of change which had gone undocumented in the history books. Thirty years of change which was never taught in school. Thirty years of change which was never recorded on TV or in newsprint. Thirty years of change which people were no longer even allowed to talk about. Thirty years of change which apparently did not exist.

At first the government began to appear incompetent. Changes occurred which threatened people's freedom, but the danger was ignored. The government were believed to be too incompetent to be dangerous. Almost unchallenged, the government began to find excuses to take emergency powers; emergency powers which were said to be temporary but rapidly became permanent. Still there was little complaint about the erosion of civil liberty. The justice system was changed so that a trial became a formality, a chance for the judiciary to rubber stamp the wishes of the security forces. An arrest was automatically assumed to be proof of guilt. The system was not only designed to be harsh, give greater power to the security officers, save time and money but also to rid society of those who might be considered to be a drain on its resources: the elderly, the sick and infirm, the poor, the homeless, the non-conformists, the criminals, the immigrants and anyone who dared to disagree with The Party.

Today people live in fear. I should say people survive in fear as it cannot really be classed as living. People are unable to talk about reality, living a life of denial with a total lack of trust. Only the elite are able to live a reasonably normal life: prominent Party members, those with important skills, trade or vocation and those able to make a lot of money; people who were considered beneficial to society.

"Yesterday" life had been reasonably good and people were content. "Today" life is full of dread and fear, but for every yesterday and today there is always a "Tomorrow"! It could be days, months or years away but tomorrow always comes and, when it comes, who knows what it might bring.

Come tomorrow change will happen, maybe for good, maybe for evil but it will come!

Come tomorrow the lamb could become the lion or the mouse!

Come tomorrow we could be facing freedom or devastation! Who knows? But come tomorrow change must inevitably come!

Chapter 2.

THIRTY MINUTES TO BETRAY GRANDAD

The grandfather clock in the living room struck the half hour. That meant it was half past four and it also meant that Tom could expect his grandson any time now. Josh always called in on his way home from school on Thursdays to have a drink, some cake and a natter with his grandad. Tom was making himself busy in the kitchen while he waited. The back door was always left unlocked, for easy access when Tom was expecting visitors. It made things easier as Tom wasn't too quick on his feet these days. The clock had hardly stopped chiming when Josh walked in, right on cue.

"Hi grandad. How are you?" the boy asked.

"Arthritis is playing up a bit but I mustn't grumble," said the old man. "All part of getting old. Anyway, how are you and your dad? Not seen your dad in … oh … must be three weeks at least."

"We're both fine grandad."

"The kettle's just boiled. Do you want a cup of tea, Josh, or would you rather have a cold drink? I've got some carrot cake as well if you want a piece."

"Yes, I'll have a piece of cake please grandad. Actually, have you got any cola?"

"As it happens Josh, I have. It's a bit hard to come by these days, with the shortages and all, but I managed to get a bottle yesterday. It's a bit expensive but I know how much you like it. I'm having a cup of tea anyway but you can have a glass of cola with pleasure."

Tom continued to make the tea, cut the cake and pour Josh's glass of cola. Josh pulled up a chair and made himself comfortable at the table.

"Everything OK at school Josh?" the old man asked.

"Yes! They've been teaching us how to be good Party members."

"That says everything about The Party," said the old man. "If you have to be taught how to be a good Party member. If you believe in something, you don't need to be taught how to believe in it."

"Actually grandad," said the boy, "it's very strange that we are taught history and politics up to the early twenty twenties, just after we left Europe and we are taught modern history and politics, over the last couple of years, but there's a thirty-year gap in between which we are told nothing about; absolutely nothing. It's almost like those thirty years didn't exist. Perhaps you can tell me about it. I've heard you mention things to dad occasionally but he usually just tells you to shut up."

"Your dad has always been afraid of getting into trouble with The Party. Many years ago, The Party made it illegal to talk about the events of that period. I do discuss them occasionally with a few of my old mates, in private, but you have to be very careful about who you are talking to. The Party takes a very dim view of it. You can get into all sorts of trouble by saying the wrong thing to the wrong person."

Joshua Kerley, Tom Chadwick's grandson, was a bright and inquisitive fourteen-year-old. He was usually very happy and outgoing but somehow, he had seemed different over the past few weeks. He seemed a bit broody and introspective as though there was something on his mind. Tom was a bit unsure whether to tell the boy what he wanted to know or not. It could be dangerous if others got to hear about it; dangerous for Tom and for Josh himself, but he knew he could trust Josh. Josh was his grandson after all and they had always got on really well. If he couldn't trust Josh, then who could he trust. Of course, he could trust him. He just had to make sure that Josh kept his mouth shut and didn't inadvertently say anything about their conversation to anyone else.

Tom looked very serious and concerned. "Josh, if we talk about this, you have to promise me that you won't speak to anyone else about it. If you do, we could both be in very serious trouble. I mean it Josh!"

"Of course, I won't say anything grandad. My lips are sealed," Josh replied.

"So, what exactly do you want to know about?" asked the old man.

"Well, I'd really like to know just what happened in those missing years of history and why it has been covered up and buried."

The old man began cautiously at first. "Do you know about Brexit?"

"Yes, we are taught about that," replied Josh. "It was when we left the European Union. I think it might have been in 2020."

"That's spot-on Josh. Well done. It was 2020 and when we left the European Union there were problems, particularly regarding trade, which the government failed to get to grips with. Things were made worse by failure to deal with climate change, a series of avoidable "natural" disasters, fragmentation of political parties, disunity of the people and a lack of accountability by the government of the time.

Things really started to deteriorate from 2021 onwards. Trade started to unravel completely. European markets and suppliers were lost. Instead of trying to rebuild that trade, the government turned its back on Europe altogether. We pinned our hopes on favourable trade deals with the U.S.A. and when they failed to materialise the economy started to collapse. There were shortages of imported foods and essential supplies. Fortunately for the government of the day, the Conservative Party, the opposition had become so badly fragmented, with leftist and moderate factions only interested in fighting each other, that they were unable to successfully oppose the government. In an attempt to increase its strength and ensure that they continued in government, the Conservative Party combined with a host of smaller right-wing parties. Many of the parties such as The Brexit Party, UKIP, BNP, the National Front and Britain First were more extreme right wing, nationalistic and in some cases even fascist. They formed a new party, The United Conservative and Nationalist Party or U.C.N.P., which we now just refer to as The Party. To accommodate the more extreme parties, the UCNP itself became more and more aligned to the extreme right wing.

Many businesses collapsed but we became the most successful in the world at three pretty despicable things," continued the old man, "arms production, waste disposal and providing a tax haven for the rest of the world.

We supplied almost the whole of the world with weapons, including chemical weapons, biological weapons, weapons of mass destruction and nuclear weapons, regardless of who was buying them or what they would be used for. We supplied weapons which enabled other countries to kill hundreds of thousands of people, some soldiers but many civilians. They fought wars, revolutions, carried out atrocities, murder and genocide all using weapons manufactured and supplied by Britain. We supplied weapons which were, in some cases, used against our own friends and allies. We even happily supplied weapons which were so lethal, so powerful and so uncontrollable that they were totally forbidden under international law. We didn't care. It was business.

We imported waste from all over the world. It was brought in by the shipload and large areas of the land and sea were used for waste disposal, no matter how toxic that waste was. We became known as The World's Trash Can.

Ridiculous tax laws enabled mega rich foreign companies and gangsters to make massive tax savings and launder their money while British citizens were taxed to the hilt.

Desperate for a cheap supply of power, but not prepared to put money or resources into renewable energy, the government backed fracking on a massive scale. At one point it looked like fracking would be stopped, but then the government made a U-turn. Fracking was never successful in providing cheap power but it did help to cause several large earthquakes. Three particularly bad ones happened in Bradford, Sheffield and Preston.

In 2028 there was a huge explosion at the nuclear power plant in Torness. More than two hundred and fifty people were killed outright by the explosion. Many more died later due to the effects of radiation exposure. Thousands of people had to be evacuated and moved into refugee camps. In fact, the explosion made it necessary to evacuate an area with a radius of thirty miles around the power station. That is an area of more than two and a half thousand square miles. The evacuated, contaminated area was used for storing much of the imported rubbish. Initially, it was put into landfill but later, as quantities increased and it became more difficult to keep up with the demand, it was just dumped on the ground. The country which got rid of its coal tips in the nineteen seventies was now building huge open rubbish tips, vast waste mountains, in the east of Scotland. These tips included both harmless and toxic waste. The authorities did not care as the circle of land around Torness would never be inhabited again. Some of the rubbish was also deposited in huge trenches dug in the sea bed near to Torness. However, that was proving too expensive so much of the waste was just dumped into that area of the North Sea. People who had been evacuated after the Torness explosion were moved into refugee camps and so-called temporary accommodation in a twenty square mile area to the south of the evacuation zone. As far as I'm aware, they have still never been properly rehomed as The Party didn't want them mixing with the general population.

There were many demonstrations and some rioting in protest at what was happening. People were calling for an election." Tom continued. "That caused The Party to take emergency powers. First, they abolished all elections until all unrest had settled down. Later, they passed a bill stating that a general election would only take place when it was deemed necessary by the government. That was soon followed by a ban on all other political parties. All opposition parties were deemed to be subversive and, as such, membership was made illegal. To avoid any further demonstrations, it was made illegal to have a gathering of more than twelve people under any circumstances, except for government members, security officers, hospitals, places of work and schools. Even weddings were restricted to very close family only, as the twelve-person rule was applied. Funerals had already been stopped as the state took possession of any bodies. No-one was allowed to be buried or cremated privately. That could only be done by the state. Even transport was hit by the new law. Trains were abolished as it was impossible for them to operate with no more than twelve passengers. In some places, new metro links were set up with single carriage computer driven rail vehicles carrying a maximum of twelve passengers. The old buses and coaches were scrapped and replaced with a network of minibuses carrying a maximum of eleven passengers plus the driver.

The government stopped referring to itself as The Government. It was only referred to as the UCNP or more commonly just The Party.

When the old king died, King Charles the Third, the monarchy was abolished and the Royal Family were given a large cash settlement to become commoners.

The press had fallen more and more under the control of The Party. Any independent newspapers were closed down and the reporters were arrested. By 2027 the only news left was Party propaganda. There were always rumours and some underground news reports that got through. That is when The Party made it illegal to discuss any events that occurred between 2023 and 2053. That's why you're not taught anything in school from that period and that's why this conversation has to stay strictly between us. I mean it Josh. If you repeat any of this, we are both in deep shit."

"You can trust me grandad! What about climate change? What problems did that cause over those years?"

"Well, I've told you about the big earthquakes in Bradford, Sheffield and Preston. There were lots of minor ones as well but we heard that around fifteen hundred people were killed in those three alone. We were pretty sure that they had been triggered by fracking although the frackers and The Party tried to whitewash them all as just freak phenomena. Global warming was pretty well ignored, although to be fair that was pretty much the situation worldwide. Too many people buried their heads in the sand and ignored it. When the sea rose, large areas of land were flooded permanently. It was estimated that twenty per cent of the U.K. land mass was lost under water. Most of London and much of the Thames Valley was permanently flooded. That was why the government and the trading centres were relocated to just outside Birmingham, where they are now. Birmingham was believed to be very unlikely to suffer severe flooding and it was safely away from the areas that had suffered earthquakes. They stayed clear of the city centre to avoid the air pollution."

"You can't blame The Party for the floods grandad."

"OK. Climate change was an international problem, but we never tried to do our bit or to persuade the rest of the world what we all knew needed to be done. When the floods came, as they were obviously going to do, The Party did nothing to try to control the situation. There was no new flood barrier schemes or pre-emptive relocation of vulnerable communities; nothing except moving the government from London to Birmingham.

They ignored warnings about air pollution and now so many inner-city areas are virtually no-go areas without face masks and sometimes even breathing apparatus. Your grandmother died of pneumonia caused by air pollution. Of course, the authorities denied that pollution was the cause. She couldn't get any proper medical treatment either due to The Party having destroyed the NHS."

"What was the NHS?"

"The NHS was the National Health Service. It provided free health care for everybody and was funded by the government but The Party decided that it couldn't afford to keep it going any longer. That's why we ended up with the system we have today. The privileged get free treatment and the rest of us have to rely on charity medical centres, run by volunteers, with few or no resources.

Anyway, as I was saying, we couldn't get any proper care for your grandmother so she was just left to die, just like your mother."

"My mum?" Josh asked, quite shocked at the mention of his mother's death. His father had never talked about how his mother had died.

"You were just two years old," continued the old man. "That's why you can't remember it. You would have had a little brother but there were problems with the birth. We couldn't get any proper medical help. Your mum and your brother both died because those bastards who were supposed to be running the country had destroyed the NHS. I lost my wife, my daughter and a grandson. Of course, everything was covered up. The death certificates just said they had died from natural causes." Although not a man given easily to tears, Tom found his eyes getting very moist and his vision cloudy as he thought about what he had lost.

"Sorry grandad," said Josh. "I didn't mean to upset you."

"It's alright Josh," said Tom, drying his eyes and blowing his nose. "It's still a bit raw, but after all these years I just feel so angry about it."

Having pulled himself together, the old man continued. "It became more and more difficult to get genuine news and information and now all we get is Party propaganda. All social media was closed down in2025."

"What was social media, grandad?" asked Josh.

"It was a way of contacting people online," continued the old man. "Facebook, Twitter, WhatsApp and several others. It was a way of sending messages to a lot of people in one go. You could contact a small group, dozens, hundreds, even thousands depending on how many people you had connections with. Letters were banned as it took up too much time for the authorities to open them and read them. I believe all e-mails and text messages are checked by The Party and sometimes edited or even deleted. Now people are even afraid to talk in case what they have said gets back to The Party. That's why your dad tells me to shut up if I start talking about the past."

Suddenly Tom was startled by the sound of an alarm signal which seemed to be coming from inside Josh's jacket. Josh pulled a radio transmitter from his inside pocket.

"That's fine Joshua. We've heard enough," came a voice from the phone. "We are coming in."

"I don't understand," said Tom in a state of confusion and more than a little fear. "What's going on Josh?"

"It's simple enough. I have become a member of The Party Youth Movement. We are expected to help to seek out dissidents and inform on them. Your unfounded rants against The Party have all been heard and recorded by my superiors. I'm sorry grandad."

"Josh, you've been brainwashed," said the old man disappointedly. "Do you know what you've done, not just to me but probably to your dad as well?"

At that moment three men burst in through the back door. All three were wearing the brown uniforms of the Government Enforcement Officers.

"Allow me to introduce myself," said the leader of the three. He was a small, dark haired man with piercing eyes, who's gaze locked on to Tom and would not release him again. In fact, it felt like those eyes were penetrating Tom's brain and reading his innermost thoughts. He tried to look away but was trapped by those eyes. "I am Chief Officer Adam Mollison of the Party Enforcement Office. My two colleagues are officers Powell and Willford. Are you Tom Chadwick?"

"You know I am," replied Tom, slightly defiant but still feeling violated by those penetrating eyes.

"Then I must arrest you for spreading dissident libel against The Party. Powell, Willford, take him to the car."

"Josh, I hope you know what you're getting into boy," said the old man as the officers took hold of him. "You've killed me Josh, just as surely as if you'd put a gun to my head and pulled the trigger yourself."

"You're being over dramatic grandad. You'll just be sent for Civil Correction. They just need to make sure you follow Party rules in the future."

"No Josh. Don't be so bloody naive. I'll be one of the old people who get arrested and disappear, never to be seen again. Your dad's not safe either." The grandfather clock struck five o'clock. "It's thirty minutes since you arrived Josh, thirty minutes to blow your whole family apart and for what? For the approval of the fucking Party and this arrogant bastard," said Tom, looking Mollison straight in the eyes with hatred and defiance.

"Enough you old fool!" yelled Mollison. "You're only making things worse for yourself. Powell! Willford! Get him out of my sight. Get him into the car. Now! If he gives you any more trouble you know what to do."

The officers frog marched the old man out, still protesting. "Josh! Don't be taken in by them! They'll kill me but don't let them ruin your life. Josh, you have to stand up to them!"

As Tom was taken out Mollison continued. "You have done well Corporal Kerley."

"Corporal sir?" asked Joshua in surprise.

"Yes of course! You deserve promotion for today's action. You should have a great career ahead of you in the force and a great future in The Party."

"My grandad will be sent for Civil Correction, won't he sir?" asked Josh, suddenly feeling very worried about his grandfather. Civil Correction was a form of brainwashing used for crimes which were not thought to be too serious.

"Most likely," replied Mollison, "although it will depend on the court. You had better go home now Joshua. I would advise you not to say too much about this to your father. You can tell him that your grandfather has been arrested but don't say anything about your part in it. You have done The Party a great service but your father may not understand."

As the boy was leaving, Willford appeared in the doorway to tell Mollison that Tom Chadwick was safely incarcerated in the car and ready to go.

"You don't really think he will get Civil Correction do you sir?" Willford enquired when Josh was out of earshot.

"Of course not!" exclaimed the Chief Officer. "The man is seventy-two years old. The only sentence he is likely to get is Age Acceleration."

This is a term used for the death penalty performed by lethal injection.

"I only agreed with the boy to make him feel better. After all, it is his grandfather. There's no point in Joshua feeling guilty about the outcome even if the silly old fool ends up dead. He brought it on himself! He should have known better and kept his mouth shut. Of course, we will need to arrest the boy's father as well and see if we can find out who the old man's friends are. They'll all need to be investigated. They may all be guilty of spreading dissident or seditious libel against The Party."

Chapter 3.

SAINT JUDE'S

The front door of Saint Jude's Medical Centre crashed open as a man rushed in carrying his wife who had collapsed. "Help me! Please help me! She's dying!"

The speed with which Sister Mary-Beth moved belied her considerable age as she pressed the alarm button to alert the emergency room and helped Frank Weedall to get his wife, Norma, onto a trolley near the door.

"I think she's having a heart attack. She had terrible pains in her chest and passed out in the car on the way here. I thought she'd died at one point."

The woman certainly did look as though she was doing her best to die. There was no movement or acknowledgement. Her face was blue-grey with large beads of sweat on her forehead despite her skin feeling cold and clammy. She was still breathing but only just and very erratically.

Within seconds, doctor Nick Kaydon and nurse Jenny Oakwood appeared and quickly pushed the woman through to the emergency room. Her husband attempted to follow but was stopped by the old nun.

"I'm sorry," said Sister Mary-Beth. "I'm sorry but you can't go through there."

"I want to be with my wife."

"I know," said the nun, "but you can't go in there while they are working on her. Believe me she's in the best possible hands. Let them do their job. As soon as they can, they'll let you know how she is. In the meantime, take a seat here. I need to get some details if you are up to it."

Sister Mary-Beth's calming voice and serene manner was beginning to help Frank Weedall to calm down a little.

"I'm sorry Sister. I know I can't go into the emergency room but I'm just so frightened that she's going to die and I won't be there with her."

"We'll do everything we possibly can to make sure that doesn't happen. Is it alright if I ask you a few questions?"

"Yes, please carry on Sister. I'm sorry."

"What is your wife's full name?"

"Norma Weedall."

"How old is she?"

"She's only forty-two. How can this happen at forty-two? She's always been so fit and healthy. She always looked after herself. She never smoked, hardly ever drank, exercised regularly and was always careful about what she ate. It doesn't make sense."

"What is your full name?" continued the nun.

"I am Frank Weedall."

"You are her husband and next of kin?" queried Sister Mary-Beth.

"Yes, that's right. We've been married for fifteen years. Fifteen years! She can't leave me now! We were supposed to grow old together. I don't think I can carry on without her."

"So, can you tell me what happened exactly?"

"She had been getting pains in her chest at times over the last couple of days. I tried to persuade her to come and get checked out but she wouldn't. She insisted it was nothing. Then just over an hour ago the pain got worse and became continuous. She was struggling to get her breath. I didn't give her any choice in the matter. I just bundled her into the car and came here. On the way here, her breathing got much worse and she passed out. I wasn't even sure if she was breathing at all at one point. Then we got here and you saw the rest."

"That's fine for now. If you wait here, I'll take your wife's notes through to Doctor Kaydon and I'll see what's going on."

Sister Mary-Beth took the notes into the emergency room where she could see that Norma Weedall was still only just clinging on to life.

"Is there anything I can do to help Doctor?" she asked.

"You can pray for her, Sister and look after her husband," was Nick's reply.

She told Frank Weedall that they were still working on his wife and she did her best to keep him calm and tried to keep his spirits up, at least as much as possible.

In the emergency room, Norma Weedall had initially stopped breathing, although at that point her heart was still beating. Nick and Jenny managed to get her breathing again fairly quickly. They had set up and attached a heart monitor.

BEEP-----, BEEP-----, BEEP-----, BEEP-----, BEEP-----,

The heart seemed fairly steady.

BEEP-----, BEEP-----, BEEP, BEEP, BEEP, BEEP, BEEE EEEEEEEEEEEEEEEEEEEEEEEEEEEEEEEEEEEEEEEE EEEEEEEEEEEEEEEEEEEEEEEEEP.

The monitor screamed to warn that she had flat lined and her heart had stopped. CPR was started immediately.

"Charging, stand clear!" yelled Nick as CPR stopped and he applied the defibrillator paddles to the woman's chest.

DUFF.

The patient's body bounced with the shock as the paddles spat their charge into her chest and CPR began again immediately.

BEEEEEEEEEEEEEEEEEEEEEEEEEEEEEEEEEEEEEE EEEEEEEEEEEEEEEEEEEEP.

"OK. Charging again. Stand clear!" came the instructions.

DUFF.

There was no response so the procedure was repeated again.

DUFF.

BEEP-----, BEEP-----, BEEP-----, BEEP-----, BEEP-----,

The heart monitor indicated that a heartbeat had returned as the heart lurched back into life.

"OK, she's back with us!" shouted Nick as he began to relax just a little. "Let's get an IV line set up as fast as possible."

The trolley with the necessary equipment was rushed over to the patient but before Nick could start placing the IV line: -----,

BEEP-----, BEEP-----, BEEP, BEEP, BEEP, BEEP, BEEP,

BEEEEEEEEEEEEEEEEEEEEEEEEEEEEEEEEEEEEEEE EEEEEEEEEEEEEEEEEEEEP.

"She's crashing! Let's start again!" yelled Nick. CPR was started again immediately and the defibrillator again prepared for use. "Charging! Stand clear!"

Once again Nick applied the paddles to the patient's chest and fired in the electric charge. Again, the body bounced dramatically, but there was no other response.

DUFF.

BEEEEEEEEEEEEEEEEEEEEEEEEEEEEEEEEEEEEEEE EEEEEEEEEEEEEEEEEEEEP.

The sequence of CPR and shocking with the defibrillator was repeated and repeated, over and over again, with doctor and nurse both getting more and more exhausted, more and more frustrated and more and more desperate. Whatever they tried, nothing would induce any response from the patient. The constant screaming of the monitor told them that they were failing, failing badly and gave no indication of recovery.

BEEEEEEEEEEEEEEEEEEEEEEEEEEEEEEEEEEEEEEE EEEEEEEEEEEEEEEEEEEEP.

Despite every fibre of his body desperately wanting to give the woman every possible chance, Nick finally gave in to the realisation that it was impossible to save her.

"It's been at least thirty minutes. I'm calling it. Time of death one thirty-five p.m."

Nick turned away from the lifeless body, only just managing to hold everything together as the emotion and exhaustion of the last forty-five minutes finally hit him. She had been rushed to Saint Jude's by her husband and now, despite the heroic efforts of Nick and Jenny, she lay dead on the emergency room table.

"You did everything you possibly could, Nick," said Jenny, trying to comfort him. As well as being a nurse, Jenny was Nick's girlfriend and she knew just how badly losing a patient affected him.

"We might have had a chance Jen, with a modern resuscitator and up to date drugs instead of having to use a crap, forty-year-old, second-hand defibrillator. How the hell are we supposed to save lives under these fucking conditions? Sometimes I feel like we might as well give up."

"You don't mean that Nick. You're feeling frustrated. So am I, but it's just a knee-jerk reaction," she said, putting a consoling arm around him. "You're a damn good doctor. You know you are. Think of the people that we've saved, people who would have died if you hadn't been here doing the best you could, even under these conditions."

"Things have to change somehow Jen. We can't carry on like this."

****

Saint Jude's was one of many charity-funded medical centres trying to provide treatment for ordinary people who failed to qualify for treatment under the so-called State Health Service. Many years previously, the National Health Service had provided good quality health care, which was free for everyone, but The Party had decided it was too expensive. The NHS was replaced by the State Health Service. The SHS ran a small number of highly equipped, highly staffed, state of the art hospitals, providing first class treatment for the senior members of The Party, the wealthy, large business owners and those who were considered important to society. Everybody else, around seventy-five per cent of the population, had to rely on health centres like Saint Jude's which relied completely on charity for their funding. Times were hard. People and businesses had little or no money to donate. The hospitals were forced to run on a shoestring. Drugs were scarce and generally old fashioned. Equipment was usually second-hand and out of date or obsolete. Nick and Jenny, like all the other doctors and nurses in the charity medical centres, worked for four days a week in the SHS hospitals to make a living. They spent the rest of the week working long hours in the charity medical centres as unpaid volunteers. Days off were generally non-existent.

Back in 2020, while the NHS still existed, the world suffered a pandemic due to a virus known as Covid-19. More than forty million people were infected and several million were killed worldwide. Many countries, including the United Kingdom, were in a state of lockdown for many months. Here in the UK the NHS struggled to cope. It was stretched to breaking point. That was the trigger for the government to decide to scrap the NHS and to develop the elitist SHS.

Worse was to come. Just nine years later in 2029 a new virus, related to Covid-19, known as Covid-29RS (Coronavirus disease 2029 Respiratory Syndrome) hit the country and much of Europe. The Party were afraid that the volunteer doctors and nurses would carry the Coronavirus from the charity hospitals to the SHS hospitals. To prevent that, they banned all SHS staff from doing any voluntary work. The charity hospitals were left with no trained staff and most were forced to close completely. The Party released no official figures but it was rumoured that more than a million people died from Covid-29RS in the UK alone, most of those because they received no treatment whatsoever. In that same period a further two and a half million people were believed to have died from non-covid related illnesses, due to lack of treatment. Eventually Covid-29RS subsided and volunteer doctors and nurses were allowed to return to the charity hospitals.

Saint Jude's had previously been a convent but was converted to a medical centre in 2031. A handful of the nuns, The Sisters of Saint Jude the Apostle, had stayed when the convent closed, to help nurse the sick. Sister Mary-Beth was the last of those nuns remaining at Saint Jude's. She still soldiered on despite her age and her own poor health.

The name of the hospital could not have been more appropriate. Saint Jude, the apostle Judas Thaddaeus, was the patron saint of lost causes and desperate situations. Trying to provide medical care at Saint Jude's was certainly a desperate situation and often a lost cause. Conditions at all of the charity hospitals were so bad that the International Red Cross and the World Health

Organisation had both offered assistance. Although assistance was badly needed, The Party would not even consider it. The offer of help was treated as an insult.

"How dare they imply that the United Kingdom could not look after its own sick?"

****

"Nick, the woman's husband is still waiting in the corridor. Do you want me to come with you to break the bad news?"

"No, it's alright Jen. It's best that I tell him on my own. Can you ask Sister Mary-Beth to ring the authorities to get them to collect the body. Right! I'll go and see Mr Weedall. It won't get any easier by delaying things."

Jenny went off to find Sister Mary-Beth while Nick went to talk to Frank Weedall who was still sitting and waiting desperately for news about his wife.

"Mr Weedall?" Nick asked.

"Yes. How is my wife, Doctor? Is she alright? Did you get her settled down? Can I see her yet?" Questions tumbled from his mouth in rapid succession as he looked for news but did not really want to hear the answers, his eyes pleading for a glimmer of hope but his mind already expecting the worst and his heart breaking.

"I'm really sorry. We did everything that we could but I'm afraid that we couldn't save her. Her heart gave out and we couldn't resuscitate her." Nick had to look down at the floor to avoid the imploring look in Frank Weedall's eyes. It was at times like this that Nick hated his job and felt such a failure, no matter how hard he'd tried or how poor the odds of success. He was there to save Norma Weedall's life and yet she was dead.

Despite having tried to prepare himself for the worst, Nick's words hit Frank Weedall like a blow from a sledgehammer. He collapsed in a battered, blubbering heap in his chair. He was a broken man, destroyed by his wife's death and confused by the events of the past hour. Gradually, he began to regain a modicum of composure,

"Thank you for trying doctor. I'm sure you did everything that you could," he sobbed.

"Would you like to spend a little time with her before they come to collect her body?" Nick asked gently.

Nick guided the weeping man to his wife's bedside. He stared in shock and disbelief at his wife lying there before burying his face on her breast, tears flowing in an uncontrollable torrent of grief and love. He remained there, motionless, for what seemed like an eternity, man and wife temporarily reunited.

Eventually Sister Mary-Beth and Jenny both entered the room.

"I'm so sorry to disturb you but I'm afraid they have come to collect Mrs Weedall's body. I have asked them to wait," said the nun.

"Thank you, Sister," said Nick. "Can you ask them to give us a few more minutes?"

As Sister Mary-Beth left the room, Frank Weedall said, "I don't want them to take her. I want to bury her myself."

"I'm sorry," said Nick gently but firmly. "It's the law. All bodies have to be taken by the authorities."

"She's not a body! She's my wife!" he yelled, becoming angry. "I should be able to decide what to do with her! What will they do with her anyway? Where will they take her?"

"I'm sorry," Nick repeated. "It's the law. I know how you feel but we can't do anything about it."

Two body collectors were waiting in the corridor with a collection trolley. They were always accompanied by an officer of the ATS, the Anti-Terrorist Squad, a paramilitary unit, dressed in their characteristic black uniform. There was one other man lurking in the corridor. This man wore a plain grey suit and could often be seen in and around Saint Jude's. He was not a patient, not a member of the hospital staff nor was he a member of the collection party.

Upon hearing raised voices, the body collectors started to enter the emergency room. Realising what they were coming for,

Frank Weedall slammed the door as hard as he could into the face of the first man, sending him crashing to the floor holding his bloodied nose. He rammed the trolley hard into the groin of the second man, leaving him crumpled with pain. A shot rang out, not from the ATS officer but from the man in the grey suit. Frank Weedall dropped like a stone and started to convulse violently before lying absolutely still. By the time he had regained consciousness he had already been handcuffed and arrested by the grey suited man and the body men were wheeling his wife, on the trolley, to the collection vehicle.

As things calmed down, Jenny turned her attention to Nick who looked as if he was carrying the world on his shoulders after the distressing events of the day.

"You need a rest babe. Let's get some coffee and take a break. You look shattered."

"I'm alright Jen. I just feel like such a failure sometimes. I get annoyed because I know we could do so much more."

"We work miracles with the resources we have Nick and you know it. If anything is a failure it's this damn government that gives us nothing to work with. How did we ever come to this and why, for God's sake, do the authorities have to take bodies away from their families? The state that poor man was in and he can't even give his wife a dignified funeral. It's inhumane."

"Steady tiger, you almost sound like a dissident. Don't forget walls have ears."

"I'll tell you what Nick, when we've finished why don't you come round to mine? You get the wine, I'll cook us a meal and then you could maybe stay over."

"That would be great Jen. It's been too long since we spent the night together." A glimmer of a smile almost forced its way onto Nick's face as it battled with the earlier misery.

Later that evening Nick and Jenny had finally relaxed with the help of a meal, each other's company and a bottle of wine. For now, the worries of the day were forgotten as they lay in a warm glow, entwined in each other's arms, on the sofa.

"Why can't life always be like this?" asked Nick.

"We can't make all the trouble go away, but maybe we could have more time like this if we moved in together. We've been together for a year now and you know how I feel about you. It makes sense."

Nick visibly flinched at the sound of Jenny's words.

"OK so it was a stupid idea," said Jenny, shaken by Nick's reaction "but we could make it work."

"Look Jen, I think it would be a great idea but we can't take that chance."

"Why not, if it's something we both want? I don't understand Nick."

"There's something that you don't know about me. I have never said anything before, to protect you. It was better, safer if you didn't know. You couldn't be hurt by something that you knew nothing about. As much as I love you, it could be dangerous to get too close and I don't want you to get hurt or get involved."

"Involved in what? What's dangerous? Nick you're starting to scare me a bit now but, whatever it is, it won't break us up. Just tell me!"

"OK. I guess I'll have to tell you and I'll understand if you think it's safer to steer clear of me in the future."

"That won't happen Nick. I promise you that won't happen. For God's sake just tell me!" Tears were starting to well up in Jenny's eyes with the fear of what Nick may be about to confess.

"You know how much I rant about this bloody government sometimes."

"That's understandable. I do myself sometimes."

"Yeah, but it goes deeper than that, Jen. I'm a member of the People's Democratic Movement."

"The PDM? Aren't they terrorists?" asked Jenny. If Nick was a terrorist and had kept it from her all this time, she began to wonder, was he really the man she thought she knew.

"That's what The Party would have people believe. We never use any unnecessary violence. We don't do anything to harm ordinary people. We are freedom fighters who just want to get rid of the cruel, corrupt bastards who run the country and replace them with a fair and caring government that, one day, will make us a democracy again. I've not been involved in any of the PDM's activities so far except for treating PDM members who've been ill or injured, on the quiet. You've probably seen a couple of them around Saint Jude's and not realise what they were. The most important thing is Jen that I don't want to put you in any danger."

Jenny realised that, despite the secrets, this really was the man that she knew and loved.

"Look Nick," said Jenny, pulling him tighter too her. "This was a bit of a shock but I can understand how you feel. We're in this together. I'm not going to run away. I'll take my chances. I want to be with you for the long haul."

"Thanks Jen."

"For what?" she asked.

"For being you. For not running away. For being here."

"You don't get rid of me that easily, Nick Kaydon. I'm going nowhere." She kissed him and held him in a way that showed him that they could not be more united if they were glued together. If she had to take on The Party she would, just as long as Nick was by her side.

Chapter 4.
THE BIRTHDAY PARTY

It was a dark, frosty night, high in the hills. Due to climate change, extremes of weather had become commonplace. Two weeks ago, the country had been bathed in sunshine with temperatures of almost twenty-five degrees centigrade. People thought that summer was on the way despite it only being the middle of April. Now the temperature had dropped to minus five degrees and snow was expected. The bitter cold temperature did nothing for the demeanour of the security officers at the scene.

Around twenty officers of the Anti-Terrorist Squad, under the command of Chief Commanding Officer Glyn Quinlan, were surrounding a lonely country farmhouse where an illegal gathering was believed to be taking place. Illegal because the authorities believed that there were more than the permitted number of twelve people in the house. Undercover intelligence had indicated that the gathering was possibly for a ninetieth birthday party for the head of the family, Tim Beardmore, who lived at the farmhouse with his wife Elsie, aged eighty-six. Chief Commanding Officer Quinlan cared nothing about the intelligence report. An illegal gathering was an illegal gathering, whatever the reason. Whatever the apparent cause for it, it could potentially be cover for a meeting of the PDM. The PDM or People's Democratic Movement was an illegal group who alone tried to oppose the UCNP and, consequently, were branded as terrorists. Even now, they could be plotting their next attack. The old man, even if he was ninety years old, could still be involved in organising terrorism or providing an innocent looking front as a cover for PDM activities. Whatever the cause, if there were more than twelve people, it was an illegal gathering. Age would not protect the perpetrators. The ATS were no respecters of age.

The ATS were hated, even by some members of The Party, for their ruthlessness and cruelty and Quinlan was one of the worst. A black uniformed paramilitary unit, the ATS took no chances. "Better a string of dead innocents than one terrorist escaping," was Quinlan's motto.

Just like all other security branches, the ATS were armed with KOS hand guns, the Legend Kill or Stun twelve millimeter. Officers of other units kept their weapons set on Stun as default and only switched them to Kill if necessary. The ATS officers' weapons were permanently set on Kill and they always shot to kill.

Quinlan and his officers had been observing people coming to the farmhouse for the past three hours and believed that there could be fifteen or so in the house. No-one had arrived in the past forty-five minutes, which would probably indicate that everyone who was coming had already arrived. As there appeared to be no further activity and his officers were getting increasingly restless after spending three hours in the bitter cold of the night, Quinlan decided to move in.

Despite the fact that there had been some sounds of merriment, some music and laughter, Quinlan was taking no chances. Five officers, including Quinlan himself, burst in through the front door. At the same time, five officers burst in through the back door. The remaining officers were deployed to cover all doors and windows, with instructions to shoot to kill if anyone attempted to get away.

"ATS officers! Put your hands in the air and stay exactly where you are!" barked the CCO.

One man instinctively made a move towards the officers and was shot dead at point blank range. Another tried to break out through a window and was gunned down by the officers outside. The rest, in a total state of shock and disbelief, followed instructions and kept their hands raised. Inside the room a pile of presents, bottles of alcoholic drinks and a large banner displaying

"Happy 90th Birthday" appeared to confirm that the gathering was indeed a birthday party.

"This is an illegal gathering!" said the commander. "You should all know that so many people are not allowed to gather in a group. It puts you all under suspicion of possible terrorist activity."

"It's only a birthday party officer," said one of the gathering.

"Be quiet unless I ask you a question!" snapped Quinlan. "A birthday party could always be cover for something much more sinister. It certainly looks like you were having a party but that excuses nothing. You are all under arrest and will have to be interrogated. Who's birthday is it?"

"It's mine officer," said a frail old man sitting in an armchair, beginning to struggle to keep his hands in the air.

"Don't put your hands down until I tell you to!" yelled Quinlan, pointing his KOS directly at the old man's face.

"I'm sorry but I don't have the strength to hold them up for much longer," replied the old man.

"You'll do as you're told or suffer the consequences," barked Quinlan.

Despite the pain, the old man raised his drooping arms a little higher.

"What is your name?" asked Quinlan.

"I am Tim Beardmore sir. I live here with my wife, Elsie."

"And I presume that this is your good lady, sat here beside you," sneered the officer, turning his attention to a frail elderly woman who was sitting and weeping quietly. "Stop that snivelling woman! Mr Beardmore is it your birthday today?"

"Yes sir."

"And you are ninety years old today, is that right?"

"Yes sir."

"And who are these other people?"

"My sons, daughters, grandchildren and great grandchildren. All close family sir."

"You silly old fool!" snapped Quinlan. "You should have known better than to cause this. Two of your family are dead and the rest of you will be arrested and punished."

The old man started on Quinlan. "Why are you doing this? It was only a birthday party. You've got no right -"

He was silenced by the back of Quinlan's hand, sending the nonagenarian sprawling out of his chair and colliding with a table, before landing in a pained and bloodied heap on the floor.

One of the old man's daughters went to help him up. "Leave him and stay exactly where you are!" Quinlan instructed, levelling his KOS at her. "You will all be taken for interrogation and punishment."

"It was only a birthday party," groaned the old man, still on the floor. "Why would you want to start killing people?"

"I've told you your party could be cover for terrorist activities and, even if it's not, it is still an illegal gathering and you will all be punished as appropriate."

A young boy around seven years old, Tim's great grandson, started to cry. "This little fellow will make a good place to start our interrogation." said Quinlan, grabbing the boy by the arm and terrifying him even more. The boy's mother tried to comfort him and was met by Quinlan's gloved fist punching her full in the face and sending her spinning to the ground. "Do you people never learn? Do you want more bloodshed?"

The occupants of the house were all handcuffed and deposited into vehicles, to be taken for questioning. In all, apart from the two dead, the ATS arrested fourteen people, including the old man and his wife, four other women and three children. All, including the children, were interrogated and the ATS pulled no punches with the interrogation.

Although no evidence of terrorist activity was found, all fourteen were sent for trial the next day. Quinlan was annoyed about the time which he and his unit had wasted on the case without catching genuine terrorists. Consequently, all fourteen were dealt with very harshly by the court, almost as harshly as if they had been terrorists. Chief Commanding Officer Quinlan was given a commendation for a successfully executed anti-terrorist operation.

Chapter 5.
NEW JUSTICE

The very next day after Tom Chadwick, Frank Weedall and the Beardmore's had been arrested and interrogated, they were all in court. Justice of The Party, George Grisedale was presiding, with assistance from the Clerk of the Court, Peter Denning. The courtroom was small, drab and dimly lit, with no windows and only three doors. One door led to an entrance hall and out into the street. The entrance hall was guarded by two security officers. A second door led to the Justice's chambers, where the Justice and the Clerk of the Court resided when there was a recess. The third door led to the detention block. This consisted of several tiny holding cells for the defendants, a room which was used by the officers waiting for their turn to bring charges against the defendants and the doctors' room which contained a restraining chair and the necessary equipment for the duty doctor and nurse to carry out the death penalty, known as Age Acceleration, when required.

In the courtroom, the Justice of The Party sat behind a large, imposing, ornately carved desk. The Clerk of the Court had a desk of his own, a much smaller and plainer one, to the side of the Justice's desk. There was a large, raised, wooden, box-like enclosure, often referred to as the dock. This was where the defendants stood during the trial, handcuffed to a restraining officer. There was also a small table, just to the side of the dock, which was used by the senior arresting officer. That was all. There was no jury, no witnesses, no prosecuting or defending solicitors and no public were allowed to watch the trials.

Gone were the wig and robe worn by Judges and Magistrates of the past. The Justice was dressed in a charcoal grey suit and distinguished only by a very large, very heavy and very ornate chain of office. The Clerk of the Court also wore a chain of office but this was far more modest, smaller, lighter and very plain in comparison.

The old judicial system had found it increasingly impossible to cope. There was no time for the old-fashioned trial by jury. The idea of "innocent until proven guilty" had been thrown out long ago. Instead, if the presenting officer believed that there was sufficient evidence against a prisoner, the Justice accepted the officer's word. No evidence was heard. No defence was heard. The Justice simply had to rubber stamp the verdict and decide on the appropriate punishment.

All that could be heard in the court was the clock on the wall, above the dock, ticking its way to the starting time of nine thirty. At nine thirty, on the dot, the quiet of the courtroom was broken by the voice of Justice Grisedale.

"Who brings the first case before me?"

"I do sir, Chief Party Enforcement Officer, Adam Mollison." Mollison stood with head erect, shoulders back and chest thrust forward as though this was his proudest moment.

"Who is your prisoner and why have you brought him to this court?"

"He is Thomas Chadwick and he is guilty of spreading dissident libel against The Party sir!" said Mollison.

The old man stood in the dock frail and motionless, a shadow of his former self, brought down by fear of what was to become of him and the shock of being put in this position by his own grandson.

"Are you satisfied that you have sufficient proof Chief Officer Mollison?" Justice Grisedale asked.

"We have a sworn statement from a member of the Party Youth Movement who heard him and we have a recording of his conversation."

"That is good enough," said the Justice. "He is obviously guilty. Please commend the PYM member for his excellent work. Now I need to decide on sentence. How old is the prisoner?"

"He is seventy-two years old sir."

"He is too old for it to be worthwhile sending him for Civil Correction. I therefore sentence Thomas Chadwick to Age Acceleration, to be performed immediately. Take him down officer!"

The old man almost fainted but was held up by the restraining officer. He was hurried away to the detention block and taken into the doctor's room. He was placed in a padded chair, his arms, legs and neck were immobilised by restraining straps and the doctor administered a lethal injection. The punishment was referred to as Age Acceleration because the ultimate outcome of old age is death. It was simply achieved much quicker. In fact, the whole process, from sentencing to removal of the body, took no more than half an hour. No family or friends were informed. Nobody was allowed to take the body for burial or cremation. All bodies, whatever the cause of death, were the property of The Party and were dealt with by The Party.

At all trials there were only three possible sentences: Civil Correction, Penal Neutralisation and Age Acceleration.

Civil Correction was used for minor crimes and for dissidents who it was believed could live a useful life after correction. It consisted basically of brainwashing, using some physical but mainly mental torture to break the person and then rebuild them as a loyal Party member.

Penal Neutralisation meant being sent to a penal colony for the rest of the prisoner's life. The old prison system had completely collapsed due to a shortage of prison officers, overcrowding, lack of discipline and persistent re-offending. All too often the prisoners had been running the prisons. The prisons were replaced by penal settlements on Saint Kilda, an archipelago in the Atlantic, near the North West coast of Scotland. Three islands were used; Hirta, Soay and Dun. Prisoners were deposited on the islands with only basic supplies. No prison officers were present on the islands. Prisoners were left to fend for themselves. Drones made regular flights over the colonies to observe what was happening. Gunboats constantly patrolled the surrounding sea. If anyone was found to be attempting to escape, by homemade boat or by swimming, they were blown out of the water with no questions asked and no attempt to catch them and return them to the colony.

In the colonies it was a case of survival of the fittest although, over the years, some communities had developed. The prisoners had to become self-sufficient although they were given supplies of timber, for building shelters and had their food supplemented by supplies of HCR. Nobody seemed to know what HCR was made from. It tasted pretty awful. It came as huge bags of a meat based, protein slurry which was usually used in stews. It could be kept, without refrigeration, for six months. There were regular air drops of HCR and timber every two weeks. The air drops sometimes triggered a spell of gang warfare as dominant factions tried to get the lion's share. All sentences to the penal colonies were life sentences, regardless of the severity of the crime. No-one ever left the penal colonies. The penal colonies were the only place where bodies were buried or cremated, rather than being taken away by the authorities. In fact, there had been rumours of cannibalism when food was in short supply.

Age Acceleration was death performed by means of a lethal injection. Perpetrators of extreme crimes such as murder, rape or terrorist activities would be punished by Age Acceleration. People who would normally have been sentenced to Civil Correction or Penal Neutralisation, but were ill or infirm, would be sentenced to Age Acceleration instead. Anyone over sixty-five years old who developed a long-term illness or infirmity would be sentenced to Age Acceleration. Anyone who was found to be destitute or living on the streets would be sentenced to Penal Neutralisation if they were well. If street living had taken its toll and they were not well they would be sentenced to Age Acceleration. Anyone undergoing Civil Correction but failing to reform or anyone refusing to accept Civil Correction had their punishment changed to Age Acceleration.

Other new crimes had been created in this time of bitter intolerance. Homosexuality, bisexuality, transgender and cross dressing had all been made illegal and a perpetrator faced Penal Neutralisation. All non-Christian religions had also been made illegal following extradition of all known Muslims, Hindus, Sikhs, Jews and followers of other religions, regardless of whether immigrants or British born. Any remaining followers who were discovered were sentenced to Penal Neutralisation. All religious or sexual tolerance had been completely destroyed.

Back in the courtroom, Justice Grisedale was already into his second case of the morning. This was also brought by Chief Party Enforcement Officer Mollison.

"Who is the defendant and why have you brought him before my court, Chief Officer Mollison?" asked Justice Grisedale.

"The defendant is Edward Kerley, son-in-law of the previous defendant. We believe that he took part in dissident discussions with Thomas Chadwick. We believe that the discussions were always initiated by Thomas Chadwick but the defendant allowed himself to listen to the ranting of the old man," said Mollison.

"Do you know if he passed on any part of these discussions to other parties, Chief Officer?"

"We do not believe so sir," replied Mollison.

"Edward Kerley," the Justice's voice boomed. "This court believes that you have allowed yourself to listen to dissident libel. Whilst it appears that you have not spread any of this libel yourself, you have not done anything to prevent the perpetrator from talking to you. There must be a possibility that your opinion may have been corrupted. I am therefore obliged to sentence you to undergo a course of Civil Correction and you will not be allowed to re-join your family until we are satisfied that any dissident or seditious thoughts have been entirely corrected and eradicated."

The defendant was taken away by his restraining officer for the process to begin immediately.

"Well done Chief Officer Mollison," said the Justice. "This kind of thing needs to be nipped in the bud to avoid future trouble and unrest."

Mollison's chest almost burst out of his uniform with pride.

The third case of the morning was brought by Chief Party Enforcement Officer Gerard Tizard. Tizard was prosecuting a vagrant, David Andrew Broadbent.

"What is the case against the defendant?" asked the Justice.

"He was found living on the street sir. When questioned, he had no money and no fixed abode. He spent most nights on a park bench in Queens Park. He admitted that he had been living rough and moving around regularly to avoid discovery," replied Tizard.

Although David Broadbent was only thirty-five years old, he looked much older and looked quite ill due to the rough sleeping. He was very underweight with a very pale, sallow complexion, sores on his face and hands and an intermittent soft cough. He looked like he hardly had the strength to stand in the dock.

"Has a doctor checked the defendant's state of health?" asked the Justice.

"He has sir," replied the officer. "The doctor believes that the defendant may have tuberculosis."

"In that case," replied Justice Grisedale, "I have no alternative but to sentence him to Age Acceleration. Take him down and deal with him immediately officer."

Again, the court was empty except for the Justice of The Party and the Clerk of the Court.

Almost immediately a new defendant was brought in by his restraining officer. This time the prosecuting officer was not in uniform. He was an officer of the DDPU, the Dissident Discovery and Pursuit Unit, who worked undercover amongst groups of non-party members, looking for dissidents and wanted men.

"Who is prosecuting?" asked the Justice.

"I am, Chief Officer Jack Kingsbury of the DDPU sir."

"And who is the defendant?"

"Francis Weedall sir."

"And what has he done, Chief Officer?"

"Yesterday, sir, I was working undercover at Saint Jude's Charity Medical Centre. The defendant's wife had just died and he wanted to take her body for burial. He was told by the attending doctor that his wife's body had to be collected and dealt with by the authorities. He said that he didn't care about the law, he just wanted to bury his wife himself. He had to be forcibly restrained to enable the body collectors to do their job."

"She was my wife, not The Party's! I wanted to bury her privately, myself. You bastards had already taken her life from me! Why should I let you take her body as well?" yelled a distraught Frank Weedall.

"Silence!" shouted the Justice. "You have no right of reply. You only dig yourself deeper into trouble. I am going to sentence you to Penal Neutralisation. Take him down and arrange transport to the penal colony, officer."

Weedall continued protesting even while his restraining officer was taking him back to his cell.

For the next case, an old man and an old woman were both in the dock, together. Each of them was handcuffed to a restraining officer.

"Who is bringing this case?" asked the Justice.

"I am sir, Chief Commanding Officer Glyn Quinlan of the Anti-Terrorist Squad. The defendants are Tim and Elsie Beardmore. They held a ninetieth birthday party yesterday evening, a gathering of sixteen people."

"Please sir, could my wife be allowed to sit down?" asked Tim Beardmore. "She can't stand for more than a few minutes sir." Tim and Elsie both looked very week and shaky on their legs. The bruises on their faces and arms revealed their experience of interrogation the night before.

"Neither you nor your wife will be allowed any special privileges. She must remain standing. You will not be in the dock for long. You held a gathering of more than twelve people. That is illegal. It also necessitated the attendance of officers from the ATS so you have seriously wasted state resources. Your party could have been cover for a terrorist gathering or it could have prevented the ATS being available to deal with a terrorist threat elsewhere. You are both guilty as charged. How old are you both?" asked the Justice.

"I am ninety years old sir and my wife is eighty-six years old," replied Tim Beardmore.

"Then I have no choice but to sentence you both to Age Acceleration, to be carried out immediately."

Elsie Beardmore collapsed and had to be carried out of the courtroom by her restraining officer, while her broken-hearted husband was led away to his fate.

There was one last case to be heard before lunch. This consisted of a family of three people, a man, a woman and a boy. The prosecuting officer was once again CCO Glyn Quinlan. The three were all from the party at the Beardmores' house on the previous night. The family were Edward Beardmore, Tim and Elsie's grandson, Edward's wife Janet and their eight-year-old son, James. Edward Beardmore was sentenced to Penal Neutralisation; his wife and son were both sentenced to Civil Correction.

Justice Grisedale commended Quinlan for his handling of the case which involved several more Beardmore family members who were due for trial in the afternoon.

With that, the Justice called for a temporary halt to proceedings. "We will adjourn now for lunch and continue in an hour and a half." Then, turning to the Clerk of the Court, he said, "You know, Peter, the judicial system works so much better now. We have tried and sentenced nine people in less than three and a half hours. In the old days that would have taken at least three weeks and then some of them may have been found not guilty and escaped justice. Much more efficient now! Much quicker! Much better!"

"It does work more efficiently sir," replied the Clerk. "I just worry sometimes that the security officers might make a mistake at some point and we may sentence an innocent person."

"Nonsense Peter! You have to trust the officers. In any case, if at some point we do sentence an innocent man that is far outweighed by the guilty men who may have got off under the old system."

"I suppose you are right sir, of course!" acknowledged the Clerk.

Chapter 6.

ON THE RUN

Doctor Nick Kaydon was about to take a break after finishing morning surgery at Saint Jude's when he was disturbed by nurse and girlfriend Jenny Oakwood.

"Nick, there are two men here insisting that they want to see you right away. I told them you were on a break but they reckon they can't wait. One of them is injured but it doesn't look like an emergency. He says you are old friends and he reckons you'll want to get him in and out as fast as possible. He gave the name of Dan Bridgewood. I don't know if that means anything to you?"

"Yes, Dan is an old friend Jen and he's right about me wanting to see him as fast as possible. You'd better bring them both in right away. Can you tell Sister Mary-Beth to make sure we're not disturbed and then can you stick around in case I need you?"

"I thought I'd better warn you as well that the guy in the grey suit, who arrested Mr Weedall the other day, is hanging around again. Will there be a problem if he sees your friends Nick?"

"There's no need to worry about him Jen. I know him. He's not what you think he is. Actually, he knows Dan as well."

"I really don't understand at all Nick but I suppose you know what you're doing. I'll go and get them," said Jenny as she went off to collect the two men and show them into the examination room. One of the men was bleeding from a head wound and in obvious pain.

Nick greeted his old friend and fellow PDM member. "Hi Dan, looks like you're in a bit of trouble mate. What's happened?"

"I'm sorry to put you at risk, Nick, coming here like this but we were on a raid and ran into the ATS We had to go over a wall to escape and I guess I'm not as agile as I used to be. I ended up doing a nosedive from six feet up. I don't bounce very well nowadays. I wouldn't have got away at all if it wasn't for Ken here." He nodded towards his companion, Ken Townsend.

"OK Dan, come and lie on the couch and I'll take a look at that head wound." Dan winced with pain as he got onto the couch. "Looks like I'd better take a look at that shoulder as well if it's that painful. Any double vision or nausea?"

"No. That's all fine."

They were disturbed suddenly by DDPU officer, Jack Kingsbury bursting into the room, despite audible protests from Sister Mary-Beth. "I've had a good look around outside Dan and I can't see any sign of you being followed so far."

"That's great. Hopefully, we've given them the slip. Thanks Jack."

"No problem, Dan. I'll keep a look out outside and I'll let you know if there's any sign of the ATS."

"But you're one of them!" muttered Jenny, getting more confused and frightened by the second. "It was you who shot and arrested that man the other day. Nick, he works for The Party!"

"Don't worry Jen, everything is OK," said Nick in his usual calming voice. "Jack is a double agent. The Party think he's a DDPU officer, undercover police, but he's actually one of us, PDM."

"Then why did you shoot Frank Weedall?" Jenny asked, still suspicious.

"Save his life you mean. Didn't you see the Blackshirts with the body collectors? I had my KOS on stun. The Blackshirt would have shot to kill if I hadn't fired first," Jack replied.

"But you arrested him. He could be dead anyway."

"He was sent to the penal colony. If we get rid of these Party bastards-" Jack stopped, paused and started again more positively. "WHEN we get rid of these Party bastards and take control, the cons will be released and pardoned anyway. I gave him the best chance that I could without blowing my cover. Anyway, I'll be outside keeping a lookout," and with that, Jack left the room.

Nick continued examining his friend. "Looks like the shoulder's just severe bruising. Give it a few days and it should be as good as new. We'd better get a dressing on that head wound though. I think it will be OK without stitching. It looks like you've been pretty lucky, although I 'd suggest it would be better to land on your feet next time."

"I'm hoping there won't be a next time, Nick. That was a bit too close for comfort."

Jenny took over bandaging Jack's head.

Suddenly Nick was shocked by a surprise question from Ken Townsend. "Has your mother been dead for long Nick?"

"About six years. Why do you ask?"

"Because her spirit is here," replied Ken, "standing beside your right shoulder."

Despite a sudden belief that Ken had gone mad, Nick was instinctively compelled to turn his head and look, as did Jenny. Of course, neither of them saw a thing.

"Ken's a psychic medium," explained Dan. "He often sees spirits. I used to think it was all mumbo-jumbo but Ken's got us out of trouble on more than one occasion with information from his spirit contacts. He's convinced me. I trust his psychic powers completely now. If Ken says your mother's here, I've got no doubt that she is."

Nick still looked a little sceptical as Ken continued. "Your mother just wants you to know that she's alright and she often comes to Saint Jude's to keep an eye on how you are getting along. She says that she's really proud of you and she thinks you do a great job here. She says that she really likes your girlfriend. You need to look after her. She's a keeper."

Jenny looked a little embarrassed.

Suddenly Ken's jaw dropped in surprise and anguish. "Another spirit has just come into the room, a man, a friend of your mother's. He's very agitated. He's come to warn you that your cover's blown. The ATS are on their way in force and they know who we all are, including you and Jenny. They know that Jack's working for us as well. We all need to get out of here right away."

At that second, Jack Kingsbury burst through the door. "It looks like the Blackshirts are coming. There are four of their cars coming down the road."

"Ken's just warned us, a spirit message, he reckons they know who we all are," said Dan.

"Then we all need to go," said Jack, "but we need to move right now! Is there a back way out Nick, some way that we can get out without being seen?"

"If we take the service stairs down to the basement, we might be able to get out unseen," said Nick. "Jen you'll need to come with us too. I know you're not really involved but if the ATS think you might know something they'll enjoy trying to get you to divulge information and you'll probably end up with the cons in the penal colony."

The five quickly took the back stairs, leading down into the basement. The basement was mainly just used for storage of supplies, not that there was much stored in there nowadays. Such was the difficulty getting supplies in these times that the most conspicuous thing about the basement was the empty space. At one end of the basement there was a hatch, with an unloading chute, opening into the grounds at the back of the hospital. Nick lifted the hatch and peered out. He could hear the Blackshirts shouting instructions as they began to search the building. He could hear Sister Mary-Beth's voice as she complained about the disruption to patient care and other staff questioning what was going on. He hoped no-one else at Saint Jude's would suffer due to his actions, not that he could do anything about that now anyway. The ATS were not the most tolerant when things didn't go their way. Fortunately, they did not appear to have anyone covering the hatch yet.

An old ambulance was parked about twenty yards away. The vehicle was a twenty-five-year-old Vauxhall Vivaro and one of the last to be produced with a petrol engine. All modern vehicles were electric. The ambulance was still used on very rare occasions so it should contain some petrol, probably not very full but enough to give them a start.

"We could use that ambulance, if we can get to it without being seen," said Nick. "The problem is the keys will probably be in the office upstairs and I doubt if the Blackshirts will let us go and look for them."

"Well, if I can get into it without being seen, I can probably hot wire it. Just one of the skills I learned in my misspent youth. Won't work with modern cars but that's old enough for me to have a good chance," said Jack Kingsbury.

A storage shed stood between the main building and the ambulance and Jack was able to use that for cover to help him get to the ambulance without being seen. He couldn't believe his luck when he found the ambulance was unlocked. There was no key in the ignition but there was a limit to how much luck you could expect. He slipped into the driving seat, still unseen and fumbled under the dashboard to find the wires that he needed. He would not try to start the vehicle until everyone was on board. He did not want to alert the Blackshirts. They only had one chance to get away without a shootout. He gave a thumbs up to signal to the others that he was ready. One by one, they each followed Jack's route, quickly and quietly, to get to the ambulance and get into the back. Dan Bridgewood was the last of the group and, just as he got to the ambulance, he was spotted by a Blackshirt who raised the alarm and fired, hitting Dan in the back. Further shots were fired but no-one else was hit as Dan was quickly dragged into the ambulance and the back doors slammed shut. Jack twisted the wires to make the engine spring to life and they roared off up the road. The Blackshirts wasted no time in getting to their cars to follow. The ambulance had a head start but the ATS cars would be much faster. There was no way that the Vivaro could outrun them. The Blackshirts were not yet in sight, in the rear-view mirror, as Jack spotted a turning into a farmyard on the left. He swung the ambulance into the yard and round behind a barn and prayed that the ATS had not seen them turn. He breathed a huge sigh of relief as he heard the

ATS sirens wailing past the farm and on up the road. He knew, however, he had only bought a short amount of time. The ATS would soon realise that the ambulance was not in front of them and they would be back for a thorough search.

Nick had been trying all he could to stem the blood from Dan's wound but it had become increasingly obvious that the gunshot had caused a lot of damage to the lungs and was causing massive, acute lung haemorrhage. Dan was fighting a massive battle for his life and losing overwhelmingly.

The farmer came out into the yard to see what was going on. When Jack asked the farmer if they could borrow his car, the farmer ran back into the house. Jack guessed what he was up to and ran after him. As the farmer reached to grab his shotgun from the gun rack, Jack's fist knocked him senseless. When he came round, the farmer found he was handcuffed to a radiator with the gun safely well out of reach.

"We need to take the car," said Jack. "When we've finished our journey, we'll leave the car where the Blackshirts will find it, so you'll get it back."

When Jack went back outside, Dan Bridgewood was desperately gasping for breath with blood trickling from the corner of his mouth.

"Come on Dan! Hang on in there, mate!" yelled Nick, choking back the tears, with his arm around Dan, cradling his head and neck. "You're not going to die. I'm not going to let you die Dan. You've got to hold on! I'm not going to let you die!" Dan Bridgewood, his face turning from pure white to grey, began to cough, expectorating pure blood. He took one last gasp as his eyes rolled back and he relaxed completely. "Dan! Dan! Wake up Dan! You can't die! Not now!" Nick yelled in desperation despite knowing that his voice fell on deaf ears, on dead ears. His old friend lay motionless, all signs of life having drained from his body.

"We need to get moving fast Nick, before the Blackshirts come back and find us." Jack was trying to shake Nick out of his grief and back into the fight for survival. "We'll take the farmer's car. A brand-new Toyota Arrow. That'll go like a bomb. They'll never catch us in that."

"We can't just leave Dan here!" wailed Nick.

"It won't make any difference to him Nick. He's dead. Come on, pull yourself together," urged Jack.

"Have you got the keys?" asked Ken Townsend.

"Don't need 'em," replied Jack. "This little baby is standard issue for all DDPU officers." He took an object from his pocket which looked a bit like a thimble and put it on his finger. "These newer cars have fingerprint recognition on the locks and on the ignition. This little tool provides a master fingerprint that overrides almost all the fingerprint recognition devices. DDPU officers are issued with them in case they ever need to commandeer a vehicle."

Jack had the car unlocked in a flash and the engine started to purr. Nick, Ken and Jenny got in and they were away. Even if they were spotted by the Blackshirts now, the Arrow was probably powerful enough to outrun them.

"We'll head for the nearest safe house," said Jack. "It won't take long in this."

As they were driving along, Jack spotted what looked like a boy running along the road. As they got closer, the boy seemed to panic and try to run across the road, right in front of the car. Jack hit the brakes hard and swerved but could not avoid the boy who rolled over the bonnet, hit the ground and lay there in a motionless heap. Nick and Jenny jumped out quickly to see if they had killed him. He was still alive but unconscious. He slowly started to regain consciousness and then, realising where he was, tried to jump up in a panic but fell back onto the road.

"Take it easy," said Nick in a soothing voice, trying to calm the boy down. "We're just trying to help you. Best if you stay as still as you can while I check you out. I'm a doctor. You're safe now. Why did you run into the road like that? Is somebody after you?"

"Blackshirts. When I saw the car, I thought you might have been them so I tried to get across the road. There's more cover on the other side, easier to hide from them," said the boy.

"Why are the Blackshirts after you?" asked Nick.

"They killed my parents. They would have killed me too if I hadn't managed to get away. I have to get away!" The boy was getting agitated and frightened again.

"It's OK. You're safe now. Calm down. We'll look after you," said Jenny gently, concerned that his fear would make his condition worse.

Nick finished his examination. "Looks like you've been pretty lucky. I don't think you've done too much damage. Let's see if you can stand." Carefully, with help from Nick and Jenny, the boy managed to get to his feet. "You'd better come with us. We're running from Blackshirts too. We'd better get going before they show up. I'll check you out more thoroughly when we get to the house we're heading for. We'll all be safe there. What's your name son?"

"Jonathan, Jonathan Patterson," replied the boy, calming down as they all got into the car and drove on.

Soon they arrived at the safehouse. It was a very large farmhouse which appeared to be deserted, despite the fact that it was currently occupied by three other PDM members. It was at least three miles away from any other house, on a very secluded road. The Blackshirts never normally went anywhere near it. The house stood in its own grounds which were completely surrounded by a high hedge and trees. Access to the grounds was via a locked gate. Fortunately, as Jack and Ken had been there quite often in the past, they had keys to the gate. Crossing the grounds there was a wide, straight, central drive. There was also a narrower track which followed the line of the hedges. Luckily, Jack knew that he needed to take the narrow track. The main drive was booby trapped with land mines in case of unwanted visitors.

As the Arrow pulled up alongside the house, it was watched and covered by Idris Llewellyn, a middle aged, six foot five inches tall Welshman. Idris was a former sergeant in the Welsh Guards before they were disbanded. He recognised Jack and Ken as soon as they got out of the car.

"What's up Jack? Ken?" asked the big Welshman. "Are you in trouble?"

"Taffy! Am I glad to see you! We're on the run from the Blackshirts. They almost caught us. They killed Dan Bridgewood. We'll need to stay for a while," said Jack. "Look, I'll introduce everybody later, but first I need to dump the car well away from here, so we don't attract any attention. We had to steal it, so the Blackshirts will know the registration by now. Can you follow me in your car? I'll leave this one about five miles away and then you can bring me back. While we're gone, can somebody get the boy into bed. I ran him over and he needs to rest. Nick and Jenny here will look after him. Nick's a doctor and Jenny's a nurse so he'll be in good hands."

"Sure thing, Jack. I'm sorry to hear about Dan. He was a good bloke. The other lads will take care of your friends. Let's go and get rid of your car."

With that, Jack and Idris drove away, leaving the others to settle into their new home for the time being.

Chapter 7.
REVELATIONS

By the time Jack Kingsbury and Idris Llewellyn got back safely from ditching the car, Nick had given Jonathan a more complete, more thorough examination and, having decided he was suffering only from severe bruising and mild concussion, had got him safely tucked up in bed. Nick and Jenny took it in turns to check on the boy, but he was soon fast asleep. Exhaustion took its toll even more than the trauma of the day's events.

There were two other PDM members already at the safe house. Derek McCarthy, sometimes known as Del, was a short, tubby scouser who, like most scousers, thought himself to be a bit of a comedian. He was the one who always tried to keep everybody's spirits up when things got tough. The other was Graham Tucker, a grey haired, sixty-year-old ex-policeman, from the days before formation of the PEO, DDPU, and ATS. Graham was a widower. His wife had been killed in a road accident twenty years earlier. Derek had a wife and daughter, currently living safely at PDM headquarters. Ken Townsend had known Derek and Graham for several years and wasted no time in introducing everyone and filling Derek and Graham in on the events of the day.

That evening, trying to relax after a meal, Jenny and Nick found themselves alone. Jenny could see just how low and upset Nick was feeling.

"Are you alright Nick? We're safe now and Jonathan looks like he should be alright, so I guess it's Dan that's making you feel like this."

"I guess so. We went way back, me and Dan, although I hadn't seen him much recently. We were at school together and, although he was a year older than me, we were inseparable; more like brothers than friends. People thought we were joined at the hip. We did everything together. We got into all kinds of scrapes, you know all the usual kids' stuff, but whatever happened I always knew Dan had got my back.

He saved my life once. We were swimming in a lake and I got my leg trapped in some submerged tree roots. The water was quite deep and I wasn't a strong swimmer. Dan could see that I was tiring and struggling to stay afloat. I could easily have drowned but Dan kept going under the water until he could get my leg free.

The first time I went on a date, it was a double date with Dan and two sisters. It was a good job Dan was there. The girls were about as interesting as watching paint dry.

When I was about nineteen, I got into debt with some pretty disreputable people, you know the kind who'd be happy to break your legs if you can't pay and I didn't have the money for them. Dan found out and paid the debt, no questions asked. I don't even know how he got the money to do it. He was pretty broke himself."

"It sounds like you were really lucky to have a friendship like that."

"I always knew I could rely on Dan. Even today, he was the one who got shot because he made sure everyone else was safely in the ambulance first but, when he really needed me, I let him down. I owed him so much but I let him down! I let him die! I desperately wanted to save him but I failed. I let him die and then I left his body behind."

"You did everything you could Nick. Nobody could have saved him. You know nobody could have saved him. At least you were there with him at the end. I'm sure that would have meant a lot to him." Jenny put her arms around Nick and kissed him gently on the forehead as tears of grief rolled down his cheeks. She wanted so much to take away his pain and suffering but had no idea how, other than just being there for him.

****

The next morning, Nick went to check on Jonathan. Jonathan was still lying in bed. When he saw Nick, he pushed himself up into a sitting position, wincing with pain as he did so.

"Take it easy son," said Nick. "Don't try to do too much just yet."

"I'm OK. I'm just a bit sore and got a bit of a headache."

"That's what you get if you try bouncing off cars. I'll get something to ease the pain. You certainly look a lot better than you did last night, Jon. Do you feel like telling me what happened yesterday? Don't worry if you're not ready yet. We can talk another time if you prefer. There's no hurry. Just tell me when you're ready, in your own time."

"It's OK," said the boy. "I can tell you now. It probably won't get any easier to talk about it later. My grandfather came to Britain from Pakistan, as a young man, many years ago. He settled here and became a British citizen. My father was born here in the UK. The UCNP started extraditing people with foreign connections, even if they were born in the UK. My grandfather was dead by then but my father was afraid that he would be thrown out of the country. He was born in the UK, to a father who was a British citizen, but they suddenly made him an illegal alien. Dad changed his name from Dilip Patel to Phillip Patterson and moved to a different part of the country, where he wasn't known. He didn't look particularly Asian, so nobody queried it. He got married and I was born. We seemed to be safe but somehow, after all those years, the Blackshirts found out about my dad changing his name.

They came to our home to arrest the whole family, because he had escaped extradition all those years ago. There must have been about ten Blackshirts. They were convinced that my dad would know of others who were here illegally. He knew nothing but they wouldn't accept it and became angry that they didn't get the information they wanted. Dad was questioned and beaten mercilessly while my mother and I were forced to watch. When they realised that he was not going to talk, they thought that his weak spot might be my mother and they started beating her. My father begged them to stop but they said they would only stop if my father gave them information. How could he? He knew nothing. My father and I were powerless to help my mother. Our arms and necks were restrained by Blackshirts. Then their commanding officer raped my mother. I think his name was Quinlan. She begged him to stop but he carried on. He was enjoying inflicting pain and humiliation. Then the beating started again. My father somehow managed to break free from the men restraining him and lunged at Quinlan. Quinlan shot him five times at close range. Three shots into his chest and two into his head. Then they continued beating my mother, just in case she knew anything. When he decided that she was not going to talk either, Quinlan put his gun to her temple and fired twice. He blew the back of her head away completely. It just disintegrated. I presume he didn't want any witnesses and he was very angry at not getting any information. I was still held by the Blackshirts and I knew that I was going to be next. Somehow, I managed to get my right arm free. The Blackshirt on that side had a dagger in a sheath on his belt. I managed to grasp the dagger and plunge it into the belly of the Blackshirt holding the other arm. He let go and I threw myself at the window behind us. The window shattered and I fell through.

They shot at me but I was moving too fast. The window was on the first floor but luckily a hedge broke my fall. I bounced off the hedge, a bit bruised but otherwise OK and limped quickly around the corner. They couldn't get a clear shot at me. By the time they got downstairs I was well away and I kept on running as best I could. When you came along the road, I thought you might have been after me and I tried to get across the road, to where there was more cover."

"I thought we'd killed you at first. I'm really glad we didn't. How old are you, Jon?" Nick asked.

"I'm thirteen."

"Just thirteen and you've had to go through all that. Well, you're safe now, with us, although that's not much consolation. We'll look after you. Don't worry. I would imagine that you've guessed that we are PDM members. This is one of our safe houses."

"I want to join you," said a very determined Jon. "Right now, I just want to kill Blackshirts!"

"I understand how you feel son. I'd feel the same if I was you, but you're too young to start killing anybody and we're not here just to kill Blackshirts or to get revenge. Anyway, just take it easy for now, OK? Just concentrate on getting better for the moment. Everything will sort itself out in time. The Blackshirts and The Party will get what they've got coming in time."

The boy gave a half-hearted smile and sank back into the bed.

★★★★

For the next few weeks, things were pretty uneventful at the safe house. Jonathan improved each day and was soon back on his feet. With each day he became more and more fond of Jenny and particularly Nick who became almost like surrogate parents.

There was a strict rule at the house that, whether on a mission, reconnoitring or even just shopping, people only left the house in groups of two or more. It was a safety measure so that there was always backup if anyone got into difficulties. Also, if anyone got arrested, the other person could possibly alert the rest of the house and any necessary action could be taken. It was never a problem and was always accepted by the men. The same rule applied to the people remaining in the house. One person was never supposed to be left on their own. However, there had been two or three occasions, when only Jenny and Jonathan were left at the house, on which Jenny had gone out on her own. Jonathan had questioned her about it and she had said that she just needed some fresh air and a change of surroundings to avoid going stir crazy. She was never gone for long, half an hour at most. She asked Jon not to say anything to the others as she knew it was against the rules but it didn't do any harm. Jonathan agreed to her request and really thought nothing of it. He trusted Jenny completely and he did not want to rock the boat.

★★★★

One day, when Nick was on his own, Ken decided he needed to have a quiet word. "Is everything alright with Jenny at the moment Nick?"

"Jenny's fine. Why do you ask?"

"I'm sure it's nothing. Perhaps I shouldn't say anything," muttered Ken, obviously feeling very uneasy about something.

"Come on Ken. Spit it out. It can't be that bad."

"I just felt that Jenny has seemed a bit different over the last few days, a bit uneasy, as though something is bothering her." Ken paused as though he was unsure whether to continue. "And there's your mother," he continued, appearing even more uncomfortable.

"My mother? Have you seen her again?" enquired Nick.

"She appeared to me again, yesterday. You weren't around or I would have let you know at the time. She didn't explain what she meant but she said that Jenny wasn't the girl that she had thought she was. She said that you needed to keep an eye on her and you shouldn't trust her."

"Good God Ken! I don't know who's battier, my mother for coming up with crackpot ideas or you for taking notice of them. Jenny's as straight as an arrow. I know I can trust her completely." Nick was beginning to get angry about Jenny being doubted.

"That's how I expected you to react Nick. That's why I was reluctant to tell you. I don't know what your mother meant but she was adamant that you shouldn't trust her. Just keep your eyes open and be careful."

"Thanks for the warning, Ken," said Nick, calming down again, "but you've got nothing to worry about where Jenny's concerned."

Despite his belief in Jenny, Nick had noticed himself that she seemed a bit quieter and more on edge in the last couple of days. Probably being at the house was getting to her a bit. After all, despite all the precautions, you never knew when the ATS might come calling.

Later that week, Del and Idris went out shopping for much needed supplies. The house had almost run out of food and with eight mouths to feed they needed plenty. When they came back, the food was safely put away in the fridge and the freezer except for a large pack of something marked HCR.

"You've left a pack of food out on the worktop lads," said Ken. "It'll soon go off if it's left there. What is it anyway? I don't recognise the pack."

"It's some kinda meat," said Derek. "I don't know what kinda meat it contains. It doesn't say on the packet. It just says MEAT BASED PROTEIN PRODUCT SUITABLE FOR USE IN STEWS AND CASSEROLES. Meat seemed a bit scarce in the supermarket today and this stuff was dead cheap so I thought we might as well give it a try. Should be just the job in a pan of scouse. The girl on the checkout reckons most of it gets sent to feed the cons in the penal colonies and only goes on sale in the supermarket when there's a meat shortage. I didn't put it in the fridge because it says on the bag WILL KEEP FOR SIX MONTHS WITHOUT REFRIGERATION."

"Six months," said Ken in disbelief. "That can't be right. Let me have a look." Ken picked up the pack to look for himself, let out a blood curdling scream and dropped the pack as if his fingers had been burned. "Fucking Hell! Dear God, No! It can't be! No! Go away! I can't help you! Please! This can't be true! I can't help you! How can they do this?"

"Ken what's wrong boy?" asked a startled Idris.

Ken had moved away from the food and was starting to calm down although he was still shaking from his ordeal. "We can't eat that stuff! No Way! We'll have to bury it or cremate it!"

"Ken you're not making much sense boyo. What is it? What's wrong?" asked Idris.

"When I touched the food there were a dozen or more spirits that came from nowhere, came from the food, begging me to help them. All desperately wanting me to help them. Taff, all those spirits appearing because of that meat and all frantic. That meat has to be made from humans! It has to be human flesh! There's no other possible explanation!"

"Are you sure you can't be wrong about this?" asked Derek. "Surely, they can't be using human bodies as food."

"No Dell, it has to be," said Ken. "It's human! I'm certain of it."

"That could be why The Party insist on taking all the bodies," said Nick, who had heard most of the conversation. "Those bastards think they've got a plentiful free supply of food and they're turning unsuspecting people into cannibals."

Idris picked up the pack to look for more information, handling it as though it was about to blow up in his face at any second.

"There's nothing written on here other than what Del read out before except it says MANUFACTURED BY THE WILLIAMSON MEAT CORPORATION and there's an address, NOTTINGHAM ROAD, BAMFORTH, YORKSHIRE."

"We need to follow this up," said Nick. "We'd better inform headquarters. They'll probably want to investigate further. They may even want to carry out a raid on the factory."

"I'll contact them first thing in the morning," said Graham Tucker. Graham was the person who was mainly responsible for liaising with PDM headquarters. "We'd better give that stuff a decent burial in the morning too."

****

Later that evening, when everything had calmed down and Ken and Idris were having a cup of tea, Ken said, "You must all think I'm a right nutcase, the way I reacted earlier."

"I can't pretend to understand what goes on when you see your visions Ken," said the big Welshman. "I was brought up, back home, as a strict Methodist and Methodist's don't have much time for spiritualists. So, I don't understand but I know you well enough to know that you believe it and I've seen you with your spirits often enough to know that you're usually right. So no, we don't think you're a nutcase boy but next time we go shopping can we have a bit more food and a bit less drama."

Chapter 8.
BETRAYAL AT J.J. MACDONALD'S

Graham Tucker walked out through the door of the room which he had commandeered as his office.

"I've just been in touch with headquarters on the DIRC," he announced, "and they have a job for us."

DIRC was Deleted Identity Radio Communicator. It was a type of radio-telephone based on a unique form of technology developed by the PDM's communications technicians. It was the only means of direct communication with headquarters, designed to make it impossible for anyone to hack, block or trace calls. Normal phones could easily be traced by the security agencies who could also easily listen in on conversations. Every PDM safe house had a DIRC and some agents were allowed to carry a DIRC when on major missions. Calls between safe houses or between agents had to be linked through HQ and had to be made by DIRC.

"They are running out of medical supplies and they are giving us the job of getting more. We can get more for our own use at the same time. They suggested a raid on the big pharmaceutical warehouse of J.J.Macdonald's in Aveden Bridge. It's only about six miles away and they believe there will only be minimal security at night. Their intelligence reckons just one unarmed security man. They suggested that we send three men in two cars to enable us to carry what we need. Who's up for it?" asked Graham.

"Well, if it's alright with youse lads, I'd like to go. I've been hangin' around here doin' not'n' for too long. It'd be good to do somethin' useful for a change," said Del enthusiastically.

"It's about time I got my hands dirty and did something other than being the crazy, annoying psychic," said Ken. "So, I guess you can count me in."

The big Welshman joined in. "You're best staying here Graham, no disrespect intended. Jack and Nick haven't been on a raid yet so I reckon I should go with the boys."

"Right, that's settled then," said Graham. "Del, Ken and Taff will do it. I suggest tomorrow night."

"That's great," said Derek. "I reckon we've gorra good little team there, lads. It'll be good to finally get some action. You get soft sitt'n' around 'ere for too long."

★ ★ ★ ★

Later that day Nick confided in Jenny that he was disappointed not to have been asked to go on the raid. Jenny was pleased that Nick was not going as she wanted him to stay safe and not take any risks.

For the rest of the day, the house was buzzing with excitement about the coming raid but next morning things were different. The peace of the house was shattered by the sound of Idris vomiting, time after time after time.

"I thought you were never going to get out of the bathroom, Taff," said Nick to the big man.

"Sorry boyo, it must be a stomach bug or food poisoning. I've puked at least four times in the past hour. I'm tired of hugging the toilet. There can't be anything else left to throw up."

"Well, you certainly can't go on the raid tonight, Taff, that's for sure."

"I'll probably be alright later. There's no need to cancel it."

"There's no need to cancel it anyway Taff," said Nick. "I can go instead. Even if you've stopped vomiting, you're not going to be up to it by tonight. You need to get back to bed, if you can stay away from the bog for long enough."

"I'm not really happy about that, boy. I ought to be there. You don't really know what we planned," said Idris.

"Look, Del and Ken can bring me up to speed and I want to do it. It sounds like an easy enough job Taff. I've got to start sometime and this could be a good time to do it."

"OK Nick. I'm not really happy about it but I'll go along with it as long as Ken and Del have no objections."

When Nick told Jenny that he was replacing Idris on the raid she was shocked and almost hysterical. "Oh God no! You can't go Nick! You're a doctor, not a soldier! They can go to the warehouse another time when Idris is better. It was planned with Idris. They shouldn't send someone else at the last minute! I don't want you to go Nick! Please don't go! If things go wrong you could get killed! You've never done anything like this before. I'm frightened for you Nick!"

"Calm down Jen. It's alright. It was my idea for me to go instead of Taff. I want to do it."

"I'm just so worried. What if you don't come back? I can't lose you now!"

"I'll be fine. Ken and Del will look after me. They know what they're doing. We'll all soon be back, safe and sound, with the supplies and then you'll wonder what you were worrying about," said Nick reassuringly.

Jenny would have done anything to stop Nick going but she knew him well enough to know that she had no chance. She could barely hold back her tears when she gave him a final hug before the trio set off on their mission.

****

They went in two cars to enable them to carry more supplies, Derek McCarthy driving one car unaccompanied, Nick driving the second car with Ken Townsend in the passenger seat.

When they were getting near to the warehouse, Ken said, "Nick I'm getting an awful feeling about this job. It sounds crazy but I can't help feeling we should abort it."

"For God's sake Ken, what's going on in your head?" asked Nick.

"I'm sorry Nick. I don't understand it myself but I've just got a feeling that the Blackshirts know about it. It feels like there's some connection with your mother's warning the other day. I think they are going to be waiting for us."

"Look Ken, there's no way the Blackshirts can know about us coming. We can't call the op' off now. We can't go back and say we chickened out of trying to do it because you had a premonition. Anyway, if we turned back, Del's ahead of us and we've got no way to let him know. Let's carry on to the warehouse, meet up with Del and then decide. If anything looks suspicious then we just get out of there as fast as we can. If it looks OK then we carry on as planned."

"I suppose that makes sense Nick but if anything seems wrong we get out of there," said Ken, still sounding far from convinced.

Nick and Ken pulled in to the warehouse car park. Derek was already parked and out of his car, waiting.

"Is everything clear Del?" asked Nick.

"It's sound. No sign of any security out here, so should just be the one guard inside, like we were told," replied Derek.

"Ken's getting some sort of premonition that we're heading into trouble and they're waiting for us."

"There's no sign of anybody around 'ere and there's no way that they could know that we're comin', Ken. I reckon you're worryin' about not'n'. Now we're 'ere we might as well go in," urged Del.

Ken grudgingly agreed but it still felt wrong. He could still sense danger.

They took no time at all to force the lock on the main door and go inside. The building was in darkness. Their first job was to locate the security guard and put him out of action. That was their plan as they moved into the warehouse following the light of their torches but, as they moved cautiously forward, suddenly all of the lights were switched on.

The whole place lit up, revealing at least eight Blackshirts who opened fire immediately. The three fired back as they headed for the door in an attempt to get away. In the fierce gun battle that followed, Del took out two ATS officers before being hit and killed himself. Nick was hit in the shoulder but only after taking out another Blackshirt. Nick and Ken managed to make it outside but, as they went through the door, they were fired on by more Blackshirts who had been successfully hidden outside. Ken attempted to shield the wounded Nick and provide covering fire while he tried to get into the car. Ken took out another Blackshirt before being hit three times in the chest and falling in a dead heap. Somehow Nick managed to get into the driving seat and drive away despite only really being able to use one arm. A hail of shots was fired at the car in an attempt to hit Nick, the tyres or the petrol tank but somehow, with tyres screeching, Nick managed to get away. The ATS cars had been parked well out of the way to avoid being seen so, by the time the Blackshirts were mobile, Nick was long gone. Nick drove back to the safe house, blood dripping from his wound, sometimes changing direction or performing switchbacks to make sure he had shaken off any following Blackshirts. He almost passed out from the pain and loss of blood but, somehow, he made it back to the safe house.

As Nick drove into the grounds of the safe house, Jack Kingsbury was already on his way to the car having spotted that Nick was alone. Nick got out of the car, covered in blood and collapsed into Jack's arms. Jack helped him into the house and shouted for the others to help.

When Jenny saw Nick, she screamed. "Nick what's happened? You're bleeding! You've been shot!"

"It's alright Jen, it's just a shoulder wound. I'll be OK."

"Nick you've lost a lot of blood." She lay him down on the sofa and started to carefully remove his bloodstained shirt.

"What's happened boy? Where are Ken and Del?" asked Idris, expecting the worst.

"They're dead Taff. Gunned down by the Blackshirts. They were waiting for us! We were set up Taff!"

"Take it easy Nick! You'll make yourself worse if you get too worked up," said Jenny, trying to calm him down. "You can tell us about it properly when I've got your shoulder sorted but for now just rest."

"Were you followed boy?" asked Idris.

"No, I don't think so. I'm sure I shook them off."

"Just in case, Taff, you'd better go and keep a lookout outside. I'll get the car moved out of sight and then I'll join you," said Graham. "As long as the ATS are not on their way here, we can talk about it more when Nick's feeling a bit better."

Jonathan just stood staring at Nick with a look of pure terror on his face as memories of the past came flooding back. He had already lost his parents; he could not bear to think that he could have lost Nick as well.

Jenny continued to clean up Nick's wound. Although he had lost a lot of blood, once the wound was properly dressed and the shoulder immobilised, she expected him to make a full recovery.

"I'm so relieved that you weren't killed Nick," said Jenny as she put his arm in a sling. "I knew you shouldn't have gone. I told you not to go! You thought I was just being hysterical."

"I was the lucky one Jen. I came back. Ken and Del are dead."

"Just try and get some rest for a while," said Jenny.

By the time Idris and Graham returned, having satisfied themselves that Nick had not been followed, they found that Nick had fallen into a deep sleep.

"We'll need to know the full details of what happened," said Graham "but it can wait until tomorrow. Just let him sleep for now."

"I'll stay with him tonight," said Jenny, making an improvised bed out of some cushions and an armchair.

"He will be OK, won't he?" asked Jon, finding the nerve to speak for the first time since Nick came home.

"Don't worry, Jon," Jenny replied. "I'm not going to let anything happen to him. You get off to bed and I'll see you in the morning."

****

The next morning Nick seemed a bit brighter but still very low. Jenny had redressed his shoulder and the bleeding seemed to have pretty well stopped.

"We need to talk about last night Nick, if you're feeling up to it," said Graham as the others gathered around.

"I don't know how, but somehow, they knew we were coming. They had set up an ambush for us. Just before we got there, Ken said he'd got one of his premonitions. He'd got a very bad feeling about the raid and he felt that we should call it off. I talked him out of it and Dell agreed with me. Why the hell didn't I listen to Ken and take his word for it? We had a good look around outside and couldn't see any sign of the ATS. The place was in darkness. We decided to go in anyway, despite Ken being against it. When we got inside, we found Blackshirts waiting for us and there were more outside. God knows where they had been hiding. Ken and Del were killed and I only just managed to get away."

"I'm so sorry you were in that position boy," said Idris. "I should have been there, not you!"

"It wouldn't have made any difference Taff and you just weren't well enough."

"But it was my turn to take the risk Nick. I'd never have forgiven myself if you'd been killed instead of me. It's bad enough losing Del and Ken, two good blokes as well as being damn good agents."

"It certainly looks like you were set up Nick, but how could they have found out about it? Who's passed on the information? I'd trust everybody here with my life," said Jack.

"The orders for the raid came from HQ," Graham joined in. "Perhaps there's been a leak from there."

"Could they have found some way of hacking into the DIRC?" asked Nick.

"No way," insisted Graham. "HQ insist that the technology is safe. It's so advanced that it's not possible for anybody to hack into it. I rang HQ earlier this morning to warn them that it looked like there was a leak. They're going to investigate to see if it could have come from them so we'll just have to wait and see if they come up with anything."

The atmosphere at the house was very low over the next twenty-four hours, lower than it had ever been before. Doubt, mistrust, shock and grief all took their toll on everyone. Unfortunately, worse was to come next morning.

★★★★

While the group were having breakfast, Idris happened to look out of the window and saw something which caused sudden panic. Three car loads of ATS were arriving at the house. The lead car smashed the gate and drove into the grounds. Unwittingly the cars began to go down the wider central drive, the one that was booby trapped with landmines for just such an occasion as this. There was an almighty explosion as the first car drove over a mine, putting the car and five officers out of action. The other two cars stopped, their officers out and ready for action in a second. The PDM group were already armed and ready to do battle, thanks to Idris' early warning. A shootout began in which, despite the ATS casualties, the PDM were outnumbered. They had to try to run for it. Jack and Graham gave covering fire while Nick, Idris, Jenny and Jon made a dash for the car parked at the top of the narrow drive. In the process, Idris had grabbed the DIRC in case they had to ring headquarters. The intention was that, once at the car, Idris and Nick would provide covering fire for Graham and Jack to get to a second car. Unfortunately, Graham was delayed as he needed to set an incendiary device to destroy the house and, most importantly, any information about the PDM or HQ. Device in place, Jack and Graham headed for their car. Neither of them made it. Both were gunned down by a hail of shots from the Blackshirts. The bomb, set by Graham, went off in a huge explosion which devastated the house and its contents. The explosion distracted the Blackshirts just long enough to allow the four, who had been pinned down by Blackshirt fire, to jump into the car and race away, tyres screeching, with Idris in the driving seat. Jenny was the last to get into the car and Nick was convinced he had seen a Blackshirt have her fully in his sights and lined up for a shot but then decide not to fire. He couldn't understand why the officer had not taken the shot but everything was happening so quickly that he instantly put it out of his mind. Within seconds, the car had smashed its way out of the grounds and was away up the road. Six Blackshirts jumped into one of their cars and gave chase. The remaining Blackshirts, from the other car, went to check if any information could be salvaged from the burning house and to give assistance to the occupants of the first car. Three Blackshirts had been killed outright by the mine and the other two were critically injured.

Idris and the others had a head start on their pursuers and this was an area which Idris knew better than the back of his hand. With sudden sharp turns, short cuts down narrow alleyways and other diversionary action he managed to shake them off. When he was sure that the Blackshirts were no longer following, he pulled off the road and turned into the car park of an old, empty, disused factory. He parked the car well out of sight from the road. The door to the factory was easily forced and the group went inside to shelter and hide.

"We'll have to go to H.Q.," said Idris "but I'll have to ring them on the DIRC and get clearance first. They may not want us there after everything that's happened. They won't put headquarters at any risk just to help us and, let's face it, somebody from the house is a mole."

Idris walked well away from the group to make the call in private. From the expression on Idris' face, Nick could tell that the conversation was not going too well and it wasn't going to be a simple welcome.

Idris ended the call and returned to the others. "They want us to stay right where we are and wait. They're going to send two senior agents down here to meet us. The agents are going to investigate what's happened. If they decide it's safe and only if they decide it's safe, they will take us to headquarters. It'll take them about two hours to get here so in the meantime make yourselves as comfortable as you can."

Chapter 9.

SUSPICION AND CONFESSION

The four, Idris Llewellyn, Nick Kaydon, Jenny Oakwood and Jonathan Patterson, waited in the cold and discomfort of the derelict factory for the arrival of the PDM's investigating agents. All were apprehensive but Jenny appeared much more nervous than the rest and getting worse by the minute.

"Headquarters seem to be taking this all pretty seriously," said Nick. "Do they really think it's one of us?"

"Either us or one of the dead men," said Idris "and they would be pretty unlucky if one of them had informed on us and then got themselves killed. The annoying thing is that there was nobody from the house that I wouldn't trust completely."

"Do you know the guys who are coming?" Nick asked the big Welshman.

"I've met them before, Dominic Welland and Jim Donlon. They've got a lot of investigative experience. If anyone can get to the bottom of this, they will."

"This is all stupid," said Jenny, obviously irritated by the wait. "If the informer was one of the dead men there won't be any way of proving it. We are hanging around all this time, risking being found and arrested by the Blackshirts, probably all for nothing."

"Whether they find the mole or not, we won't get into headquarters. unless we are all cleared by these guys. A possible mole at HQ. puts every PDM member in danger," said Idris.

"What happens if they can't prove that we're in the clear?" asked Nick.

"I don't know for sure boy, but we definitely won't get into headquarters. I suspect we might get cut adrift to fend for ourselves and try to avoid being found by the Blackshirts."

"When are they going to get here?" asked Jenny, not hiding her irritation at all. "They're taking their time! I thought they would be here in two hours. This waiting is driving me insane."

"Relax Jenny! It's only just over two hours since I rang them. They've probably just got stuck in traffic or something. They're not going to rush too much and risk drawing attention to themselves. Being stopped for speeding wouldn't be a good idea," Taff replied. "Don't let it get to you girl. We've all had enough of waiting and wondering."

"I'm alright Idris!" snapped Jenny, who was clearly not alright. "I just want to get it all sorted out, over and done with."

Jonathan, as always when things were going badly, remained tight lipped and deep within his own thoughts. He had noticed one thing which worried him deeply. He had noticed just how nervous Jenny was becoming. Everyone was obviously concerned about the uncertainty of the situation but Jenny was visibly becoming distraught and distressed. He wondered if the others had noticed. More importantly, he wondered why.

About half an hour later, they heard a vehicle pull in to the car park. Idris opened the door a little and peered out gingerly. He saw a white van with two men getting out. He recognised them immediately and quickly let them in to the factory, checking carefully that there was no-one else around to see.

"Hello Dom, Jim. We were beginning to think you'd never get here boys."

"Sorry to keep you waiting Taff. We got here as soon as we could. It looks like we've got a bit of a nasty problem to sort out. I'd better introduce myself to your friends first. I am Dominic Welland and my colleague here is Jim Donlon."

Idris introduced the rest of the group.

"As I'm sure you know," continued Welland, "we are the investigation team from PDM headquarters. We have to find out if you have a mole and decide if you can be cleared to go to headquarters. Unless we can clear you, you won't be allowed anywhere near HQ, so we need to make sure we get to the bottom of what happened. Why don't we start, Taff, with you filling me in on what exactly took place?"

"A couple of days ago we carried out a raid on a pharmaceutical warehouse. It was a three handed job. I was supposed to go but I had to cry off at the last minute with a stomach bug. Nick here went instead of me. Nick, Ken Townsend and Derek McCarthy were the team that went. The Blackshirts were there waiting for them and had set up an ambush. Ken and Dell were killed. Nick was hit in the shoulder but managed to get away."

"I knew Del quite well. He was one of the best. His wife Charley and his daughter Madison are in bits. Someone's got a lot to answer for. Obviously the Blackshirts had been tipped off," said Dominic Welland, who noticed that a tear came into Jenny's eyes when he mentioned Derek McCarthy's family.

Taff continued. "This morning the ATS hit the safe house just as we were having breakfast. Whoever told them where the house was didn't do such a great job because they obviously hadn't been warned that the main drive was booby trapped. We had laid land mines. The leading car hit a mine and was blown up. There were two other car loads of Blackshirts. Graham Tucker and Jack Kingsbury were killed in the shoot-out. Luckily, we managed to get away."

"Could they have got any information about the PDM from the house?" asked Jim Donlon, who had been quiet up to that point although he had been carefully watching everybody's reactions as the story had been told.

"No Jim! Graham blew the place up to destroy anything that might have been useful," said Taffy.

"That sounds typical of Graham. He was a quiet man but always on the ball and reliable," said Donlon. "We've lost some good men."

"Headquarters have investigated at their end and they're convinced that they're clean. That makes it look like it has to be someone from the house," continued Welland. "Of course, it could have been one of the guys who got killed but it's not likely that the ATS would be careless enough to kill their informant."

Jenny was beginning to lose control, nervously rubbing her hands and tears starting to trickle down her cheeks.

"Was anyone ever left on their own, either at the house or outside?" asked Welland.

"Never Dom!" replied Taffy. "When we went out, we always made sure that we were in a group of at least two. When most of us were out we always made sure that there were at least two people at the house. We all knew the rules and we stuck to them."

"That's not quite true," piped up Jonathan, who had also clearly seen Jenny's reaction.

"What do you mean Jon?" asked Nick. "Do you know something? If you do, you'd better tell us."

The boy started tentatively and reluctantly. "Well … When everyone else was out, leaving me and Jenny on our own at the house, there were two or three times when Jenny went outside on her own for a while. She said that she just needed a bit of fresh air. I asked her not to, but she said she was going stir crazy just hanging around the house all the time. She said that she knew it was against the rules but it didn't really matter. It wouldn't do any harm. She asked me not to say anything because it would only cause trouble. She was never gone for long, twenty minutes at most."

"Is that right Jenny?" asked Nick. "What were you doing? What were you thinking? You knew it was wrong but you did it anyway and asked Jon to lie to cover for you. What's going on Jen?"

Jenny, who had now even started to shake, finally broke down in a flood of hysterical tears. As she started to regain a little composure, sniffing back the tears and the mucous, she began to explain.

"When we ran away, I was worried about my grandmother. I didn't have any other family to look after her. She's eighty-two and she worries about things. I wanted to let her know that I was alright but I wouldn't be able to see her for a while. I rang her on my mobile but nobody answered so I rang a neighbour of hers who used to help her with shopping and stuff like that. She told me that my gran had been arrested and taken away by the ATS a couple of days earlier. I rang ATS headquarters to try to find out what they had done with her. They put me on to their senior officer, Chief Commanding Officer Quinlan. He knew who I was without me telling him. He said that he would let my gran go if I gave him information about the next PDM raid. If I didn't give him the information he wanted, he would send her for Age Acceleration. I didn't know about the raid on the pharmaceutical warehouse then. I said I would ring him when I knew something. I couldn't let my own gran be killed. I couldn't sign her death warrant. He agreed he would hold on to my gran for a few days, to give me time to get some information. When I found out about the raid, I rang Quinlan and told him. He said he would let my gran go."

"How could you be so stupid Jen?" interrupted Nick. "If Quinlan arrested your gran, she would have gone for Age Acceleration within twenty-four hours. She would already have been dead when Quinlan was bargaining with you for her life."

"I didn't realise that! I had no idea! I thought I was saving her life! I'm so sorry!" Feeling even more distraught and afraid, Jenny continued. "I told him about the raid. That's why I didn't want you to go, Nick. I swear I would never have told them anything if I'd known you would be there! When I found out that you were going instead of Idris, I rang Quinlan again and told him that the raid had been postponed for a few days but he obviously didn't believe me. I never told him anything about the house. I didn't tell him where it was! You have to believe that!"

"When you rang Quinlan, did you ring him on a normal mobile?" asked Donlon.

"Yes of course I did! I had no other way to ring him."

"You didn't need to tell him where the house was. The ATS can trace a mobile in no time at all. They would have had your position pinpointed before the end of the first call. I guess that explains why they didn't know about the mines," said Welland.

"I'm so sorry! I never meant for anyone to get killed and I never meant to put you in danger, Nick, I swear!"

"So, we know who the mole is, now we have the problem of deciding what to do about you. We can't really let you go back to the ATS and we can't let you go free at PDMs headquarters, in case you pass on more information," said Welland.

"I promise you I won't," pleaded Jenny.

"I actually believe you," said Welland, "but we just can't take a chance on that. If the Blackshirts ever found our headquarters the PDM would be destroyed. That leaves two alternatives. The simple one would be to shoot you right now, but we're not like the ATS and I'm sure your friends wouldn't want that. The other alternative is to take you back to headquarters and lock you away in the prison block."

"How long would I be locked up for?"

"It would have to be until our fight with The Party is over," answered Jim Donlon.

"That means I could be locked up for the rest of my life."

"I won't lie to you Jenny," said Donlon. "It is a possibility. Who knows? Unfortunately, I'm afraid that's the best we can do for you."

Jenny was overtaken by a sudden fit of sheer panic and made a bolt for the door. Donlon and Welland both raised their hand guns but, before either of them could get off a shot, Jon flung himself at both men, knocking Welland's gun to the floor and taking Donlon to the ground. Welland was the first to recover, as the winded Donlon was struggling to his feet. By the time he got to the door, Jenny was already sprinting across the car park, heading for the street. Welland raised his firearm and lined up his sights on Jenny's back. He had a clear and easy shot. All he had to do was pull the trigger to stop her in her tracks. He hesitated for a moment and then relaxed his trigger finger and lowered his weapon. Jenny, oblivious to what was going on behind her, carried on running until she was out of sight.

Welland rounded on Jonathan. "Don't you ever do anything like that again young man! You've not only let a prisoner escape but you could easily have got yourself killed!"

"I'm sorry but I couldn't let you shoot her," replied the boy. "Anyway, why didn't you fire when you had the chance? You could have taken her out easily."

"I guess I'm a bit like you son. I couldn't just shoot an unarmed woman in the back. I hope she doesn't know any more secrets that will come back to haunt us."

"I don't think she'd know anything important Dom," said Idris. "She's never been told anything about headquarters. I think we're safe."

"I hope you're right Taff. If there's no risk to us it's probably best that she got away. I don't know how well she'd have coped with being locked up, possibly for the rest of her life," said Welland. "I hope she doesn't get picked up by the ATS. I don't know what kind of reception she'd get from them. She's already helped them but they'll need a lot of convincing that she doesn't know anything else and they won't forget that she didn't warn them about the landmines."

"Perhaps I'd better go after her," said Nick, feeling a need to protect her.

"Forget that idea right now!" said Welland. "You're going nowhere except to HQ with us!"

"Dom we'd better get going. Now! "Interrupted Jim Donlon. "If we hang around much longer, we could have the ATS knocking on the door. We'd best dump the car here. The Blackshirts might have the registration number. We'll drive you lads to headquarters in the van. Come on! Let's go!"

Nick was still in a state of shock and turmoil over Jenny's confession as they started their journey. He still desperately wanted to go after her and keep her safe but he knew that was impossible.

Chapter 10.
THE DAILY PARTY NEWS

It was almost three p.m. at Hoddington Brook School and a maths lesson was just drawing to a close.

"Put your books away quietly, The Daily Party News will be starting in five minutes," said Mr Rhodes, a small, elderly maths teacher, nicknamed Dusty by his pupils, who had been struggling to get them to pay attention for the past hour.

The Daily Party News was a political broadcast put out by The Party, which went on air every day at three p.m. precisely. The Party would have people believe that it was a news programme but in reality, it was pure Party propaganda and fake news, repeated over and over again in an attempt to keep people brainwashed. There was a large television screen at the front of the classroom. The set was fitted with a timer which was set by The Party and could not be interfered with. The set was automatically switched on at three p.m. and switched off at the end of the broadcast. It was impossible for anyone to manually turn the set off and in fact it was illegal to do so. Television sets with the same timers, fixed by the authorities, were compulsory in every house, office, factory, school, shop, hospital and any other building where people might be present at the time of the broadcast. There were even sets in certain places on the streets. At three p.m. every day everything else had to stop and The Party broadcast had to be watched. Small screens were even fitted in all vehicles and, when the broadcast came on, the driver had to pull over, park and watch it. No ifs nor buts, if the security forces found anyone not watching the programme there were very grave consequences. Only the security forces themselves were granted exemption from having to watch.

As he put his books away, Joshua Kerley quietly confided in his friend, Stuart Woodleigh, that he was beginning to have doubts about some of the information that was shown in the broadcasts.

"You shouldn't be saying that, Josh," said Stuart. "After all you're a Corporal in the Party Youth Movement. You've always been more committed to The Party than any of us."

"I know," replied Josh very quietly, "but I've had some doubts for a while. You know what happened to my grandad. He was arrested because I informed on him. They lied to me. I thought he would only be sentenced to Civil Correction and I didn't think that Civil Correction would be that big a deal. I thought it was just a case of re-educating him in party loyalty. How wrong was I? They sent him for Age Acceleration. I signed my own grandfather's death warrant. They sent my father for Civil Correction for no reason except he had listened to my grandad. I don't know what they did to him. Dad won't talk about it but it's left him a completely broken man. He's afraid of everything now! He won't talk to people in case he says the wrong thing and it gets back to The Party. He won't go out because he's afraid he'll get arrested again. He won't even decide what he wants for dinner in case he makes the wrong choice. I have to be the adult of the family. God only knows what they've done to make him act the way he does. How can that happen? I've destroyed my family just to get praise from my senior officer and promotion to Corporal. If the party can do that and lie about it, what else are they lying about? I don't know, but one day I'll find out. One day I'll get revenge for my family being destroyed."

"I understand how you feel Josh. I sympathise, I really do, but be careful what you're saying. Don't mention anything about this to anyone else or we could both be in serious trouble. Of course, you can trust me not to say anything Josh. I've had some doubts too but let's just keep it between us for now," said Stuart.

Joshua and Stuart had been best friends for a couple of years so Josh felt safe talking to him. Fortunately, none of the other pupils had overheard the conversation. Mr. Rhodes, not always the sharpest tool in the box and a little deaf, was also unaware of the conversation.

"All of you be quiet now! The broadcast is starting!" shouted Mr. Rhodes.

The screen lit up. There was a fanfare loud enough to wake the deepest sleeper while the date was displayed on the screen with the title, THE DAILY PARTY NEWS. This was followed by several seconds of pastoral music while some of the most beautiful views of the country were shown. Everything then cut to a man, the leader of The Party, standing in a huge office. A caption at the bottom of the screen introduced the man as PRESIDENT NIGEL VALENTINE, LEADER OF THE UNITED CONSERVATIVE AND NATIONALIST PARTY.

Nigel Valentine was a slim man, in his late fifties, clean shaven with short, grey, immaculately groomed hair. He wore a smart, expensive, light grey suit, a pristine white shirt and a pale blue tie. Despite his best attempt to appear jovial and a man of the people, his demeanour oozed the honesty and integrity of a dodgy used car salesman combined with the ruthlessness of an assassin who could strike at any moment.

He began speaking. "When The Party came to power, over thirty years ago, the United Kingdom was in a terrible, fragmented state. Drastic changes had to be made. The President at that time, President Grosvenor, decided that we needed to judge what British interests were and we should be resolute in defending them. He decided on the road he was resolved to follow, the path he had to go. He asked all who had spirit … the bold, the steadfast and the young in heart, to stand and join with him as they went forward. You, the British people, responded as you always have. The Wind of Change was blowing through the land. Thanks to that government and subsequent governments we made vast changes and huge improvements. This did not come about because of consensus. It happened because we said, 'This we believe, this we will do. It is called Leadership!

We achieved great success. Where there was discord, we brought harmony. Where there was error, we brought truth. Where there was doubt, we brought faith and where there was despair, we brought hope. We created a strong and stable government and now most of our people have never had it so good!

The Party was the future once. Now we are the past, the present and the future and will continue to be so for a very long time! I would rather be dead in a ditch than to allow this country to fall back into the state it once was!

Our successes are numerous and ongoing. We still continue to ensure that everyone can receive some level of medical care. Some of our hospitals have state of the art equipment and provide cutting edge treatment. We have massively reduced the numbers of the elderly requiring state care and nursing. We have cut the number of homeless on the streets by ninety per cent. We have reduced the number of convicted criminals who reoffend to almost zero.

While there have occasionally been shortages of some foods, we have been able to provide a vast quantity of cheap food in the form of HCR, so no-one will ever need to starve.

We have saved many of you a fortune by taking away the bodies of your loved ones, making it unnecessary for you to face the cost of burial or cremation.

There has been some talk amongst you about Climate Change, even sometimes being called a Climate Emergency. This is false information spread by people with their own agenda. The National Climate Agency has been monitoring climate, not only in the United Kingdom but worldwide, for over twenty-five years. The NCA have confirmed that there is NO CLIMATE EMERGENCY! It is true that there have been some instances of extreme weather in the last few years but the NCA are confident that these are only due to natural climate variation. If anything could be done about them, we would already have done it. THIS IS NOT A CATASTROPHIC SITUATION AND WILL SETTLE DOWN NATURALLY IN TIME! Anyone putting forward views about the climate, other than the official view of The Party, will be dealt with MOST SEVERELY!

Three months ago, the North West was hit by a severe storm. Some people referred to it as Hurricane Edwina. Rumours were spread indicating major damage and even some deaths. These rumours were entirely false and again were spread by people with their own agenda. The storm did cause some minimal damage to property but no lives were lost. I repeat NOT ONE LIFE WAS LOST! In fact, the storm never reached hurricane status and the emergency services were completely in control of the situation. Once again, I must warn you that anyone spreading these slanderous accusations WILL BE SEVERELY PUNISHED!"

In fact, Hurricane Edwina, named after the Vice-President, had wreaked devastation on the North West coast. The truth was that over a hundred people were believed to have been killed. An estimated fifteen million pounds worth of damage had been caused by severe winds and flooding. The only response from The Party had been denial of the truth. The emergency services had done their best, helped by some off duty Brownshirts, the general public and even the PDM, but had been overwhelmed. No official government help had been provided and the only government response was denial.

The President continued. "We continue to maintain peace and prosperity in the land. A peace which is only broken on occasions by that group of anarchistic terrorists, the PDM. The Vice-President will tell you more about that but THE RULE OF LAW MUST PREVAIL OVER THE RULE OF THE MOB as we strive to make Britain a country THAT WORKS FOR EVERYONE!"

This was followed by a long spell of canned applause, until the camera cut away to show a woman. The caption at the bottom of the screen introduced her as VICE-PRESIDENT EDWINA SYKES, DEPUTY LEADER OF THE UNITED CONSERVATIVE AND NATIONALIST PARTY.

Edwina Sykes was a very attractive woman in her late forties. She had very sleek black hair, pulled back tightly and fastened at the back in an immaculate bun. Her face was quite heavily made up. She was dressed in a close-fitting charcoal grey suit and a royal blue silk blouse which revealed just a hint of cleavage. Her aura was a mix of seductive dominatrix and ruthless high-powered business woman. She spoke with a soft, cultured but nevertheless powerful voice.

The Vice-President continued from where the President had left off.

"There is one very large problem which we must eradicate immediately and we can only do that with your help. That problem is the so-called People's Democratic Movement. Make no mistake, the PDM are not of the people and they are not democratic. They are terrorists, thugs and murderers. They cost you, the taxpayer, billions of pounds every year by their blatant destruction of state, public and private property. They constantly carry out murderous unprovoked attacks on security forces and innocent civilians. Only three days ago, they planted a bomb in a school in Derby. The explosion killed three teachers, twenty-seven innocent children and severely injured many more. A large part of the school building was also destroyed. What kind of people wage war on young innocent children? The root cause of their threat is their extremist ideology itself. A twisted ideology which has no aim except annihilation of our society. This extreme world view is their gateway and violence is their ultimate destination. We must successfully wipe these foul devils and their ideology from the face of the earth. While they have been murdering the innocent, our brave security forces have been tirelessly waging war on them. The good news is THAT WE ARE WINNING AND WE WILL PREVAIL!

We will not stop until they have all been destroyed! To assist with this, one of our brave heroes has been promoted to take charge of the war against the PDM. Former Chief Commanding Officer Glyn Quinlan of the ATS has been made Commander of all security forces and has been admitted to the Inner Circle of Ministers of The Party, the small group who, along with President Valentine and myself, have the responsibility of ruling and protecting our country. I will leave you with the words of The Declaration of our great country."

The Declaration had long since replaced the National Anthem.

"Please all stand and repeat the words with me:

I DECLARE THAT I LOVE MY COUNTRY!
I LOVE THE PARTY!
I will always do everything in my power to uphold THE PARTY!
I will never doubt the LEADERS OF THE PARTY!
I will always protect THE PARTY from criticism and danger, whether this comes from an external power, internal terrorists or from my fellow citizens!
I will always believe in THE PARTY!
I will always defend THE PARTY, right or wrong!
I will always put THE PARTY before my family, my friends and myself!
MY COUNTRY FIRST!
MY PARTY FIRST!"

The boys had all stood up to loyally proclaim The Declaration with their right fists clenched against their left breast, directly over their heart, in a gesture of love and loyalty.

Finally, the broadcast came to a conclusion with more pastoral music and more shots of the beautiful British countryside.

Every day people watched The Party propaganda. Every day people stood, fist on heart and repeated The Declaration. Despite all this brainwashing, Joshua was beginning to have very strong doubts about the truth, so was Stuart. They were not the only ones.

Chapter 11.

BROOKSLADE AIRFIELD

PDM investigators Dominic Welland and Jim Donlon were in a van with Idris Llewellyn, Nick Kaydon and Jonathan Patterson, on their way to PDM headquarters.

"Where are we going?" asked Nick. "I've no idea where H.Q. is."

"No-one's supposed to know until they need to go there," replied Dom Welland. "The less people who know, the safer it is. Taffy's been there a couple of times in the past."

"Yes, but not for quite a long time, boy, although I don't suppose it'll have changed much," said the big Welshman.

"You'd probably be surprised Taff. The tech boys have taken over part of it and they seem to be performing miracles with some of the stuff they are working on. The Party could be in for a shock soon but you'll find out about that all in good time. We've recently set up a school as well, with the families living there. There are quite a few children over quite a wide age range, all needing an education or at least as much of an education as we can provide. It's difficult to cover a full range of subjects as we have so few teachers. Charley McCarthy, Del's widow, organised some of the mothers to set it up and they do a pretty good job in the circumstances. No doubt Charley will want to see Jon once you're settled in."

"I don't want to go to school, I just want to fight Blackshirts!" exclaimed Jonathan.

"Time enough for that when you're a bit older son. For now, you need to keep up with your education. Boys your age are not allowed to fight for us but you'll get your chance soon enough," continued Dom. "We're headed for Brookslade, a small village in North Yorkshire, between Ripon and Thirsk. Headquarters is set up at a disused airfield near the village."

The airfield and it's attached barracks had been built in 1936 and was initially used for training new RAF recruits. During the Second World War it was used by Bomber Command for night bombing raids. After the war it reverted to being a training establishment until 1992 when it was transferred from the RAF to the Army Air Corps, being used by 12 Regiment of the AAC. In 2016 it was taken over by the Royal Logistics Corps before finally being closed down completely in 2031. It was left empty and unused, to become derelict. The airfield's two runways were ripped up so that no planes could land there but the buildings were just left empty. The buildings consisted of several large hangars, a large workshop, storage buildings, an office block, a canteen with a large kitchen and barracks. There was also an accommodation block consisting of flats, built to house the families of service men, now housing the families of married agents. All of the buildings had fallen into a state of disrepair but had provided the basis of a base for the PDM when they moved in four years ago. While they had carried out repairs on most of the buildings to make them habitable and utilizable, they had resisted making obvious visible renovations to hide the fact that the base was occupied. H.Q. was in fact home for two hundred and twenty PDM agents. Wives and children increased the total number of people living on the base to three hundred and sixty-six.

The hangars were used to store vehicles, weapons, equipment and explosives. They also provided some additional workshop space for the technicians and mechanics, in addition to the workshop block. The land itself had become overgrown with bushes and dense undergrowth, apart from the vehicle tracks, as nature had taken over the airfield. One side of the airfield was fairly close to the main road between Thirsk and Ripon. Fortunately, it was well shielded from the road by several dense rows of pine trees which provided more than adequate cover. Another side of the airfield was hidden by Brookslade Wood, a large forest of oak, ash, yew and sycamore trees. The rest of the perimeter was hidden by Brookslade Wood Farm, a large dairy farm run by Sam Jarvis and his two sons, Jacob and Michael. Although they were not actively involved, the Jarvis family were staunch supporters of the PDM and did all that they could to help keep headquarters secret, including getting food supplies from a nearby farmers market to avoid arousing suspicion. Occasionally they would pick up supplies in Brookslade, the village about a mile and a half away, but usually only if they were buying small quantities.

Headquarters could be accessed by driving through the yard of Brookslade Wood Farm. However, to avoid arousing suspicion, it was usually accessed via a rough track between the trees in Brookslade Wood.

The set-up was potentially fraught with danger and yet worked very well. Three hundred and sixty-six people and all the necessary equipment were successfully hidden away right under the noses of the ATS and they never suspected a thing. Headquarters and the people in it could only survive by maintaining very strict discipline. There were rigid restrictions on how many people could be outside at any one time, to avoid attracting unwelcome attention. Everything was hidden away. Nothing was left out in the open. If any drones or aeroplanes approached, the base's radar picked them up in plenty of time to make sure nothing could be seen from the air. All windows were fitted with heavy blackout curtains or shutters which had to be closed whenever lights were switched on. Outside lights were all shielded to ensure that light could only shine directly downwards but these were turned off if the radar picked up any approaching drones or aircraft. The same applied to lights in the hangars and workshops which were also blacked out. The use of mobile phones or any other kind of communication device, apart from the DIRCs, was forbidden under any circumstances, to avoid calls being traced. Admission to headquarters had to be authorised in advance. Any PDM agents not based at Brookslade had to get permission for access to headquarters and that could only be done via the DIRC. Anyone who turned up without authorisation put themselves in serious danger as sentries were prepared to shoot first and ask questions later.

There were hundreds more PDM agents out in the field, living in safehouses or in their own homes, but H.Q. was the place where all PDM actions were organised and authorised. This was the place where plans were made, plans which hopefully would lead one day to The Party being overthrown. As yet, the PDM were not strong enough to do that on their own. They would need help and a lot of it, but they never stopped believing that one day it would happen. One day people would be released from the oppression of the Valentine regime; from the oppression of The Party.

"It shouldn't take us long now," said driver Jim Donlon, "only about another fifteen minutes. The boss will want to see you as soon as we arrive, Commander George Richmond. He's a good bloke but strict on discipline. He has to be to avoid the ATS breaking us. We'd be sitting ducks if they ever found out where headquarters was. He really cares about his men and the public. I informed H.Q. what had happened before we started out. I'll ring them again a couple of minutes before we arrive. To turn up without being expected is a good way to risk ending up dead."

George Richmond was a tall, statesmanlike fifty-five year old who appeared more like a politician than a fighting man. Reality was different to image. In his time, he had fought in many actions for the PDM. In fact, he had been quite a hero. He had been the leader for the past five years, five years in which the PDM had become far more organised and efficient. Every agent had the utmost respect for George Richmond.

Donlon made his call on the DIRC and was told to drive into headquarters by the route through Brookslade Wood. As they entered the premises, a hangar had already been opened so that they could drive the van straight in, out of sight.

They were greeted by Alex Munroe, a small, wiry Glaswegian nicknamed Jock. Jock Munroe was well known by Dom Welland, Jim Donlon and Idris Llewellyn. Taff introduced him to Nick and Jonathan.

"I'll show you guys to your quarters and let you get settled in," said Jock. "The boss wants to see ye in an hour so I'll come and collect ye then. Taff, I've arranged for you to share a room with Nick and the wee laddie, so you can help them find their feet."

"I'm not a wee laddie!" exclaimed Jonathan angrily.

"Steady on son," said Alex. "No offence intended! It's just my way of saying that you're a boy. I can see that you've got plenty of spirit. That'll keep you in good stead around here."

The barracks, which had originally consisted of long, open, communal, dormitory type bedrooms, had been divided by wooden partitions into smaller rooms. Jim Donlon and Dominic Welland already had their own quarters. Idris, Nick and Jon were shown to their room.

"I'll let ye get yerselves settled in," said Alex. "I'll come back in an hour to take you to the guvnor. I'd better warn you, he's not in a great mood today."

"Alright boy," said Taff. "Thanks for the heads up. We'll see you in a while."

The room provided little in terms of comfort although it was adequate, three single beds, a small table with four chairs, three lockers and a cupboard. It wasn't much but it was home for the foreseeable future.

Later they were taken for a debriefing with George Richmond, as they expected. He welcomed them to headquarters and they told him their version of the events at the house. He had already been informed by Welland and Donlon but he wanted to hear the story first hand.

"You've certainly had it pretty hard in the last couple of days," said the Commander. "Hopefully, things will stay quiet for a few days while you settle in. How are your quarters?"

"Not as comfortable as the safe house but we'll be fine," replied Nick.

"Get used to it," said the Commander. "You could be here for a long time."

"At least the food will probably be better," said Idris. "Graham Tucker was a good bloke but a pretty awful cook. His culinary skills weren't up to scratch."

"I don't think you'll have much to complain about on that score," replied Richmond with a smile. "Our cooks work wonders with our supplies. The rules here are pretty similar to those at the safehouse but there are some extra ones regarding keeping everything hidden from sight. Blackout curtains have to be drawn before any lights are turned on. Lights have to be turned off before external doors are opened. Vehicles are never parked in the open. They are always driven straight into a hangar. That sort of thing. It might seem a bit daunting at first but you'll soon pick everything up."

"Excuse me asking sir," Nick started very tentatively, "but I can't help worrying about Jenny, even after all she has done and I know Jonathan feels the same. Could I have permission to go and look for her, to check if she's alright?"

"I've heard how close the two of you had become Nick and I can only imagine how you must be feeling at the moment but it wouldn't be safe to go back right now. The Blackshirts will still be sniffing around and we can't risk you getting caught. Let things settle for a few days and then I'll reconsider your request. Tomorrow you and Jon will need to see Charley McCarthy to sort out Jon's education. We need to make sure the children get as normal a life as possible while they are here. Now, I don't know about you lads but I'm getting pretty hungry and it's time for dinner so I'll take you to the canteen. We all eat together here. I can start introducing you to the others as well," said the Commander.

Chapter 12.
CHARLEY, MADDY AND THE SEARCH FOR JENNY

The school was based in part of the block of flats, alongside the airfield, which also provided accommodation for some of the families. It did not provide a lot of space for the classes but it was more than adequate as there were only thirty-two children of school age. The biggest problem was that those thirty-two children were spread over the whole age spectrum, from five-year-olds to sixteen-year-olds, making teaching very challenging. Charley McCarthy, widow of Derek McCarthy, had done an excellent job in organising some of the agent's wives as teachers. Some of them, like Charley herself, had previous teaching experience but some had to learn to teach on the job. Some of the technical staff also helped with the older children, when their expertise was useful and they were able to find the time. Despite the difficulties, Charley had managed to pull everything together to enable the children to have a decent education.

Nick knocked on the door which he had been told was Charley's office. He and Jonathan had gone to see her about Jonathan's schooling. Upon hearing a voice calling, "Come in!" Nick opened the door and the pair entered the office. Charley McCarthy sat behind her desk. She was petite, trim and very attractive, with shoulder length, wavy, auburn hair and a smile that could charm the birds from the trees. When she spoke, she had a very slight, attractive Merseyside twang, nowhere near as strong as her late husband's scouse accent.

"Hi, I'm Charlotte McCarthy. People call me Charley," she said as she stood up to shake hands with Nick and Jon. "You must be Jonathan and Nick. When I said call me Charley, that goes for you too Jonathan. We don't stand on ceremony around here. You don't need to call me Mrs. McCarthy. The same goes for the other teachers. As long as we are treated with respect, the names are not important. So, Jonathan, tell me what subjects you would like to be taught. Obviously, Maths and English are compulsory. We're a bit limited in some subjects but, if you tell me what you're interested in, I'll see if we can cover it."

"Well, I guess science subjects mainly and maybe I.T. I'm not really keen on languages or history and stuff like that."

"I think we can do that. The techies and the mechanics here give us a hand with the teaching when they have time. That's a massive help with physics, I.T., electronics and engineering. They have no teacher training but what they don't know about their own field of expertise isn't worth knowing and they seem to really enjoy interacting with the students. I'm trained to teach biology so that's no problem. How does that sound?" asked Charley.

"That sounds OK, better than I was expecting," replied Jonathan.

"Jon wasn't keen on going back to school. He wanted to be more active with the PDM," added Nick.

"Time enough for that when you're older young man. First you need to look after your future," said Charley. "Let the adults take care of the fighting."

Jonathan smiled at Charley's comment, a fake smile out of politeness.

"While you're both here," continued Charley, "there's someone else that I'd like you both to meet and she loves to meet new people."

She got up and went into the next room. When she came back, she was guiding a young girl by the hand. The girl pulled up a chair and sat beside Charley.

"This is Madison, my daughter, Maddy for short," said Charley.

Nick noticed that Maddy's eyes were permanently closed as though she was blind.

"Hello Maddy, I'm Nick and this is Jonathan. We're very pleased to meet you," said Nick.

"I'm afraid she can't hear you," said Charley. "She's deaf-blind. She's been like that since she was born and before you say you're sorry, we don't allow pity, neither self-pity nor pity from other people. We just learn to cope and make the best of life."

Nick noticed that Charley was signing into Maddy's hand and Maddy returned the signing.

"Is that how you communicate with her?" asked Nick. "That must be difficult."

"It's tactile sign language," said Charley. "She can't see me signing, like a sighted deaf person would, so she puts her hands over mine so that she can feel what I'm signing and then she does the same to me. Sometimes she uses Tadoma."

"What's that?" asked Nick.

"She puts her thumb on my lips, her little finger on my throat and the other fingers along my jaw, then when I speak, she can feel the vibration and recognises the words. She tends to use that more when she is with people that she knows and is comfortable with. I've already told her that you and Jon are here and she's asked me to say Hi for her."

More signing continued before Charley continued the conversation. "She just asked me if she can feel your faces. It's her way of getting to know you. She feels the contours of your face and then she can recognise you next time, from that and from your smell."

"What do you mean from our smell?" asked Nick, a bit shocked.

"Everybody has their own personal smell that is unique to them. Most of us don't notice it but Maddy's sense of smell is really highly developed to compensate for her other senses, so she can recognise most people that she knows by their smell. It's a bit harder with you and Jonathan, because there are two of you, but she'll cope with it and she'll know the next time either of you are around."

Nick put his head forward so that his face was close to Maddy. Her hands found his face and she felt it all over. Her touch was so gentle that it felt like little more than a cobweb touching his face. When she had finished, she signed to her mother.

"She says that she likes you and you have a very kind face," said Charley.

Maddy repeated the same procedure, just as gently, with Jonathan.

"She says that she likes you too," said Charley, "but she can sense a bit of anger. I heard that you said you wanted to kill Blackshirts. I know what they did to your family so it's not surprising that you're angry but don't hold on to that hate Jon. Let it go or it'll eat away at you."

"How old is Maddy?" asked Nick.

"She's six and, as I said, she's been like this from birth. She was premature. I was only thirty-four weeks pregnant when she was born. It was touch and go as to whether she would survive for a while. She's healthy now and she's happy, that's the most important thing. Well, I won't keep you any longer, unless you've got any more questions. Maddy and I have got classes to get to."

"No! Everything's fine," said Nick.

"Thanks for coming to see me and I'll see you in school tomorrow, Jon, nine o'clock sharp."

"Thank you, Charley," said Nick. "Will you say goodbye to Maddy for us?"

After leaving the office, Nick said to Jonathan "I expected you to put up more of an argument about going back to school. What changed your mind?"

"When I realised what Maddy was having to learn and cope with I thought it's not going to do me any harm to go back to school. I think Maddy and Charley are both amazing."

Nick smiled.

★★★★

Jonathan soon settled into his new school and Nick soon settled into his new life at Brookslade but there was something still worrying them both. They were still concerned about Jenny. In spite of what she had done, Nick in particular needed to know that she was alright. He had waited for a couple of weeks before asking George Richmond once more for permission to go and find her.

Again, the Commander refused permission on the grounds that he thought it was too risky.

Later that day, Nick was talking to Idris in the privacy of their own quarters. He told Idris that, despite having been refused permission again, he had decided to go anyway.

"Are you mad, boy?" asked Taff. "Have you got a death wish? If the Blackshirts don't get you, the boss could throw the book at you when you come back! If you find Jenny, what are you going to do with her? She won't come back here just to be locked up! If you stay there, you'll be picked up by the Blackshirts in no time! For God's sake see sense boy! George Richmond wouldn't have said no if he hadn't realised the danger!"

"I don't care Taff! I have to know what's happened to her! I can't just carry on without knowing!"

"You're handling this all wrong Nick," said Idris. "I must be as mad as you boy. If I can't stop you going then I'm coming with you."

"Why put yourself at risk Taff?" asked Nick. "It's not your problem."

"If you run into the ATS you've got back up. You know we're not allowed to go anywhere alone. If you've got me for back up then you've broken one less rule. I can confirm that you've had no contact with Blackshirts if the boss doubts your loyalty. The boss has known me a lot longer than he's known you."

"Taff, I can't ask you to do that," said Nick.

"You're not asking me, boy, I'm telling you that's the way it is! If I can't stop you from going then I'm coming with you! We'll need to take a DIRC. We can ring the boss when we're on the way back. It'll give him chance to calm down a bit before we get back and it could be a bit hairy trying to get back in here if nobody's expecting us," said the big Welshman.

"Thanks Taff. You're a good friend. I owe you one. I reckon we should set off after breakfast tomorrow. I won't say anything to Jonathan. I don't want him to worry."

****

The next morning the two borrowed one of the cars, picked up a DIRC and set out on their journey. Nobody queried what they were doing or where they were going as they left H.Q. It was always much easier to get out than it was to get back in.

The journey was uneventful. There was no sign of the ATS on the way. The first point of call was Jenny's flat. They found no-one there. Most of Jenny's clothes and belongings appeared to still be there but there were signs that someone had been rummaging through the drawers and cupboards, as though the place had been searched, probably by the ATS. They found nothing to indicate where Jenny might be but, if the ATS had searched the place, things did not look good.

Nick decided to try Saint Jude's. If he could find Sister Mary-Beth she might know something. As they walked into Saint Jude's, Nick saw Sister Mary-Beth in reception. She rushed over to him.

"Doctor, what are you doing here? It's not safe! We still have visits from DDPU officers occasionally. If they find you here, we're all in trouble!" exclaimed the old nun.

She quickly ushered Nick and Idris into a small side room where they would not be disturbed or overheard.

"This is Idris," said Nick. "He's a friend of mine. Sister, I wondered if you have any idea where Jenny is. I've tried her flat and she's not there but it looks like it's been searched."

"Some time after you all left," said Mary-Beth, "Jenny came back here. She told me the full story of what she had done. I think she wanted to get the burden off her chest. She was truly sorry and very distraught. She wanted to come back to work here as a nurse. I advised her against it and told her she was putting herself in danger but she wouldn't listen. I think she thought it was the only way to make up for what she had done.

Well, the very next day, when she was on duty the ATS turned up and arrested her. They had a particularly nasty officer in charge called Quinlan. Quinlan started yelling at her, ranting about losing good men and some explosion. Something about a mine that Jenny should have warned him about. He gave her a nasty beating. I tried to stop him but I got a black eye and a blooded nose for my effort. He was out of control. I don't see the devil in many people but Quinlan certainly had the devil in him. Poor Jenny suffered his anger and, when he had finished, he arrested her and took her away. He was yelling at her that she would get the death penalty. She would go to court and then for Age Acceleration next morning. I wish I could have done more to protect her, doctor. I tried, I really did, but that man is pure evil."

"You couldn't have stopped him, Sister. I know you did what you could. I'm thankful that he didn't do more to you. At least I know what happened to Jenny now and nobody can hurt her any more. I'm sorry for putting you at risk by coming here but I didn't know where else to go," said Nick.

"That's alright doctor," said Sister Mary-Beth. "I'll just make sure the coast is clear in reception before you go. That Quinlan needs to be stopped. Hopefully, God will punish him."

"If God doesn't punish him, Sister, there's a whole lot of people queueing up to do the job for him."

Nick and Idris got safely away from Saint Jude's.

****

On the journey back, Idris said, "That old nun is a formidable character. There aren't many around like her."

"No Taff, they broke the mould when they made Sister Mary-Beth. She's afraid of nothing and nobody, not even Glyn Quinlan. One day Quinlan will get what's coming to him. I'll make sure of that, especially now he's been made head of all of the security forces," said Nick, the sorrow of Jenny's loss temporarily being held in check by his anger towards Quinlan.

Idris used the DIRC to ring headquarters to warn them of their imminent arrival. After a severe tongue-lashing over the phone, he was told that they should both present themselves to George Richmond the moment that they got back to H.Q.

Inside the Commander's office, George Richmond laid into them in no uncertain terms. He stressed that they had put themselves and headquarters at risk and that anything similar would not be tolerated in the future. He told them that he would be justified in putting them in prison for deliberately disobeying his orders. He said that he understood why Nick had acted so stupidly, although that was no excuse, but for someone as experienced as Idris to go along with it was indefensible. Nick tried to defend his friend and take the full blame himself but Richmond was having none of it. His full anger was still directed at both men. In the end they were both ordered back to their quarters, unpunished for the time being but with a warning that the Commander would be watching them and they would suffer greatly if they dared to step out of line in future.

If facing George Richmond was hard, Nick had to face the equally daunting task of telling Jonathan about Jenny's death. Nick found Jon in the recreation room, a large room next to the canteen, used for down time. It contained a large TV, a pool table, a snooker table and two dart boards. It was Jonathan's favourite place to go when he wasn't busy. Nick explained what had happened to Jenny as carefully and as gently as he could. The boy appeared to take it in his stride but Nick knew that he was just bottling up his grief and building up an even greater hatred for the new Commander of Security Forces and Minister of Security, Glyn Quinlan.

Chapter 13.

NICK LEARNS MORE

Nick sat alone in the canteen, staring into a large mug of cold tea, the milk starting to congeal into a fine skin on top.

"Good morning, Nick! Do you mind if I join you?"

Nick was startled and brought back to reality. "Oh! Hi Charley! I'm sorry I didn't see you come in. Aren't you teaching this morning?"

"I'm on a break so I thought I'd have a change of scenery and come here for coffee instead of sitting in my office." Charley sat down and continued the conversation. "Actually, that's not strictly true. I heard about Jenny and I thought I'd see how you are doing, you and Jon. I guessed you might be in here."

"I'm surprised you care. After Del getting killed, I couldn't blame you if you thought Jenny just got what she deserved."

"There's not a day goes by when I don't wish Del was back here with me but that's not going to happen. Nothing that happened to Jenny will ever bring Del back! Jenny made a stupid, naive mistake. All she wanted was to save her gran, not to put anybody in danger and certainly not to get anyone killed. She didn't deserve to die for it. What happened will never stop you loving her and grieving for her. I know what you must be going through and that's why I was concerned about you," said Charley.

"I thought you'd probably hate Jenny," said Nick, "and maybe me too for taking her to the safe house."

"Like I said," continued Charley, "Jenny made a mistake, a pretty catastrophic mistake but she never meant for anybody to get killed. Why should I hate you? You couldn't have known what was going to happen."

"I should never have taken her with me to the safe house!" said Nick.

"You did what you thought was the best way to keep her safe, Nick. It wasn't your fault! Sometimes things just go wrong, especially if you're with the PDM. Had you been together long?" asked Charley.

"We'd been a couple for around six months. We were thinking of moving in together just before we had to run away from Saint Jude's and go to the safe house. How about you and Del?"

"Del was already on the fringe of the PDM when we met. He was involved but not in a very active way. That was seven years ago. I fell for him almost as soon as I set eyes on him. He seemed different to anyone I'd ever been with before. It wasn't long before I fell pregnant with Maddy. We decided the safest thing would be to see if we could move to headquarters. Del wanted to be more involved with the PDM anyway and he thought Maddy and I would be safer here. We got married and came here just before Maddy was born." Just a hint of a tear glistened in Charley's eyes.

"How do you cope with it?" asked Nick, starting to feel a bit ashamed for wallowing in his own grief and self-pity.

"I keep busy and it helps to have Maddy to look after. I wouldn't be without her for the world. There's not a day goes by that I don't miss Del and it hurts like crazy, but each day gets just a little bit easier to get through than the last. You will get through this Nick! We both will! How's Jon coping? I've not noticed much in his classes."

"I wish I knew! Jon always plays his cards close to his chest! When he's hurting most, when he really needs to talk about things, he just shuts down and says nothing," said Nick. "It worries me that he won't let me in."

"I'll keep a closer eye on him at school and see if I can find a way to help. I know Maddy misses Del a lot, although I'm not sure if she really understands that he's never coming back. At least it helps that Del had been away at the safe house for about a month before he died. It would be much harder for her if she was used to seeing him every day.

I'd better get back to work! My break should have finished ten minutes ago! Nick, if you ever feel like you need to talk, I'm a pretty good listener and you know where to find me."

"Thanks Charley. That means a lot. You're a good friend."

"I mean it Nick! Any time you need to talk, I'm here," said Charley, with an encouraging smile as she headed off back to school.

Nick felt like a pathetic, self-centred idiot. Charley had been through just as much as he had and yet she was looking out for him and Jonathan while he was just feeling sorry for himself.

When Nick got back to his quarters, Idris was there. Nick told him about his conversation with Charley and how he thought she was a marvel coping with her own bereavement, looking after Maddy, running the school and still making time to care about other people.

"If you ask me, Nick, it sounds like you're a little bit smitten with our school ma'am," said Idris with a half joking, half knowing little wink.

"Don't be stupid Taff!" exclaimed Nick, getting irritated. "She's grieving for Del and I'm grieving for Jenny! We're just friends!"

"Oh, I know. She's too much of a lady and you're too much of a gentleman for anything to develop yet. You both need time to heal, but I know a spark when I see one and you two have a connection."

"Taff you're getting this all wrong!" said Nick, although he could feel himself starting to blush a little. He changed the subject. "We've never really talked have we Taff?"

"What do you mean boyo? We talk all the time. We live together," said Idris.

"Oh, sure we have conversations but you never tell me anything about yourself or your past. Who is the real Idris Llewellyn?" asked Nick.

"What do you want to know?" queried Taffy.

"Where do you come from? Have you got any family? You've never mentioned any. How did you come to join the PDM?" came a bombardment of questions from Nick.

"Originally, I came from Aberystwyth. My dad had been a miner, a strict Methodist and a staunch Trade Unionist until he died in 2001. I joined the Welsh Guards when I was eighteen. I loved the army life but in 2025 The Party scrapped the army, as we knew it, completely. Britain was no longer involved in international affairs so we didn't need an army. Instead, the army was replaced by the security forces: the PEO, the DDPU and the ATS, as they were only interested in enforcing the authority of The Party.

While I was in the army I got married to Agnes. Agnes was beautiful. She had the body of a model, the face of an angel and the grace of a swan. I thought the world of her. We had a son called Aled. We were happy. I thought we were the perfect family. When I left the Guards, I was getting angry about the injustices that people were suffering under the rule of The Party so I joined the PDM. Although I wasn't involved in much, Agnes worried about it. She asked me to leave the PDM but I wouldn't. I guess I was too selfish. I put my principles before my family. That's when she told me that she'd been having an affair with the manager of the office where she worked. He was being transferred to an office in Cardiff. Agnes was going with him and taking Aled with her. She said her new bloke made her feel safe while I just made her worry about a visit from the ATS. She didn't want me to visit Aled when they moved in case anybody linked them to me and the PDM. They moved to Cardiff and I've never seen Agnes or Aled since. If I'd realized just how much it meant to her, I might have left the PDM but instead, when they moved to Cardiff, I moved north and became more involved with the PDM. I hope Agnes and the boy have been happy in their new life. There's never been anyone else since. After all this time, I guess I'm married to the PDM now."

"I'm sorry Taff! You didn't deserve that," said Nick, putting a comforting hand on the Welshman's shoulder. "Perhaps one day you'll be able to see your son again."

"No chance boy. Apart from the risk, Agnes never let me know her address when she moved. I wouldn't have a clue where to start looking for him."

"I'm sorry Idris," said Nick. "I had no right to get you to drag up your past like that."

"It's alright boy. It's been a long time. There's been a lot of water under the bridge since then. Almost everybody here has been through a lot of suffering over the years. It goes with the territory.

George Richmond lost three brothers and his mother back in the two thousand and twenties. The ATS had only recently been formed and wanted to make a reputation for themselves. There was a protest march against the policies of The Party. George, his two older brothers and a younger brother all joined the protest. It was a completely peaceful protest but the Blackshirts started firing at the crowd. They claimed that terrorists in the crowd started shooting first but George denies that completely. The ATS started shooting unarmed protesters just to show that they could. All three of Georges brothers were killed. George was wounded and lucky to get away. He found out later that his mother had been arrested. When she wouldn't tell them where to find George, they beat her and sent her for Age Acceleration. That's why you won't find anyone more passionate about getting rid of these fucking bastards than George Richmond.

Jock Monroe lost his father because he dared to speak out against the government. He was arrested and sent for Age Acceleration. There are many, many more. Everyone here has a story to tell. Everyone has a reason to hate The Party."

"I'm sorry Taff! I never realized," said Nick, feeling guilty and selfish for brooding about his own loss.

"One day The Party and the Blackshirts will pay for what they've done," said Idris. "We've got to keep believing that boy."

Chapter 14.
OPERATION ARMAGEDDON

Nick was bored. Having nothing better to do, he was lying on his bed contemplating a dirty mark on the ceiling above him. He thought it looked a bit like a swan, but then it also looked a bit like a flat hand with the index finger raised. While he was trying to make up his mind, his peace was shattered by Idris rushing in to the room.

"Oh, there you are Nick," said the big Welshman, sounding a little excited. "I've been looking for you everywhere boy. I should have known to try the most obvious place first."

"What's up Idris? Why did you want me?" asked Nick.

"Fred Whitlow has just told me that the boss wants us both in the Ops Room in fifteen minutes. Fred reckons there are around twenty of us who need to be there. Sounds like there's an op being organised, something big judging by the number of people involved." Taffy's enthusiasm was already building with the thought of what lay ahead. "It's quite a while since we had any major action. I wonder what George is planning."

"Well, there's only one way to find out Taff," said Nick, as calm and as matter of fact as ever.

Idris and Nick joined the others in the operations room, a large room with a screen and projector, maps, a large flip chart and several rows of chairs. As Fred Whitlow had said, there must have been around twenty men, all sitting and wondering what was going down. Commander George Richmond and his deputy, Mark Grigson, stood at the front by the demonstration aids.

"Right gentlemen! Make yourselves comfortable and settle down!" said Richmond. The chatter stopped immediately. The Commander continued. "I know you're all wondering what's going on. I think you all knew the late Ken Townsend. He was a bit strange sometimes but a good agent and a psychic medium. I know some of you have always been sceptical but a lot of his premonitions have been proved right over the years. Ken was convinced that the authorities were using human bodies to make HCR. In case any of you don't know, HCR is the food that is sent to the penal colonies, to feed the convicts. It's occasionally on sale in supermarkets when there's a meat shortage. There is nothing on the packaging to say what is in it. All we really know was that it is produced by The Williamson Meat Corporation in Bamforth."

A few of the men seemed sceptical and were getting a bit fidgety.

"I know it seems pretty unbelievable but, as I said, Ken was absolutely convinced. We've been keeping round the clock obs on The Williamson Meat Corporation. A huge juggernaut truck takes a delivery of something to the factory every night at around four o'clock in the morning. It always takes the back roads and always arrives at the same time, when there's nobody around except the factory's security men. Whatever they are carrying, they clearly don't want it to be seen. We've not been able to find out where the truck comes from but we suspect it does the rounds of the body collection places, the places where we always thought bodies were cremated.

We've only got circumstantial evidence to back up Ken's idea, but it's enough to convince us that we need to get into the factory. If we're right, the factory and any HCR already produced will have to be destroyed.

We do know that lorries take the HCR from the factory to a huge storage facility at North Briddingtop Airfield. That is the stock of HCR waiting to be flown out to the convicts. There is also a storage facility in Hedgebury. We believe that is where HCR is kept for supplying supermarkets when necessary. If we are right about what's going on, we'll have to destroy both stores of the stuff and we'll have to do that on the same night that we hit the factory, so that we don't give the ATS any warning. If they get any idea of what we are up to, they'll step up security and make it a lot more dangerous."

Mark Grigson, who had been pointing out the targets on a large map while Richmond was talking, now took over.

"The raid on the factory will be a seven-man operation, three drivers and four men to actually go inside. Idris, I want you to lead the operation. Nick, I want you to go in as well. Your medical knowledge might be helpful. If you can get into the office, bring back any documents you can find which will prove what HCR actually is. We want photographs as well. You're going to get in by hijacking the delivery truck and driving in. There are normally two men in the truck, a driver and a mate. No guards travel with them, so the hijack shouldn't be too difficult. The factory has to be put completely and permanently out of action so, Dennis, you'll deal with the explosives and Pete will help with the demolition."

Dennis Wheatington was the PDM's top demolition expert. There was nothing that Dennis couldn't blow up, given a little bit of time and the right equipment. The other man going into the factory was Pete Trattley, an engineer who was very skilled in decommissioning machinery.

"The raid on the factory," continued Grigson, "will be given the code name Operation Armageddon. The raid on the airfield will be a six-man job and will be called Operation Meat Loaf. You will need to cut through the perimeter fence. The store is right by the fence. There may be some armed security guards close by so be prepared for any action. That's why we have to carry out the raid before the ATS have any warning. The raid on the supermarket storage facility will be Operation Cornflake. It will be a five handed job. We don't expect much security there but, as always, be prepared for anything.

We go tonight. Idris, we'll wait for word from you that Armageddon has been successful and that we're right about the HCR before giving the go ahead for Operations Meat Loaf and Cornflake. The teams will be in place awaiting your call. There's obviously no point in carrying out those ops if it turns out that we are wrong. The Commander and I will speak to you in your separate groups to go through the details."

The Ops Room was buzzing with excitement. The men couldn't wait to get into action as George Richmond and Mark Grigson went through everything in great detail, making sure all were prepared as thoroughly as possible. Success of the operations was important, massively important, but the most important thing was to get all of the men back with no casualties if possible.

Operation Armageddon, as Mark Grigson had said, was to be a seven-man, three car operation. Idris was the leader and would go into the factory along with Nick, Dennis Wheatington and Pete Trattley. The three drivers would be Fred Whitlow, Jordan Lorder and Tim Collinson. The three cars would transport all the agents and would be used in the hijacking of the body transporter. The juggernaut would then be used to gain entry into and exit from the factory. They would then dump the truck at their rendezvous point and transfer to the cars, kept safe and ready by their drivers, for the journey back.

****

At around three thirty a.m. Joe Snark was driving his gigantic body transporter along the quiet back road that led to the factory of The Williamson Meat Corporation. He couldn't wait for his shift to be over as it had been a gruelling and somewhat gruesome night, picking up bodies from numerous collection points around the country. His mate and co-driver was Jason Gibling. It was important not to attract attention to the truck and its grotesque cargo so the pair always took the minor roads, rather than the quicker, more direct route. Up ahead they could see two cars, effectively blocking the road, looking as though they had collided and spun. One car door was open, with a man lying on the ground as if he had been flung from the car. The drivers of both cars were slumped over their steering wheels, apparently not moving. Joe pulled up and jumped out of the truck quickly to see if he could help any of the supposedly injured men.

Jason got out of the truck more slowly and shouted to his partner. "I'll ring for help Joe!"

"OK Jase!" Joe shouted back to his partner.

At that moment, a third car pulled up quietly, right behind the truck so that it was impossible to reverse or to turn around. Before Jason could use his phone two men, Idris Llewellyn and Pete Trattley, pulled their weapons and ordered him back into the truck. As Joe looked back, wondering what was going on, the man on the road, Nick Kaydon, pulled out his weapon and ordered Joe to stay right where he was. Jason had his arms put behind his back and wrists bound together with gaffer tape. He also had tape stuck over his mouth as a gag. Idris opened up the back of the truck and was overwhelmed by the smell which greeted him, the unbearable, putrid smell of rotting, putrefied human flesh. It certainly was full, absolutely full of human bodies in various states of decay. The bodies were in a huge central vat. There was room on each side of the vat for a man to get to the controls of the tipping mechanism, to enable the hideous cargo to be unloaded. Idris forced Gibling into the back of the truck, at gunpoint and got in himself along with Dennis and Pete. Nick ordered Joe back into the driving seat and got in beside him, in the front passenger seat. He kept his gun discretely hidden under his jacket, poking hard into Joe's ribs as a constant reminder of the danger if he failed to cooperate. The other three moved the cars to allow the truck to continue on its way and then drove off to the rendezvous point.

"You're going to drive us into the factory," said Nick, giving Joe an extra hard poke in the ribs with his KOS.

"The security guards know us. They'll want to know why Jase is not with me," said Joe.

"You tell them that Jase is off sick. He has a nasty bug and I'm covering for him until he's better. Have you got a family?" Nick asked.

"I've got a wife and two boys," replied the nervous driver.

"If you don't cooperate, you'll have a widow and two orphans," said Nick. "Do you understand? Oh, and if anybody tries to get into the back, your friend will be dead long before they get the doors open."

"Alright! I'll cooperate, but you must be crazy to think you'll get away with this," said Joe. "Even if you get in, the security men will see whatever you're doing on the CCTV. You won't get out again."

"You'd better hope for your sake and your mate's sake that we do," said Nick.

Joe drove the truck right up to the barrier. Two security guards occupied a box beside the barrier.

"Hi Joe! Where's Jase?" shouted one of the guards.

"He's off sick Ted!" shouted Joe. "He's got a really nasty bug, headache, vomiting and the squits so I've got Alan with me tonight."

"Hi Alan," said the guard.

"Hi Ted," replied Nick, raising his hand in acknowledgement.

The guard took a long, inquisitive look at Nick, so that he would recognise him in the future.

"Alright lads, you can go through," said Ted, raising the barrier to allow them into the yard and operating the remote control which opened big double doors to enable them to drive right inside the factory. The doors closed automatically behind them. They were in! The first phase of the operation was successful!

Once inside the factory, Joe manoeuvred the truck so that it was backed up to the unloading chute. He and Nick, Nick's gun still out of sight, got out of the cab and tried to look busy for the CCTV cameras. Without making himself visible on camera, Pete Trattley sneaked out of the back of the truck and quickly found the main cable for the CCTV. He clamped a Circuit Repeater SB2 on to the cable.

The circuit repeater was a device, developed by the PDM techies, which caused the CCTV to play back the last thirty seconds of recordings repeatedly in a continuous, seamless link. Once attached, all that could be seen on the TV screens was the events of that thirty seconds, over and over again. That done, the team could do whatever they wanted without being seen until the gadget was removed. Hopefully, the guards wouldn't spend so much time watching the screens that they would become concerned about not seeing Nick and Joe actually doing very much.

As they had driven through the doors, the truck had triggered a sensor which switched on every light in the factory, revealing its gory contents. The bodies in the truck were tipped down a chute which fed into an enormous cauldron where the initial cooking of the bodies began. The semi-cooked bodies were then fed into a crushing unit, which crushed and blended everything into a fairly fine paste. At this point, other additives were delivered from an overhead hopper and mixed in before the human slurry passed into another cauldron for its final cooking. Finally, the people paste went through a refrigeration area, to cool it as quickly as possible, then in to the packing plant where it was packed into large bags and stacked on pallets.

Joe was gagged and his wrists bound with gaffer tape, just like Jason, but only after removing his baseball cap and bomber jacket. Before gagging Joe, Idris had obtained the necessary information from him about how to get out of the factory. Joe did not require too much persuasion to give up the information. Idris only had to convince him that they would only have three minutes to get out, once the timer had been set, before the whole place went up, killing the drivers and agents if they were still inside.

Joe and Jason both safely out of action and incarcerated in the truck, the team rapidly set to work. Dennis Wheatington, with the help of Pete Trattley, set explosive devices at all strategic points to destroy the whole mechanism of the plant. Incendiary devices were set to destroy the unloaded bodies, any remaining body parts already in the system and the vast pile of bags of HCR already stacked on pallets awaiting transportation. All had to be completely destroyed as well as the building itself. Finally, it was all linked up to one timing device. Once the timer was set, they would have just three minutes to get to safety before The Williamson Meat Corporation became an inferno hotter than Hades.

While the explosives were being set, Nick headed for the office which was situated on the left, up a short open staircase. He found a locked filing cabinet which he forced open quite easily. Looking through documents, he suddenly stopped and let out a scream of anguish. Idris, who had been photographing the plant in all its grotesque detail, rushed into the office.

"What is it, Nick? What's wrong?"

"THE FUCKING BASTARDS!" shouted Nick. "How could the bastards do that? This is a lot worse than we thought Taff! That stuff lasts so long because they're adding fucking GDN93."

"What's that?" asked Idris.

"GDN93 used to be used as a preservative in many foods. Then they discovered that it was carcinogenic and hepatotoxic, even in small amounts and it was banned," continued Nick. "In other words, they stopped using it because it caused cancer and liver failure. They are not only putting it in HCR but the bastards are using it at twenty-five times the concentration used before. That's why this fucking stuff can be kept for so fucking long. They are not just making people cannibals; they are killing them as well. Anybody eating this fucking shit is signing their own death warrant." Nick grabbed a sheaf of documents and stuffed them inside his shirt for safe keeping. "Time to get out and destroy this fucking pestilential Hell Hole!"

The whole operation was carried out in barely more than five minutes. Jason and Joe, who had been locked in the back of the truck, were now joined by Dennis and Idris, but not before Dennis had set the timer for the detonation and Pete had removed the circuit repeater from the CCTV. Nick, who had been seen by the guards and was known by them as Alan, got into the driving seat. Pete, who was about the same size as driver Joe Snark, put on Joe's bomber jacket and baseball cap and climbed into the front passenger seat. He sat slouched down, with the baseball cap pulled right down over his eyes, trying to look like Joe.

Nick drove the truck up behind the double doors and sounded his horn four times, the signal that Joe had said was used for the guards to release them. The doors swung open, Nick drove out and up to the barrier.

"What's up Alan?" asked the guard suspiciously. "How come Joe's not driving?"

"I think he must have that bug that Jase went down with, Ted. He almost passed out for a few minutes. That's why it took us a bit longer than usual. I'd best get him back home as soon as possible."

"Right you are," said Ted. "Sorry you're feeling bad Joe!" he shouted.

Pete said nothing but raised a hand in acknowledgement as he kept his head well down. The guards raised the barrier. Nick drove out and away as fast as he could, away from the pending inferno.

After releasing the truck, Ted turned to the other guard. "Something doesn't seem right, Harry. Normally Joe would have to be nearly dead to let anyone else drive his truck out of here. Perhaps I'd better call the ATS and get them to stop the truck for a check."

Ted had just picked up the phone when all hell was let loose, an explosion so vast that both guards were knocked completely off their feet. The factory was enveloped in total conflagration which ripped it apart, destroying everything inside.

Nick could see the factory go up in his rear-view mirror as he drove along, flames leaping high into the early morning sky, giving it a red glow. Large columns of acrid black smoke billowed up and there was a pervading smell of cremated barbecue.

"That's some firework display," said Nick. "It's a pity we can't hang around to watch it."

Idris got on the DIRC to call headquarters. "Operation Armageddon is complete and successful. Meat Loaf and Cornflake must go now! I repeat, Meat Loaf and Cornflake must go now!"

They quickly got to the rendezvous point where all three cars were waiting and transferred to them. Joe Snark and Jason Gibling were left, still bound and gagged, in the back of the truck. The team's journey back to headquarters was safe and uneventful, marred only by the stench of putrid, rotting human bodies which had infiltrated their clothes, invaded their nostrils and even exuded from their pores. Nasty as the smell was, it served as an indelible reminder of just how evil and vile the Valentine regime was and exactly what the PDM was fighting for.

By the time they were safely back at headquarters, showered and changed, in a vain attempt to get rid of the smell, the teams from Operation Meat Loaf and Operation Cornflake had returned. Both teams had been successful in achieving their goal. All stocks of HCR had been successfully destroyed. Their spirits were dampened by one unfortunate, tragic event. Operation Meat Loaf had indeed turned into a gun fight, just as Richmond and Grigson had warned. During the battle one member of the team, Dewi Griffice, had been shot and killed. Dewi was a fellow Welshman and a friend of Idris. Everyone else had got back safely and unharmed. The loss of one man in such a big and important action was not an unexpected price to pay, but the loss of any man was too much. It was a sad Idris who turned up for the debriefing next morning, having lost a long-standing friend.

At the debriefing, George Richmond praised all of the men for the job they had done, with a special mention for Dewi Griffice. Idris showed the photographs he had taken to the Commander and the men. Nick showed Richmond the documents which he had taken from the factory and explained to the men the significance of GDN93 being added. The documents showed that HCR actually stood for Human Carcass Reconstitution. When he heard about the use of GDN93, George Richmond was worried. They had destroyed the stock of HCR but how much was already out there in the pipeline? How many people had already bought it from the supermarket and had it stored in their kitchen? That could be a lot as the stuff had a six-month shelf life. How much of it was stored in the penal colonies? What alternative food supply would the cons have when their supply of HCR ran out? Most important of all, how many people were already in the process of dying from the effects of HCR and what could be done about it? Somehow people had to be informed. The technicians had been working for some time on a new communication system which would enable them to make TV broadcasts.

The biggest difficulty was that the equipment had to be mobile, otherwise the ATS would be able to trace its whereabouts. It also needed to use a signal which could not be blocked. The techies had made great progress but work on it would have to be speeded up to enable information like this to be spread as quickly as possible. They also needed to find some way to inform the cons and possibly get a temporary supply of alternative food to them. The authorities would still have to feed the convicts, even if they could no longer give them HCR, but no doubt they would be in no rush to do that.

★★★★

That afternoon, Nick met Charley McCarthy in the canteen.

"I heard you and Idris were on a raid last night," said Charley.

"Yes, that's right, but I can't really say too much about it at the moment," replied Nick.

"No! That's OK! I wouldn't expect you to tell me anything! I just wanted to say I'm glad you came back safely," said Charley, beginning to blush noticeably, as though it was more than just a polite comment.

She really did care about his safety. She'd had years of worrying about Del when there was any action and now, she was worrying about Nick. Nick thought how pretty she looked when she blushed. In fact, he had noticed how pretty she looked any time.

"Unfortunately, we lost one man," said Nick. "Dewi Griffice! I don't know if you knew him. He was a friend of Idris."

"No! I don't think I know him. How's Idris taking it?" asked Charley.

"You know Idris. He's putting on a brave face, but I can tell it's got to him. I suppose it's only natural for him to be upset."

"Well at least he's got you to help him get through it, Nick. He's lucky in that way."

Knowing that a man had been killed reminded Charley just how much danger Nick could be in at times, as could all of the agents. She really hoped that he would stay safe.

Chapter 15.

OPERATION TAKEAWAY

George Richmond had been worrying for days about what the PDM could do to help the convicts on Saint Kilda. In fact, he had been worrying ever since Operation Armageddon had revealed the vile, repulsive truth about Human Carcass Reconstitution, or HCR. Convicts would be dying from its toxic effects and still unwittingly eating it. Operation Armageddon had successfully destroyed the stock of HCR in mainland Britain but who knows how much of it was already stored on Saint Kilda? He had to do something to help and he had to do it as soon as possible. Even now, it might already be too late. The Commander had spent hours discussing it with his second in command, Mark Grigson.

Saint Kilda was an archipelago, consisting of several small islands, which was part of the Outer Hebrides. The largest island was Hirta, which was home for most of the convicts. There were also penal colonies on two smaller islands, Soay and Dun. Other islands in the archipelago were unoccupied, some being little more than rocky stacks protruding from the Atlantic Ocean.

Somehow the people on Saint Kilda had to be warned and had to be provided with an alternative temporary supply of food.

It would be impossible to reach Saint Kilda by sea. The sea surrounding the archipelago was constantly patrolled by gunboats, to prevent any escape attempts, with a mandate to shoot to kill first and ask questions later. Also, there was no way of knowing how the convicts would react to a boat landing on their shores. They may well hijack it to use it in an attempted escape, leaving the crew high and dry, stranded in the penal colony. The mountainous terrain of the islands made it impossible to land any sort of plane, even if the PDM had one. There was only one possible way of getting anything on to Saint Kilda, it would have to be airdropped. The only possibility was to drop warning leaflets and food by air. In fact, that was the method used by the authorities to get supplies to the convicts.

The PDM had no planes of their own and there was no way that any commercial aviation company could be hired to do that job. No-one would make that flight for money. The only other alternative was to hijack a plane. The PDM had the personnel who could fly a plane if they could procure one. Two agents had a lot of previous flying experience with the Royal Air Force, which had been disbanded in 2030 as drones took over from manned aircraft in providing the country's defence. Declan Dunleavy was a former Squadron Leader and Max Nedwell a former Flying Officer. Both men had a lot of experience flying combat aircraft.

George had the idea of hiring a commercial aircraft and pilot to transport a fictitious cargo, filing a flight plan to an airfield as close as legitimately possible to Saint Kilda. The plane would then be hijacked. The hijackers would follow the registered flight plan for as long as possible, breaking away at the last possible moment to head towards Saint Kilda.

Mark Grigson was strongly opposed to the idea. There were just too many risks involved. First of all, they could be sussed when they tried to hire the aircraft and pilot. Then the hijack might fail or be spotted and the mission stopped before they had even taken off. Once the plane left its registered flight path, drones would almost certainly be scrambled to search for and destroy it. There were frequent routine reconnaissance flights by drones over the penal colonies anyway, which would have to be avoided. Finally, even if the cargo was successfully dropped, the crew still had to fly back to mainland Scotland, land somewhere undetected and rendezvous with agents who would transport them back to headquarters.

Despite his fears, George Richmond was so determined to go ahead with the plan that finally, reluctantly, Mark Grigson agreed. They spoke to the two former pilots who both thought the plan was feasible and were keen to give it a try. Richmond made sure that they were under no illusions about the risks involved but both men were determined to give it a go.

A freelance commercial pilot, Tim Sharnwood, with his own plane, a Cessna 405 Gypsy, was hired by a fictitious business man to transport cattle feed and machinery parts from Hannant Clough Airfield to Stornoway Airport.

Hannant Clough was a small commercial airfield near to Sheffield. Stornoway Airport was on the Isle of Lewis, one of the larger islands in the Outer Hebrides. It was a journey of around four hundred and seventy miles. It still left a further journey of seventy miles from Stornoway to Saint Kilda and a return journey of one hundred and twenty-five miles from Saint Kilda to a disused airfield near Ullapool, the rendezvous point for the agents' return.

The Cessna 405 Gypsy was a little outdated now but it was still more than capable of doing the job in hand. It was a later development from the Cessna 208 Caravan. American built, it could easily carry two crew and fourteen passengers, although to carry that many people would have been illegal. It had been adapted for use as a cargo plane and also had a roll up door in the middle of the port side to enable it to be used for sky diving. It was powered by a single Pratt and Whitney turboprop engine with a cruise speed of two hundred knots, roughly two hundred and thirty miles per hour, a range of fifteen hundred miles and a maximum cargo weight of one and a quarter ton. It was certainly no match for the drones with which it might have to contend.

In reality, the cargo was large sacks and wooden crates containing rice, beans, lentils, grains and flour. Each large container was filled with numerous five-kilogram bags to enable easier distribution. It was impossible to attach parachutes to all of the goods, so the intention was to fly as low as possible to drop the containers. The outer containers were certain to burst open on impact with the ground, but hopefully the smaller packs would stay intact.

The sacks were labelled as cattle feed and the crates were labelled as machine parts, all for delivery to the Isle of Lewis, in case of inspection before take-off. There were also three large sacks of leaflets warning about HCR, one to be dropped on each island.

The Cessna Gypsey stood fuelled and ready to go, near the runway at Hannant Clough Airfield. The PDM agents loaded the cargo while Tim Sharnwood went to file the flight plan. Officially, Dunleavy and Nedwell were flying with the goods to assist with unloading and transport on arrival at Stornoway. When Sharnwood returned, with the plane ready to go, he was overpowered by the two agents, knocked unconscious, gagged, bound hand and foot and shut inside a nearby storage shed. That done, Dunleavy and Nedwell jumped into the cockpit. Declan Dunleavy started the Cessna's engine and switched on the plane's radio. They were also carrying a DIRC to maintain contact with George Richmond. They hoped that the real pilot would not be found too soon and the mission stopped before it had really started, as they started to taxi towards the runway.

Dunleavy was on the radio immediately. "Hello Control, this is Bravo Whiskey Echo Two One Seven requesting clearance for take-off. Repeat, Bravo Whiskey Echo Two One Seven requesting clearance for take-off. Over."

"Bravo Whiskey Echo Two One Seven this is Control. You are clear for take-off. Repeat, you are clear for take-off," came the reply.

The engine roared as the Cessna turned onto the runway, with a quick brake check on the way. As it started along the runway, there was a rapid surge in the engine as the plane charged forward and up, up into the sky, climbing constantly. The course was set for Stornoway. The plane levelled out at twenty thousand feet. For the time being, Declan Dunleavy and Max Nedwell could relax as they were following their official flight plan.

Declan used the DIRC to report back to headquarters. "Hello HQ. Dunleavy and Nedwell safely airborne. Operation Takeaway safely underway. Over."

George Richmond replied. "Good to hear that, Dec. Good luck. Over and out."

The journey was uneventful with just a couple of calls from Air Traffic Control checking the Cessna's position.

As they were approaching the Isle of Lewis, instead of requesting permission to land they reduced altitude to just under five hundred feet in an attempt to avoid the radar and keep Air Traffic Control guessing where they were heading.

"This is where the fun starts Max," said Declan as he changed course for Saint Kilda.

"Let's do this Dec," replied Max.

After disappearing from the radar screen, they could hear Stornoway Air Traffic Control on the radio.

"Bravo Whiskey Echo Two One Seven please report your position. This is Stornoway Air Traffic Control. Bravo Whiskey Echo Two One Seven please report your position. Over. ***** Come in Bravo Whiskey Echo Two One Seven. Over. ***** This is Stornoway Air Traffic Control. Bravo Whiskey Echo Two One Seven please report your position. Over." With each repeat of the message, the voice of the controller became more and more agitated and frantic.

Both men prayed that the drones would not be mobilised yet, although they knew that it would not be long.

Declan kept the altitude at just under five hundred feet, as that seemed to be keeping them under the radar, all the way to Saint Kilda, dropping to fifty feet as they started to pass over the islands. As they crossed the coast of Soay, Max opened the roll up door and started to push out some of the cargo. The plane swept from the north over Soay, Hirta and Dun, with Max dumping the rest of the cargo. Declan needed all of his experience to be able to keep the plane so low over such mountainous terrain.

As the last sacks were dropped and Max closed the cargo door, Declan reported back on the DIRC. "Hello HQ. Operation Takeaway successful. All cargo away. Repeat, all cargo away. On our way back. Over."

"That's great news Dec," said George Richmond, allowing himself a slight smile. "Have a safe journey home, lads. Over and out."

Declan began to turn the plane on to the course for Ullapool and climbing steadily back towards five hundred feet. As he turned, he spotted two drones, still some way off but closing in fast. He didn't know whether they had been scrambled from Stornoway when they dropped off the radar, in which case they would be armed and ready for battle, or they were on a routine reconnaissance flight, which could mean that they were not armed. Any hope of them not being armed was immediately destroyed as the Cessna was hit by laser cannon fire, damaging the port wing.

"Mayday! Mayday!" Declan yelled into the DIRC. "Under fire from drones. We have been hit. Will have to ditch! Repeat, will have to ditch!"

Declan shouted to Max to get his parachute on, as he struggled to turn back towards Hirta and climb to one thousand feet, a safer height to jump from.

"I'll hold it as steady as I can while you jump!" shouted Declan, trying to put on his own parachute. "Once you're clear I'll follow you."

Within seconds, Max had got the cargo door open and jumped. As the canopy of his chute opened, Max heard the drones firing again. This time a direct hit on the Cessna Gypsy caused an explosion, leaving a fireball crashing into the Atlantic Ocean. Declan had no chance to jump.

Max drifted down safely, hoping that the drones didn't turn their attention to him. They didn't bother. There was no need. If he wasn't claimed as a victim of the ocean he could only get to the safety of a penal colony, from which there was no escape.

As he hit the water, Max knew that he had to get out of his parachute fast, before the wet silk dragged him down. He managed to struggle free from the harness and jettison his chute. After a few seconds to get his bearings, he struck out for the shore. He had come down in Village Bay, not too far from the coast of Hirta. He had to battle hard against the sea, his sodden boots and clothing dragging him down. On two occasions, Max almost succumbed to the unforgiving ocean but just managed to keep battling on, driven by sheer willpower and determination to survive. Finally, he reached dry land, a small beach, where he lay exhausted, breathless and bitterly cold but thankful to still be alive.

As he looked towards the land, he saw a random selection of dwellings. There were some old cottages, ghost buildings left from a hundred and fifty years previously, when the island was home to crofters. There were also some wooden shacks and some crude, very basic stone shelters. As he gained a little more strength and composure, he realised that a crowd had gathered above him, at the top of a steep, stony slope.

A smaller group of eight or nine men, all armed with heavy wooden clubs, had come much closer to him and surrounded him. Max knew he was in imminent danger. One man stood out from the rest, with gruesome tattoos on his arm and neck. He appeared to be the leader. He looked angry, more than angry, he looked psychopathic. He looked like a man intent on murder.

"Can you help me?" asked Max.

"He wants us to help him, Dante!" sneered a very tall, bald man.

"Help him?" queried the tattooed man. "The only help he'll get from us is help into an early grave, Grainger."

"We dropped some leaflets warning you about HCR," said Max "and some food, dried food that you can boil up."

"I know!" said Dante, producing one of the leaflets and tearing it up. "You're spreading lies. Your leaflets are all lies. You're going to ruin my business. If people stop eating HCR, you could put me out of business completely. We can't have that now, can we?"

"You don't understand!" yelled Max. "That stuff is toxic. It'll kill people!"

"No! You don't understand!" said Dante. "We're toxic! We kill people! Finish him lads but not too quickly and make it hurt. You have an audience to play to. Give them a good performance."

★★★★

Back at PDM headquarters George Richmond had been listening on the DIRC. He had heard Dec and Max trying to jump from the plane and he had heard the explosion as the Cessna Gypsy was blown apart by cannon fire. Had either of the men managed to get clear before the explosion or had they been destroyed along with the plane? If they had jumped in time, had they landed safely or had they drowned in the rough, ice-cold water of the North Atlantic? If they had made it to dry land, what kind of reception had they received from the convicts? In short, were they still alive or were they dead? There was no possible way of knowing and no possible way of rescuing them and bringing them back home, even if they had survived. With a heavy heart, George sent out a message on the DIRC to recall the car waiting at Ullapool for the rendezvous.

Operation Takeaway had been a success in terms of trying to help the convicts, but a total failure in having almost certainly lost two good men, two heroes who took on the mission when they knew the odds were heavily stacked against them. Declan and Max had successfully delivered their cargo but if the convicts ignored the leaflets and continued to eat HCR the mission would have all been for nothing. It had been George's call and right now it felt as if he had made the wrong call. He deeply regretted his decision and wished he had taken more notice of Mark Grigson's reservations. He was beginning to doubt his ability to lead the PDM. George had always given everything for the cause. He had always given everything for his men and loved the men under his command like a father. The men had all respected him and given him everything in return. His aim had always been to keep any losses to an absolutely unavoidable minimum and yet he felt like he had sacrificed Declan Dunleavy and Max Nedwell and for what?

Chapter 16.

GEORGE HAS A WOBBLE

George Richmond sat in his office, staring at the wall. After Operation Takeaway he had serious doubts about his ability to lead the PDM and, having taken a couple of days to mull things over, he felt no different. He had been frustrated by the fact that, after all the years of fighting, there still seemed no chance of defeating the UCNP. The Party had a stranglehold on the country. The PDM were nowhere near strong enough to defeat them without an uprising by the people. The people were too complacent, too scared or too brainwashed by constant propaganda to help. A people's uprising was made even more difficult by the law banning gatherings of more than twelve people.

Mark Grigson entered the office. "Are you alright boss? You look awful. Have you got something on your mind?" he asked.

"Mark, I'm seriously thinking of resigning as Commander! I'll still stay in the PDM and do whatever I can to help of course, but I think it's time to put someone younger in charge. We're getting nowhere at the moment and I can't see that changing in the foreseeable future. Maybe a younger head at the helm can steer us to greater success."

"You're still feeling bad about Declan and Max," said Mark. "You did what you had to do! Alright it didn't come off as we'd have liked, but that wasn't your fault. We had to try!"

"It was a bad plan from the start. You had the sense to see it," said George.

"Yes, I was against it, but it was easier for me to hold back because I didn't have to find a solution. You didn't have that option. You were stuck between a rock and a hard place and you had to do something."

"It was the wrong decision Mark and I've made too many of those lately," said George. "I've decided I need to call a meeting of all the men to vote on a new leader and I'll be recommending that you take over as Commander."

"If you do that George, I'll refuse to accept command!"

"Then the men will just have to vote for a new leader from amongst themselves!"

"We need your experience, George!" said an exasperated Mark.

"I'm going to call for a meeting of all agents tomorrow and I am going to resign then!" said a very determined George Richmond.

★★★★

Nick and Charley were having coffee together in the canteen, something which seemed to be happening much more often recently. They enjoyed each other's company.

Idris, having just been served a mug of tea, went over to their table. "Do you two mind if I join you?"

"Of course not, Taff," said Charley with her usual smile. "Take a seat."

Idris sat down and continued. "I've just been talking to Jock. He told me that there's a meeting of all agents been called for tomorrow and it's to discuss and vote on a new Commander. Apparently, George Richmond wants to stand down!"

"Surely not! That can't be right!" said Nick in astonishment. "In any case, if George had to pack it in for any reason, Mark Grigson would automatically take over surely."

"You'd think so boy but, according to Jock, Grigson's adamant that he's not taking the job," said Idris.

"I don't know much about how the PDM is run but it appears to me that George Richmond has the total respect of all of the men. He can't just throw that away," said Charley.

"I've been with the PDM long enough to have served under three different Commanders and George is the best we've had!" said Idris.

"Maybe you need to let him know that," replied Charley, taking a gulp of her coffee.

"Are you sure that Jock's not got this all wrong?" queried Nick.

"Jock has got his finger on the pulse, Nick. He usually knows what's going on before most people. There's definitely a meeting tomorrow anyway, ten a.m., so something big is happening," said Taff.

"If George does stand down and Mark Grigson won't take the job, who's left as a contender for next Commander?" asked Nick.

"There's no obvious stand out candidate," said Taff. "I suppose Jock Munroe could be a possibility, maybe Dom Welland, Jim Donlon or even Fred Whitlow. They've all got plenty of experience, but they're no George Richmond!"

"How about you, Idris?" asked Charley. "You've certainly got the experience."

"No! I'm no leader!" said the big Welshman.

"You did a good job when you led Operation Armageddon," said Nick.

"It's one thing leading an op," replied Idris, "but that doesn't make me capable of running the whole shebang. No, I'm not the next Commander!"

"If push comes to shove, I reckon Mark Grigson will take it on," said Charley. "I reckon he's only turned it down to put pressure on George to reconsider."

"There speaks a very wise woman. Brains as well as charm and good looks," said Taff, giving Nick a sly wink.

"Flattery will get you everywhere Idris," replied Charley, smiling and blushing slightly.

★★★★

It was decided that it was easiest to hold the meeting in the canteen. The tables were all stacked and moved out of the way with the chairs set out in rows. All of the agents, whether active in the field, engineers or technicians, were present. Mark Grigson was chairing the meeting. He and George Richmond sat at a table, at the front of the room.

Grigson called for order and began. "I suppose word has got round by now, but for anyone who hasn't heard, we've called this meeting to decide who will be the new Commander of the PDM. George feels that he wants to stand down."

There were groans, mumbles and mutterings as the men were shocked to have the rumours confirmed.

"Settle down lads! You'll all have a chance to have your say! As I said, George has decided that he wants to stand down as Commander. He has asked me to take over but I have refused, because I think he is the better man for the job. Consequently, we are going to have to vote for a new leader. Is anyone prepared to nominate somebody for the job?"

The room was silent.

"Come on lads!" continued Mark. "I don't like this any more than you do but we have to have a Commander. Nobody will be offended if you nominate someone else instead of them, but we need nominations so will somebody start the ball rolling?"

Dominic Welland stood up to speak. "I think we'd all like to know why you want to resign George. We've never known you to walk away from anything."

There were general mutterings of agreement from the gathering.

George got to his feet to reply. "I'm not walking away from anything Dom. I'll still be here in an active role. I just don't think I'm the right guy to lead you any longer. I think I've lost my edge. We've lost too many men of late and I have to take the blame for that. Perhaps I'm just past it. Age catches up with all of us and I just think a younger man, with new ideas, might have more success."

Idris raised himself up to his considerable height. "George you're no more past it than I am, or any man here. You've got more experience than any of us and, most important of all, you have the respect of every single one of us. I've never heard one single complaint, from anyone, about your leadership. Oh, I know things have not gone as well as they might have done in the last few weeks, but that's not your fault. Things go wrong sometimes. Agents get killed sometimes. We all know that and we're all prepared to take that risk, otherwise we wouldn't be here. You've always looked after us and done your best to keep us safe. We all know that and we all appreciate that. That's why we want you to lead us. You're still the best man for the job. We know you are even if you have doubts. You're the only man for the job! No offence to you Mark!"

"None taken Taff! I absolutely agree with you!" said Mark Grigson.

"Operation Takeaway was a big mistake and my stupid idea cost us two good men," said George.

"That was no fault of yours George," continued Idris. "You had no choice. You couldn't have just sacrificed the people on Saint Kilda and done nothing! We had to try something. The odds were always against Dec and Max but they knew that and they were still prepared to try. They were prepared to try for you George, because that's how much these boys are prepared to follow you."

"I just get so fucking frustrated that you are all putting your lives at risk and, after all these years, we're no nearer to overthrowing this fucking Valentine regime. We'll never be strong enough to get rid of The Party unless we get the support of the people and that's not going to happen any time soon. I don't want to send men to their death for nothing any longer."

"Actually George, we've had a bit of a breakthrough that might help," said Phillip Holgrave, generally known as Pip, a diminutive man with long, unkempt, straggly grey hair and a grey moustache. He didn't look at all like an agent. That was because he wasn't really. Pip Holgrave was a boffin. He wasn't just a technician. He was head of the electronics techies. In his field he was the best. "I was going to tell you about it this morning anyway, but I think it's best to discuss it in private, after the meeting, with you or the new leader if we have one. I'll just say that this is big and it should make a difference."

George was intrigued, despite his intention to resign.

"Look George," said Dom Welland, "let's take a vote to see what the lads think before we start nominating a new leader. Does anybody here think they would want to stand as Commander?"

No hands were raised.

"Does anybody think that George Richmond should be replaced?" continued Dom.

No hands were raised.

"Come on lads, don't be shy. Nobody'll think badly of you. Put your hand up if you think we could do better than George Richmond as Commander," continued Dom.

Still no hands went up. Not a single one. Not even any movement.

"How many of you want George to reconsider and stay on as Commander?" asked Welland.

Immediately every hand in the room shot up, without even a second of hesitation.

"That looks pretty unanimous to me George," said Dominic. "Every single man here wants you to continue as Commander because every single man here knows that you're the best man for the job. No, you're the only man for the job. So, what do you say, boss? Can we persuade you to carry on? We're all behind you, as you can see."

"I don't know what to say, lads." George could feel his eyes starting to well up. "With loyalty like that, I guess I've got no alternative but to carry on. I just hope you've made the right decision. I hope I've made the right decision and I hope I don't let you down."

"You won't let anybody down George!" said Mark Grigson. "I'm glad that's settled and we can get back to business as usual."

"Talking about business as usual," said Commander George Richmond, "do you want to come to my office in an hour Pip and we can talk about your new breakthrough."

"I'll be there George," said Pip Holgrave. "You'll like what I've got to tell you!"

It was a very relieved group of men who began moving chairs and tables back to their usual positions.

★★★★

Pip Holgrave knocked on the door of George Richmond's office. He was pleased about George staying on as Commander but most of all he was bursting with excitement about his imminent news.

"Come in Pip! It's open," shouted the Commander.

"Thanks for seeing me, George," said Pip, as he sat down. "First of all, can I say that I'm really pleased that you decided not to stand down? It wouldn't be the same working for somebody else."

"Thanks Pip! That means a lot!" said George. "Now you seem quite excited about something so you'd better tell me all about it."

"You'll like this George," said Pip, bubbling over with enthusiasm. "You know we've been working on MUB2. MUB1 was just a crude prototype but MUB2 is the business!"

"I'm sorry Pip but all your abbreviations and stuff leave me in a haze," said George. "Can you explain it to me from the start?"

"OK! MUB stands for Mobile Untraceable Broadcasting. In other words, equipment to enable us to transmit programmes and messages via the TV, like The Party do now with The Daily Party News, but it's mobile and it's almost impossible to trace where we're broadcasting from. I say almost impossible to trace because they would have to be really clever and, even if they were capable, it would take them at least a couple of hours. As I said, MUB1 was just a prototype but with MUB2 we seem to have gotten rid of all the gremlins. Of course, we can't be completely certain until we've actually tried it in the field, but I'm ninety-nine point nine per cent sure it's going to deliver the goods.

We need to set up a small room as a filming studio. Then we film what we want to broadcast and record it on to DVDs in advance. We've developed broadcasting equipment small enough to fit in the boot of a car, wired up to controls in the car's glove box and what looks like a normal CD player. We take the car somewhere safe, insert the DVD into the false CD player and broadcast whatever is on the DVD. The Daily Party News is broadcast every day at three p.m. TV sets are fixed to automatically turn on at three and people can't turn them off, so The Party has a captive audience. If we broadcast at three p.m., our baby will block The Party's broadcast and show ours instead. The Party can't do a thing to stop it being seen. If we want to broadcast at a different time as well, we will need to have a message at the end of the broadcast to tell people when the next broadcast will be. People will have the opportunity to watch that broadcast if they want to but they can't avoid the three p.m. broadcast. That means that we can break the cycle of constant lies and brainwashing from The Party and we can tell people the truth.

Now, as I said, it's almost impossible for the position that we are broadcasting from to be traced. It can possibly be done by an exceptionally good electronics expert, given enough time, but it would take at least a couple of hours, maybe more. That's why the equipment has to be mobile. The car parks up, we do a half hour broadcast and we will be packed up and gone long before our position can be traced. We broadcast from a different place each day, following a completely random pattern so there's no chance of the ATS guessing where we're going to broadcast from next. We've also put the equipment into two cars, so we can easily broadcast from opposite ends of the country on subsequent days, using one car one day and the other car the next day. Unless the ATS happen to be in the right place at the right time by a complete fluke, purely by a lucky guess, they have no chance of finding the broadcasting car. I suggest we have a crew of three men in each car, a technician and two agents to share the driving, set up obs while we're broadcasting and manpower just in case the ATS do find us and we have to shoot our way out. As I say though George, a shootout could only happen if the ATS got incredibly lucky.

The equipment is astoundingly powerful for a mobile unit and the broadcast will reach the whole of the UK. It will even send out a strong enough signal from underground, up to a reasonable depth of course, you couldn't use it from the bottom of a mine. That means, for example, we could easily broadcast from a railway tunnel or an underground car park, which gives us more options of hiding safely when broadcasting."

"Wow!" said George, totally amazed and feeling somewhat shell-shocked by Pip's enthusiastic revelation. "That sounds almost too good to be true. We can finally let people know the truth about what's been going on. If we can use that to get enough people on our side then maybe we can get enough support to finally change this sorry mess. When will it be ready for us to start?"

"It's ready to go right now! Two cars are fully equipped. You just need to get the broadcasts recorded on to DVDs, pick the crews, decide where to make the transmissions from and we're good to go!" said Pip, beaming with pride at what he and his team had achieved.

All George Richmond's recent self-doubt was now a distant memory, forgotten in the excitement of this new venture. This could be exactly the breakthrough that the PDM had been waiting for.

Chapter 17.
THE END OF THE BEGINNING OR THE BEGINNING OF THE END?

The next two days were spent working frantically hard in the newly created and adapted film studio at PDM headquarters. It was little more than a small office but perfectly adequate for requirements. The schedule was relentless but, by the end, six broadcasts were in the can, on disc, ready to begin broadcasting the following day. Two broadcasting teams had been chosen and fully prepared. Team A consisted of Pip Holgrave with Idris and Nick. They would make the first broadcast. Team B consisted of Mike Riches, another electronics boffin, backed up by Jock Munroe and Tim Collinson.

The first broadcast, made by Pip's team, would be from Tyneside. They would then stay at a safe house near Lincoln before making their next broadcast, two days later, in Ipswich. Finally, they would stay at a safe house in Cambridge before making a final broadcast from Coventry on Day Five. They would then return to H.Q. for a well-earned rest with a new team taking over.

Team B, Mike's team, would start by broadcasting from Bristol on Day Two. They would stay in a safe house in Hereford before broadcasting from Chester on Day Four. They would then go to a safe house in Southport before making their final broadcast, on Day Six, from Carlisle. They would then also return to H.Q. to be replaced by a new team.

For the time being any information was on a strictly need to know basis. Anyone who was not directly involved was told nothing. That would no longer be the case once broadcasts had started. A meeting was arranged, in the canteen, at two forty-five p.m. on the day of the first broadcast. Everyone was instructed to attend; agents, technicians, wives, girlfriends, in fact all adults had to be present. Only children were excused. The whole place was buzzing with excitement and anticipation. Something big seemed about to happen and, although nobody appeared to know what, the general consensus was that it was expected to be something good.

That evening Nick called to see Charley, as he did quite often nowadays. Although they were still just friends, they both felt that they were getting closer and yet both were afraid to admit it in case it spoiled their friendship. Sometimes Jonathan would accompany Nick, as he and Maddy were building up a strong friendship, but on this occasion Nick went alone. Eventually the conversation got around to the events of the following day.

"Do you know anything about the meeting tomorrow, Nick? What's it about?" asked Charley. Nobody that I've spoken to seems to have any idea. That's odd in itself because there are usually some rumours and speculation. Nobody's talking at all, which makes me think that it's something pretty important."

"Yes! Actually, I do know about it but I can't say anything except that I won't be there," replied Nick, wanting to tell Charley all about it but knowing that it was more than his life was worth. "In fact, I won't be around for a few days, so can you keep an eye on Jon while I'm away?"

"Yes of course I will, with pleasure. I've arranged for Jon and a couple of the older children to look after the younger children while we are all at the meeting tomorrow, so it had better not go on for too long. Jon can come and stay here while you're away, if he wants to. Maddy loves spending time with him. I don't suppose you can tell me where you're going or what you'll be doing, but I hope it's not anything dangerous," said Charley, suddenly looking very anxious.

"No! I'll be with Idris and Pip Holgrave. It's all perfectly straightforward and there shouldn't be any danger so there's no need to worry." Despite not wanting to worry Charley, Nick couldn't help feeling pleased that she cared enough to worry about him.

"I can't help worrying Nick. I couldn't stand it if anything happened to you!" Charley blushed a little as she realised she was letting her guard down.

Nick had become much more than a friend despite her attempts to suppress her feelings. When they met, they were both struggling to cope with bereavement. Charley had lost Del and Nick had lost Jenny. Even in better times, the uncertainty of life with the PDM was not a good background on which to base a relationship. Yet, despite all that, she now realised that she was falling for Nick.

"It'll be fine," said Nick with a reassuring smile. "If anything does go wrong, which it won't, I'll have Idris there to look after me. Just make sure you don't miss that meeting tomorrow. It's definitely something that you'll want to be there for!"

Nick desperately wanted to take Charley in his arms but he held back, still not sure of what she wanted and so afraid of destroying the relationship that they did have.

****

The next morning Pip, Nick and Idris set out on their seventy-mile journey, a journey which could turn out to be the most important in the entire history of the PDM so far. The three were bouncing with excitement, like three little children on an outing, especially Pip Holgrave. Although it had been a team effort, the broadcasting equipment had been Pip's idea. It had been his baby from start to finish and now that baby was reaching maturity. Finally, today, it would all come to fruition. Just under two hours later they reached Arderne, a small village a few miles from Newcastle Upon Tyne. Idris, who was driving, turned off the main road and went down a narrow lane leading to The Drum and Trumpet, a derelict pub with a car park at the rear. The Drum and Trumpet had been empty since the ban on gatherings, to which its dilapidated condition bore testimony. Idris pulled the car round behind the pub and parked so that it could not be seen from the road. It was about half past two, half an hour to broadcast time and probably ideal timing. Any later and it would have been a rush to be ready on time. Any earlier would have increased the risk of being spotted by a routine ATS patrol which had struck lucky.

Pip wasted no time in opening the glove compartment to reveal the control panel, turning the equipment on and giving everything a final check. Idris and Nick took up positions where they could watch the road without being seen. Absolutely nothing could approach anywhere near The Drum and Trumpet without Nick or Idris knowing about it. Pip was shaking with excitement and expectation as he inserted the recorded disc into its drive and waited for the correct time.

At precisely three o'clock Pip said to himself, "Let's get this show on the road." He switched on the jamming equipment and pressed the button marked BROADCAST. Finally, he started to relax as he watched the broadcast on the small TV screen fitted in the car, as in all vehicles. History was being made. This was a massive advance by the PDM and a huge step for the country. It was a truly momentous occasion, probably more momentous than anyone had yet realised.

★★★★

Back at PDM headquarters, everyone had gathered in expectation and curiosity about what was to come. Tables had been removed from the canteen and chairs arranged in rows to accommodate everyone. A large TV screen stood at the front of the room.

"We're going to watch The Daily Party News," announced George Richmond, with a cheeky smile on his face.

A groan escaped from the unimpressed audience as the fanfare rang out and the title flashed up on the screen. Was this really what they had all been summoned for? They did not remain unimpressed for long when they realised they were no longer watching Nigel Valentine. Instead, they were now watching Commander George Richmond. A spontaneous cheer rang out as everyone's interest intensified. At the end of the broadcast, a beaming George Richmond was given a standing ovation as he gave full credit and thanks to Pip Holgrave and his team.

★★★★

It was almost three p.m. and pupils at Hoddington Brook School were waiting for The Daily Party News to begin.

"Not again," said Joshua Kerley to his friend Stuart Woodleigh. "Every day it's the same old thing. What a great job this shit government is doing and what bastards the PDM are. I'm not sure I believe any of it anymore and we certainly don't need to keep hearing it day after day after day."

"Quiet Josh or we'll both be in trouble," replied his friend.

"Kerley and Woodleigh shut up or you'll be going to see the headmaster!" shouted maths teacher Mr Rhodes. Fortunately, although he had heard the boys talking, he had not actually heard what they were saying. Had he done so, the boys would probably have received a greater punishment than just going to see the headmaster.

The screen lit up, the usual fanfare began, the pastoral scenes were shown and the title, THE DAILY PARTY NEWS, was displayed on the screen. Then something very strange happened. Instead of President Valentine being on the screen there was a different person, a man who the boys had never seen before. This grey-haired man looked a little bit dour and yet had a kind, honest face. He looked like someone that you could trust. His manor was statesmanlike. He appeared to be as different to Nigel Valentine as a man could possibly be. He introduced himself as Commander George Richmond, the leader of the People's Democratic Movement, confirmed by his title displayed on screen.

"For many years," George began, "The Party have fed you with lies and propaganda daily. I have come here today to set the record straight and to tell you the truth!"

"Oh dear!" said Mr Rhodes, getting in a panic. "I don't think we should be watching this! The Party wouldn't like it! I'll have to turn it off!"

"You can't turn it off sir! The set's fixed so that it can't be turned off!" shouted Stuart.

"Oh! Yes! Yes, you're right!" mumbled Mr Rhodes, getting into a complete flap. "Well then perhaps you should just not watch it. Just ignore it!" he jabbered, getting more stressed by the second.

"But we want to watch it sir!" shouted Josh. "We need to watch it! We need to know what's really going on."

"You don't understand the trouble that we'll all be in if you watch it. Please trust me on this," pleaded the teacher.

"Look sir, you've tried to turn it off," argued Josh, "and you can't, so you can't stop us watching it."

Mr Rhodes, now breaking out in a cold sweat and visibly shaking with fear of the consequences, was forced to concede defeat.

The programme continued. "First of all, let me refute the lies that you have been told about the PDM. We are neither terrorists nor anarchists, as The Party would have you believe. We are freedom fighters, trying to get freedom from the tyranny of this government for you. We have never hurt or killed innocent civilians! We have never destroyed public, private or state property unless it was absolutely necessary. We were recently accused of planting a bomb in a school in Derby, killing children and teachers. That was a lie! It never happened and we would never do such a thing!

Every day people disappear without family or friends having any idea where they have gone. Every day people, who The Party wish to eliminate from society, are killed or sent to penal colonies with no right of protest or appeal.

The President states that he has reduced the numbers of the elderly requiring state care. To achieve these hugely reduced numbers, the elderly and the infirm have been euthanised by Age Acceleration for no good reason other than to prevent them from being a burden on society.

President Valentine says that he has cut the number of homeless by ninety per cent. That is because he has made homelessness a crime and punishment has often been Age Acceleration or deportation to a Penal Colony.

He has boasted that he has reduced the number of criminals who reoffend to almost zero. That is because offenders are sentenced to the Penal Colony for the rest of their lives. If they never get back into society they can never reoffend.

Now I have to tell you about something that you will find totally shocking and upsetting, even nauseating, but I have a duty to tell you the truth and we cannot allow this to be covered up any longer. The President has frequently boasted that he has provided cheap food, in the form of HCR and he has dared to claim that he has saved you money by taking away the bodies of your deceased loved ones, saving you the cost of burial or cremation. The reality is so abhorrent that I can hardly bear to tell you about it, but unfortunately, I have to. HCR stands for Human Carcass Reconstitution. HCR is produced from the bodies of your loved ones. I know that you will find it almost impossible to believe but unfortunately it is the truth. To prove it we recently carried out a raid on a factory owned by the Williamson Meat Corporation, the company paid by the government to produce HCR. The photographs which we are going to show you were taken to verify what was happening. If any of you are watching with young children, you may want to get the children to look away now."

While George continued talking photographs were shown on screen, the photographs which Idris took on the night of the raid showing the bodies, the machinery and the documents which were found by Nick.

"Not only was HCR made from human bodies but it also had large quantities of GDN93 added to it as a preservative. GDN93 was used in minute quantities in food many years ago. It was banned when it was discovered to be both carcinogenic and hepatotoxic. It can cause cancer and liver failure. Despite it being banned, it was added to HCR in much larger quantities than it had ever been used before. GDN93 is the reason that HCR can be kept for six months without refrigeration. I am very proud to say that this factory is one thing that we did genuinely blow up and destroy. At the same time, we also destroyed all known stocks of HCR. Unfortunately, because it can be kept for so long, some of you may have a stock of it in your own kitchen. If that is the case, I implore you not to eat it. Please burn it or bury it but you

MUST NOT EAT IT! Apart from making you an unwitting cannibal, eating it repeatedly WILL KILL YOU!

President Valentine boasts about the quality of the State Health Service. The truth is that the SHS only serves a quarter of the population. The other seventy-five per cent of you have to rely on charity hospitals which are not fit for purpose. Despite heroic work by volunteer nurses and doctors, people are frequently dying due to the lack of adequate treatment.

For far too long you, the people, have had no say in your government. Worse than that, you daren't even talk about the government for fear of being arrested. We want the country to return to being a democracy, with people able to choose their own government and being allowed to talk openly about politics. We want you to have the freedom to gather in groups again, to go to the pub, hold parties, funerals, weddings, sporting events. We want to give you back your freedom but we can't do that without YOUR help. The time has come to rise up against The Party but we can't do that on our own!

What I have told you must have been an enormous shock and almost impossible to believe. Take some time to deliberate on it. UNFORTUNATELY, IT IS THE TRUTH! Keep watching your TV set for our broadcasts at this time each day. We may also announce different times for broadcasts later. Whenever we can, we will bring you more programmes to keep you informed of the truth."

As the broadcast came to a close Mr Rhodes was still in a flap. "Ignore everything you've just seen and heard! You never watched it! It's obviously all lies! The Party won't be happy if they think you've watched it! I'll be in trouble if they think I let you watch it! This is all so bad! Say nothing about this afternoon to anybody! It never happened! Remember that boys, it never happened! You didn't see anything!"

"That all makes so much sense," Josh said quietly to Stuart. "I'm inclined to believe the PDM."

"Me too," replied Stuart. "I can't wait to see the next broadcast."

"Well, we won't have too long to wait. It sounded like there'll be another one tomorrow."

"As long as they don't find some way to stop us watching it," said Stuart. "Dusty will have a nervous breakdown if he has to go through that again. He's obviously terrified of the authorities."

Although the two boys had been talking in barely more than a whisper, their conversation had been overheard. Fortunately, they had been overheard by a friend and fellow pupil, Shane Whiteliff.

"If this is all true, we can't just ignore it and leave things as they are," interrupted Shane.

"What can WE do?" asked Stuart.

"I don't know yet but we seriously need to think about it!" replied Shane.

"He's right Stu," said Josh, looking very thoughtful. "We've got to do something!"

Others all around the country had taken the information on board but were not quite so prepared to talk about it yet, BUT THE SEED HAD BEEN SOWN!

Chapter 18.

GERMINATION

On their arrival back at headquarters Pip, Nick and Idris were treated like heroes, such was the impact of the broadcasts, both on the morale of the PDM and the anticipated reaction of the public. Mike Riches, Jock Munroe and Tim Collinson were treated with the same reverence when they returned the following day. Replacement teams were already prepped and ready to take over as soon as the equipment had been checked. Everyone realised it was a team effort. Many had played their part already and many would in the future but, just like the first moon landing, people would always remember the pioneers who were the first to step forward and put their heads above the parapet. Despite the temporary adulation there was one person who Nick was desperate to see.

In the days when he had been away, when he was not actually busy with the matter in hand, Nick had been constantly thinking about Charley and their relationship. He could not get her out of his head. He was worried that Charley might have had second thoughts while he was away, that she might think the developing relationship would destroy the great friendship that they had. He wondered if they might feel uncomfortable when they met, after their last conversation. He had no need to worry. Charley had been waiting anxiously for his return. The moment she saw him, the smile on her face said everything as she threw her arms around him. Neither of them cared if anyone else was watching as their embrace turned into a passionate kiss, the first they had shared but definitely not the last, as both were overcome by the joy of being reunited.

"I'm so relieved that you're back safe," said Charley, resting her head on Nick's shoulder. "I was so afraid that I might lose you."

"There's no way that I'd let that happen. I'm afraid you're stuck with me, like it or not!" Nick reassured her, remembering how she had lost Dell and the fear she must have of that being repeated.

"I like it!" she replied. "You're quite a hero you know, you Pip and Idris. You wouldn't believe how much it's lifted everybody's spirit."

"How's Jon been?" asked Nick, coming slightly back to reality.

"He's been fine. He's really proud of you, you know. I think he always has been but he's even more proud than ever now. Jon and Maddy have been great together, almost like brother and sister rather than just friends. He's so protective of her and you can tell that she feels safe and relaxed whenever he's around.

I've been so nervous about you coming home. I wasn't sure how things would be for us when you got back but we're good, aren't we?"

"Yes Charley! We're good! In fact, we're great!" Nick reassured her as they kissed again.

Idris, who had stood so quietly that Nick and Charley had not even noticed his presence, gave a discreet cough.

As Nick and Charley jumped apart, Idris laughed. "I'm so glad you two have finally admitted how you feel about each other. The rest of us have known it for months."

"How did you know, Taff?" asked Nick. "We weren't even sure ourselves."

"It was as plain as the nose on your face boy!" said Idris, still grinning. "I felt like banging your heads together, more than once."

Charley blushed with embarrassment, making her look even more attractive. At least for the time being the couple were relieved and happy in their newly discovered relationship.

★★★★

Josh, Stuart and Shane were discussing the events of the past week, away from prying ears, as they walked home from Hoddington Brook School. The three mates all lived in the same direction so walking together would not arouse any suspicion but it was important that their conversation was not overheard.

Despite the persistent worrying and vocal disapproval of teacher "Dusty" Rhodes, nothing could prevent the boys watching all six of the PDM broadcasts so far. The three were now convinced that the PDM's version of events was the truth. The other pupils were starting to voice a similar opinion, although Josh did not trust them all. He had once tricked his own grandfather into giving himself away, to Josh's eternal shame. How could he be sure that he was not going to be the victim of similar deceit? He knew he could trust Stuart and Shane, but there were several others that he had doubts about. The less they knew about his thoughts, for the time being, the better. For now, all ideas had to be kept strictly confidential, although a time would soon come when they would need to go more public. Support for the PDM was certainly growing. There were even beginning to be some mutterings of discontent from some adults, although Joshua's father was still too afraid of his own shadow to say anything against The Party.

"Alright," said Josh, "we know now that The Party have been lying to us. We have to find some way of helping to change things! We have to help to get The Party out of office. We have to change this fucking rancid government!"

"Any idea how?" asked Shane. "It's not like WE can suddenly start a revolution!"

"No! That would need the adults to join with the PDM to fight the government and that's not going to happen!" said Stuart.

"The adults are scared shitless of what The Party, particularly the fucking Blackshirts, might do so they sit back and just accept it, all the shit that we are getting! Maybe we could give them a push to get things started," continued Josh.

"What do you mean?" asked Stuart, getting worried about what he might be getting into. "How can we give them a push? We can't fight anybody! We don't have any weapons and we're not trained to fight! We wouldn't have a clue! We wouldn't stand a chance!"

"Suppose we organized a demonstration," suggested Josh. "A peaceful demonstration! Just us, just children! If we were unarmed the Blackshirts would have no reason to attack us. They wouldn't see us as a threat, just a bunch of kids being a nuisance. Sure, we would be breaking the law by holding a large gathering. Some of us might even be arrested but there would be no excuse for them to use violence. Maybe, if our parents saw what we were doing, they'd want to join in and rise up against The Party."

"That all sounds pretty risky," said a very nervous Stuart. "You can't be sure the Blackshirts won't use violence. They won't give a damn who gets hurt or even killed!"

"It could be worth it," said Shane, getting fired up by Josh's enthusiasm. "We'd need to take them by surprise though, so we'd have to be careful how we organize it. We'd need to make sure word didn't get out until we were ready."

"So, are we agreed then?" asked Josh. "Are we going to do it?"

"I'm really not sure about this at all, Josh!" said a very reticent Stuart.

"Well, you can count me in!" said Shane without a moment of hesitation.

"Okay, you guys have convinced me," said Stuart with new found confidence. "You can count me in as well! Let's do it!"

"It'll take a little time," said Josh. "We need to sound people out carefully and make sure who we can count on."

"Agreed," said Stuart, "but we can't take too long to organise it or word will get out to the authorities and they'll stop us before we've even got started."

****

The Party had been in turmoil since the PDM's broadcasts had begun. The first couple of broadcasts had just made them angry but when they realised that the broadcasts were going to continue, they went into panic mode. Headless chickens was the perfect description, with everybody playing the blame game.

Nigel Valentine had called for a meeting with recently promoted Commander of Security Forces, Glyn Quinlan. The frosty meeting took place in President Valentine's office.

The President was pacing the floor with nervous anger as he started on Quinlan. "I told you after their first broadcast that this had to be stopped immediately Commander and you agreed to do just that! We have now had six broadcasts and they obviously intend to continue. So far, you've failed pathetically! What's going on? I sincerely hope that you are going to tell me that you can put a rapid stop to the broadcasts! How can they possibly broadcast their transmissions and block ours?"

"Mr President," whined Quinlan, "they've obviously developed some technology which we just don't yet have. Our electronics experts are working hard to solve the problem but so far, they are nowhere near success. We've tried everything we possibly could to trace where the broadcasts are coming from, but they are very clever. They don't broadcast long enough for us to pinpoint the site. We've only been able to narrow it down to an area, a town or city, but nothing more precise than that. To be able to trace them more accurately we would need the broadcasts to last much longer and they obviously know that. What makes it more difficult is that the broadcasts come from a different area each day. On day one they broadcast from Newcastle-upon-Tyne, day two from Bristol, day three from Ipswich, day four from Chester, day five from Coventry and then today from Carlisle. They can't possibly have that many transmitters which must mean that they have some kind of mobile unit. If so, it is clearly far more advanced than anything that we have. I would expect it to require an extremely large vehicle which would stand out like a sore thumb, but our patrols have seen nothing suspicious. Then we have the pattern: Newcastle-upon-Tyne, Bristol, Ipswich, Chester, Coventry and Carlisle. There is no pattern to it at all! They are travelling many miles and apparently doubling back on themselves to avoid detection. Consequently, we have no way of working out, or even guessing, where they might broadcast from next. We fixed all of the TV sets, for our own broadcasts, so that they had to be on at three p.m. and the sets could not be turned off. That unfortunately means that it is pretty much impossible to stop people watching the broadcasts."

"ENOUGH OF YOUR EXCUSES COMMANDER!" yelled Valentine, banging his clenched fist hard on his desk in temper and frustration. "We have to stop them no matter what it takes! Failing to do so is NOT an option! NO MATTER WHAT IT TAKES COMMANDER!"

Quinlan thought for a moment. "If we switch The Daily Party News to a different time and keep changing the time of it, at least we should be able to avoid them jamming our broadcasts. Of course, not everyone will be watching at the right time, but we will still reach many of the people.

We can get engineers into as many homes as possible, as quickly as possible, to remove the automatic switch on devices from the TVs. Of course, it will take time to get to all of them. In the meantime, we make it illegal to watch the PDM broadcasts, with Age Acceleration being the penalty for anyone caught doing so. We can follow that up with random spot checks on houses, at the times of the PDM broadcasts, to catch any perpetrators. Fear of the death penalty should frighten most people enough to stop them watching. I'm afraid it's really only damage limitation but that is the best we can do until our electronics experts can find a permanent solution."

"Then get to work Commander!" said Nigel Valentine. "Find these broadcasters as soon as possible but, in the meantime, come down on those watching with your full might! Let them feel your anger and your will! Make them afraid to watch the PDM! Exert your authority with an iron fist! That's why you were given the job!"

"Rest assured the ATS will do whatever's necessary, Sir!" said Quinlan with the swagger of a man who was about to do what he was best at and what he enjoyed most. He intended to terrorise anyone who dared to follow the fortunes of the PDM.

Chapter 19.

A VOICE FROM THE PAST

Joshua Kerley was chilling, listening to music in his bedroom, unwinding after a hard day at school when his phone rang. He answered it to hear a warning voice, a voice which sounded familiar and yet one which he could not place.

"Is that Joshua Kerley?"

"Yes, it is," answered Josh.

"Joshua, the ATS are coming for you. They know what you have been planning, you and your friends. They are on their way now. You probably only have about half an hour to get out of there."

"Who is this?" asked Joshua.

"That doesn't matter and it's probably best that you don't know. You and your father both need to get out of there quickly! Trust me! You have no time to lose." The call ended abruptly.

Although he could not put a name to the caller, Josh was convinced that the call was genuine and that he knew the caller. The voice had been very matter of fact, lacking in emotion and authoritative. Josh rushed to tell his father who was sitting in the living room, struggling to decide what to watch on TV. These days Edward Kerley found it very difficult to make a decision about anything.

"Dad, I've just had a phone call warning me that the Blackshirts are on their way here, NOW! We need to go. It's me that they're really after but I don't want them to hurt you again. We both need to get out of here right away!"

"No point in running son! They'll find us whatever we do! They can't be beaten. We're done for!" said Edward, sounding like a rabbit caught in car headlights, too scared to move.

Josh thought he had better warn Stuart and Shane. If the ATS knew about Josh they were sure to know about his friends. He wasted no time in ringing both and arranging to meet them outside a derelict pub, The Purple Goblin, about half a mile away. He stuffed some spare clothes and some food into a rucksack as quickly as he could and went back to tackle his dad again.

"Dad, I have to go!" said Josh. "Now! Before the Blackshirts get here! Please come with me!"

"You're right, son," said Edward. "If they're coming for you then you have to go. You'll have a much better chance without me. I'm staying here. They'll get me wherever I go! I've got no chance of getting away. I'll just sit here and wait for them but you go. Good luck son!"

Josh knew he had no chance of persuading his father to change his mind and run. He hated leaving him behind but there was no alternative. Josh had to go.

"Take care dad," said Josh, his eyes beginning to well up. "I'm gonna miss you."

"Get out of here Josh! Now! Before it's too late! Don't let them hurt you the way they hurt me!" shouted Edward, as his son was going out the door.

About twenty minutes after Josh had left, Edward heard someone hammering on his front door and knew, of course, it was the ATS. Frozen with fear, he remained sitting in his armchair unable to move to the door to let them in. The wooden frame splintered as the door was kicked in and the Blackshirts entered.

"Why didn't you open the door?" asked the officer in charge.

"I knew you would get in anyway whatever I did. I didn't need to open the door," replied Edward, shaking and rocking in his chair with fear.

"I am Chief Commanding Officer Woodwill of the Anti-Terrorist Squad." Hugo Woodwill was the new replacement for Glyn Quinlan, following Quinlan's promotion to his government role. "Are you Edward Kerley?"

"You know I am," replied Edward, his feeble voice reaching hardly more than a whisper.

"Where is your son, Joshua?" demanded Woodwill.

"He's gone!" said Edward, with a faint smile of bravado.

Woodwill despatched three officers to search and ransack the house.

"You won't find him!" continued Edward. "I told you he's gone, well away from here. He had a phone call to warn him that you were coming."

"Phone call from whom?" demanded Woodwill.

"I have no idea," replied Edward. "Someone just rang up and said that the ATS were coming."

"Do you have any idea where he will have gone?" continued the CCO, becoming angry at the thought of Josh slipping through his fingers.

"I have no idea," replied Edward Kerley, beginning to rock in his chair again as his fear was building.

The officers returning from their search confirmed that Joshua had indeed gone and they had found nothing to indicate where he might have run to.

"In that case, Edward Kerley you are under arrest!" CCO Hugo Woodwill smiled a twisted, sadistic smile.

Edward's fear had now developed beyond the rocking stage as he began to hug himself tightly and shake uncontrollably.

"What are you going to do to me?" he stammered, hardly able to get the words out.

"We will take you away for interrogation and, when we have finished with you, you will go for Civil Correction," sneered Woodwill.

"I can't go through that again! I can't!" sobbed Edward, tears running down his face as he rocked and shook.

"Then you should have stopped your boy from getting into trouble and you should tell us where he is! You have brought this upon yourself!"

"I didn't know what was going on. I thought he was a good boy. I've done nothing!" pleaded Edward.

His nerve and all reason now completely deserting him, Edward sprang from his chair. Surprise enabled him to knock Woodwill to the ground and grab the officer's handgun from its holster. For a second, he just stood there with the gun in his hand before putting the muzzle into his own mouth and pulling the trigger.

"The stupid, cowardly fool," muttered Hugo Woodwill as he wiped the spattering of blood and brain from his uniform.

****

Joshua Kerley and Stuart Woodleigh had been waiting outside The Purple Goblin for their friend Shane Whiteliff for over an hour.

"Shane must have been picked up by the Blackshirts," said Joshua. "There's no way that he would be this late unless he'd been arrested."

"Unless they don't know about Shane and, if they've not turned up to arrest him, he's decided to stay put," replied Stuart.

"If that was the case, Stu, surely he would have let us know. He has both of our phone numbers. I'd try ringing him but we might get one of the Blackshirts answering. No! He must have been picked up!"

The boys had been watching the road like hawks for any sign of Shane or any sign of the ATS. Suddenly Stuart spotted what they had been dreading.

"Josh there's two ATS cars coming down the road! We need to get out of here!"

The boys thought about making a run for it but a third car started pulling in to the car park at the rear of the pub. If they attempted to run now, they were bound to be seen. The pub was locked, bolted and barred securely except for the hatch on the entrance to the cellar. They quickly lifted the hatch, dropped into the cellar and prayed that they had not been spotted. The cellar contained several empty barrels, from the days when the pub was open and thriving. It also contained an enormous bunker, used to store logs. In its heyday, the pub had boasted cosy log fires. The logs and sacks to carry them upstairs were kept in the bunker.

The Blackshirts found the unfastened cellar hatch and entered to search the pub. They passed through the cellar and up the stairs to search the rest of the building. They even checked the old wood store.

"This is a waste of time," they overheard amidst the noise of stomping feet and banging doors. "They're not here. They've clearly flown the coop, unless the lad gave us duff information."

"The Chief was convinced the info was genuine. He said the boy's been very helpful lately."

"Well, we must have got here too late then. They're not here now so we'd best not waste any more time on them."

"I suppose you're right but the Chief won't be happy, not happy at all!"

The boys heard what sounded like the Blackshirts leaving but they remained in their hidey-hole for some time to be sure they were not walking into a trap.

'So, Shane has dobbed us in,' thought Josh, annoyed with himself for trusting his so-called friend.

Certain that they were alone again, the boys emerged from the wood store. One officer had actually looked into the bunker, but a covering of empty sacks and a few logs had been enough to prevent them from being seen.

"We can't stay here," said Josh. "They could come back any time."

"Do you know the old Saint Dominic's Church? It's been closed and boarded up for as long as I can remember, but I was nosing around there a few weeks ago. There are a couple of places where the boards are not very secure and we should be able to get in quite easily. It's easy to get to without being seen. Just about a mile walk, through woods all the way."

"Sounds good to me! What are we waiting for?" said Josh. "Let's hide in there tonight. It'll give us chance to get some rest and plan what to do next."

The journey to Saint Dominic's was uneventful except for tripping over the occasional tree root in the dark as neither boy had thought to take a torch. It was easy to gain access to the church, just a case of removing one of the boards which covered the doors and windows. Once inside, they found candles and matches. They quickly lit two or three candles. The empty candlelit church had a very eerie feel but at least they were safe there, for the time being anyway. They ate some of the food they had taken with them and soon fell asleep, both overtaken by the exhaustion of the night's events.

****

Josh awoke early although Stuart was still asleep. As he lay awake, Josh was turning things over and over in his mind. It looked like it must have been Shane who betrayed them. If not, why did he not turn up at The Purple Goblin and how would the Blackshirts know where to look for Josh and Stuart? How did he let Shane fool him so easily? He had been convinced that Shane was loyal to their cause. Shane always seemed so keen on the idea of the demonstration. Why did Shane change sides or was his apparent enthusiasm always just a ploy to ensnare Josh and Stuart. He wondered what had happened to his dad. Josh wished that he had been able to persuade his dad to escape with him. Who knows what the Blackshirts might have done in a bid to persuade him to give them information, information which he didn't possess. At the very least he would be taken for Civil Correction, the same Civil Correction which had previously left him broken, mentally scarred and from which he had never recovered. Josh was also wondering who the mystery caller was. Who had warned him to get out and why? It sounded like an older man. He knew the voice but he just couldn't place it. Who could Joshua possibly know who might be privy to information about the activities of the ATS?

When Stuart woke up, the boys shared the remains of their food for breakfast. They decided it was safest to stay put, in the church, for the time being. They had the basic essentials: a water supply, a toilet, somewhere to hang out and to sleep. Although the electricity had been disconnected, they had a plentiful supply of candles for light. The one important thing that they did not have was more food. Josh decided that he would wait until school was over and then he would ring Lorna. Maybe Lorna could bring them some food that evening.

Lorna Duncan was Josh's girlfriend and had been for about six months. She was very much a tomboy, despite having a pretty, dark haired, dark eyed, feminine appearance. That contradiction was what Josh liked most about her. She wasn't spooked easily. She seemed to take everything in her stride. She had played a minor role in trying to organize the demonstration so Josh was worried in case Shane had sent the ATS to her as well. He thought it was very unlikely as her involvement was only minor, otherwise he would have warned her at the same time that he had warned Stuart and Shane.

Josh rang Lorna at around five thirty, hoping that no-one else would be around to hear when she took the call. She recognised the number immediately.

"Josh! I'm so glad it's you! I was terrified that you might have been dead! I was so worried when you and Stuart weren't in school today. Shane was saying that he wondered if you had been arrested by the Blackshirts," she gabbled excitedly.

"Calm down, Lorna," said Josh. "We can't talk for long in case you're overheard but Stuart and I are hiding in Saint Dominic's Church, you know, the old church ruin."

"Yes, I know the place," she replied, becoming a lot calmer.

"I really don't want to get you involved babe but we need food. Do you think you could bring us some?"

"Yes, I'll get onto that right away. Do you need anything else?"

"A torch would be useful. Lorna, please be careful and don't say anything to anybody about this. Most important of all, don't say anything to Shane when you see him tomorrow."

"Okay Josh! I won't be long!"

"Thanks Lorna. Please take care babe. See you soon." Josh put the phone down. He really didn't want to risk getting Lorna involved but he didn't know where else to turn for an ally.

★★★★

It was little more than an hour later when Josh received another phone call from Lorna. "Josh, I'm outside the church. How do I get in?"

Josh stepped out of the side door from which he had removed the boards. "I'm here babe. Come this way."

They both entered the church and, once inside and despite the presence of Stuart, Lorna gave Josh a big hug.

"I'm so glad you're safe!" said Lorna. "It was such a relief when you rang. I thought you might have been dead! When the two of you didn't turn up for school this morning, Shane kept saying that he was worried you may have been arrested. I decided to go to your house at lunchtime to see if you were alright. I knocked but nobody answered. When she heard me, your next-door neighbour came out to tell me that the Blackshirts had called at your house last night. She thought that she had heard a gunshot and she said that the Blackshirts carried somebody out in a body bag. Josh I was so scared that it was you in that bag!"

Despite his usual stoicism, Josh found himself crying uncontrollably. "I asked him to come with me! I begged him to come with me but he wouldn't! I had to go. I couldn't wait any longer," he sobbed. Regaining a modicum of self-control, he continued. "My dad wouldn't leave the house. He was too afraid to. He must still have been there when the Blackshirts arrived. They must have killed him! It must have been my dad in that body bag!" He sniffed hard and wiped away the tears with his palm as anger began to take over. "The fucking bastards! Why did they do that? He wouldn't harm a fly! He was too afraid to harm anyone. Those bastards! I'll get even with them! If it takes the rest of my life I'll get even!"

Knowing that any display of affection now was the last thing that Josh would want, Lorna just stood with a comforting hand resting on his arm.

"And all this has been caused by fucking Shane," said Stuart. "It has to have been Shane!"

"I don't understand," said Lorna. "What's Shane got to do with it? He seemed most concerned when you didn't show up this morning."

"I got a phone call last night, I don't know who from, warning me that the Blackshirts were coming for me. I rang Stuart and Shane to warn them. We agreed to meet up at The Purple Goblin. Shane never showed up but the Blackshirts did. We were lucky to get away. Shane must have tipped them off. If not, why did he not admit to you that he knew we were on the run? That proves that he's responsible for this."

"I suppose we have to call the demo off. No doubt the Blackshirts will know all about it and be ready for us. Shane was pushing for it to take place on Friday. It's a pity if we do have to cancel it, because support really seems to be growing today. Strangely, wondering about you two appears to have caused a lot more interest," said Lorna. "Dave Bridlane seems really keen to get involved. He's got two brothers, Paul and Ryan, who both go to Saint Erasmus High. They've been spreading the word there and it looks like the Saint Erasmus kids want to join in. Shane also wants them to try to get the primary school kids to join us."

Saint Erasmus High School was less than half a mile up the road from Hoddington Brook School. It was right next to Saint Erasmus Primary School.

"Why on earth does he want the kids from the Primary involved?" asked Josh.

"Shane reckons that it'll be safer if we have the primary school kids with us. He said that even the Blackshirts won't harm little children."

"That's rubbish!" exclaimed Josh. "The Blackshirts won't care how young the kids are. They'll be in too much danger! Lorna, you've got to try to talk them out of that! You've got to try to stop the primary kids getting involved!"

"I'll do my best Josh but Shane seems to be pushing pretty hard for it," replied Lorna.

"Hopefully," said Josh, "the demonstration can still go ahead on Friday without the little ones. Don't say anything to Shane but I intend to be there!"

"Count me in as well!" said Stuart. "I'd love to see Shane's face when we both turn up!"

"Is that wise?" asked a concerned Lorna. "If the Blackshirts recognise you, you might be singled out as a target."

"That's a chance we'll just have to take," said Josh with a smile of determination. "What do you say Stu?"

"Too right mate!" replied Stuart, emboldened by his friend's enthusiasm. "There's no way that we're going to miss it!"

Lorna's attention turned to the bag that she was carrying. "I've brought you food. I've brought bread and butter, cheese, ham and some cold chicken. I've got a carton of milk and a couple of cans of cola. Oh, and I've brought you a torch and some spare batteries. Tell me if there's anything else you need and I'll try to bring it tomorrow."

"Thanks babe, that's great!" said Josh.

"Very much appreciated!" agreed Stuart.

"Now you'd better not hang around any longer," said Josh. "We don't want you arousing any suspicion or putting yourself in danger."

★★★★

Later that night, Josh was still thinking about the warning phone call. He was convinced that he knew the voice and couldn't get it out of his mind. Suddenly he had an epiphany.

"Stu, I know who rang me yesterday! I knew the voice was familiar. It was Chief Officer Mollison of the PEO! I'm certain of it!"

"Adam Mollison? Chief Officer of the Party Enforcement Officers? The guy who tricked you into shopping your grandfather? Why would a Brownshirt officer want to help you?" asked Stuart.

"I don't know," said Joshua. "Maybe he felt guilty about what happened to grandad and wanted to do something to make up for it. Maybe he's not as enamoured with The Party as we always assumed he was. Who knows? I'm certain it was him!"

Joshua wondered if it might prove to be useful to have an ally in the Party Enforcement Office if indeed that was what he had.

★★★★

Shane Whiteliff was on the telephone to Chief Commanding Officer Hugo Woodwill.

"Getting rid of Josh and Stuart doesn't seem to have put anyone off holding the demonstration. Most of them seem keener than ever. A few more have stepped up to help to organize it. I can give you some more names if you want to arrest them."

"No. There's no need! I think we'll let them all gather for the demonstration and then we'll teach them a lesson that they'll never forget! Just make sure that the little children go along. I might also need your help to flush the other leaders out when the time comes. Well done, Shane! You have done well!" said the Chief Commanding Officer.

Chapter 20.
DEMONSTRATION AND REVOLUTION

It was Friday morning at Hoddington Brook School. All of the pupils had gathered in the classroom as usual, all that is except Joshua Kerley and Stuart Woodleigh. The demonstration was planned to start at nine thirty. Everyone was bursting with excitement yet almost manic with fear and trepidation in anticipation of what was to come; everyone except Shane Whiteliff. Shane appeared as cool as a cucumber. Only Lorna knew the real reason for Shane appearing so calm. Only Lorna knew that Shane was a traitor. That knowledge made Lorna even more nervous as she sat watching the clock. The clock ticked and the minute hand moved one minute on.

"That's nine thirty! Time to get the show started!" shouted Shane enthusiastically.

"Yeah! Let's do this, folks!" added Dave Bridlane, trying to match Shane's apparent bravado.

Despite protests from their teachers, the clamour of excitement increased as the pupils left the classroom and grew to a crescendo as classes met in the entrance hall. They headed out through the front door, to face who knows what in the street, to begin the demonstration. The sudden feeling of being more exposed outside dampened the buzz just a little and made most feel even more apprehensive, but the street seemed surprisingly quiet. The pupils felt relieved that there were no Blackshirts waiting for them. Around six hundred and fifty pupils gathered and began to march towards Saint Erasmus High.

"Paul and Ryan should be bringing the Saint Erasmus kids out by now," said Dave Bridlane.

"I'm surprised there's no ATS or PEO here to stop us," said Lorna. "I can't believe that we've managed to do this without them finding out."

Two figures suddenly emerged from across the road and ran to join the crowd.

"Josh? Stuart? I didn't think we'd see you two here today, but I can't tell you how glad I am that you are!" said Dave with a big welcoming grin.

"I'm really pleased to see you both too," said Lorna. "It looks like we're all ready now!"

Shane stayed silent.

"We wouldn't have missed this for the world!" replied Josh. "There's no show without Punch! Good to see you too Shane!"

Shane still said nothing but gave a sheepish smile.

"We had a quick scout around on the way here," interrupted Stuart. "There's a lot of Blackshirts and Brownshirts in the area. They're not here now so I can only imagine they intend to confront us after we've joined up with the guys from Saint Erasmus."

"I guess we always knew we'd have to face them at some point, so don't worry about that until it happens," said Shane, finally finding his voice.

Moving along the road they soon met up with the pupils from Saint Erasmus; four hundred and fifty from the High School and two hundred and fifty from the Primary School.

"Hi bro's!" said Dave Bridlane when he met up with his brothers, Paul and Ryan. "You've done a great job getting everybody to turn out."

"Why have you brought the Primary School kids?" asked Josh.

"Shane's idea!" said Ryan Bridlane,

"Shane reckoned it would stop the Blackshirts from reacting too harshly," added his brother, Paul.

"Stupid idea if you ask me," said Stuart. "It won't make any difference to what the Blackshirts do and, even if it did, only cowards hide behind little kids."

"Well, they're here now, so we can't do much about it except protect them as best we can," said Josh.

Shane still stood tight lipped, looking extremely uncomfortable.

The relative peace was soon shattered by the sound of marching men, the sound of military boots stamping on concrete and tarmac, as the security forces amassed to confront the demonstrators. Three hundred Blackshirts and three hundred and fifty Brownshirts, all in full riot gear, armed with firearms and batons, gathered under the command of Chief Commanding Officer Hugo Woodwill and Chief Officer Adam Mollison respectively.

The PDM had heard a rumour about the demonstration and had sent thirty agents, under the command of Jock Munroe, to try to protect the children. They had not expected such a display of force by the authorities, not against children. Outnumbered by more than twenty to one, Jock was unsure of what to do and so they stayed out of sight and waited.

Hugo Woodwill, assisted by a microphone and loud speakers, addressed the crowd. "You stupid, stupid children! What do you think you are doing? You are acting against The Party and breaking the law! Surely you knew that we would not allow that! Are you not afraid of the consequences? You should be! I can see some of you shaking with fear and yet you have been foolish enough to let your leaders lead you into this! I will give you one chance to disperse and go home, NOW! If you don't accept that opportunity, you will suffer the consequences and I guarantee that you will regret the decision to stay!"

Although the children were all now frightened out of their wits, none of them moved. Every child stood in defiance.

"Very well! So be it!" Woodwill's voice boomed out from the speakers. "You have brought this upon yourselves! You will regret being so stupid."

Upon Woodwill's instruction, an ATS snatch squad of around a dozen men waded into the demonstrators, wielding their batons and cracking skulls as they went, to grab six of the youngest primary school children. The terrified five and six year olds began to cry and scream as they were dragged back to the CCO.

"We have some little piglets!" continued Woodwill with delight. "Some little squealing piglets! I know how to stop them squealing, permanently! I want your ringleaders to give themselves up right now! If they do not, I will slaughter one of the little squealing piglets every sixty seconds!"

Josh and Stuart stepped forward and were immediately handcuffed.

"Where are the rest of your leaders? Are they too cowardly to come forward? Are you trying to take me for a fool? Do you expect me to believe that only two people organized all this? I want the rest of the ringleaders and I am running out of patience! You obviously doubt that I will carry out my threat!"

Woodwill grabbed one of the terrified infants and shot the child at point blank range, tossing the limp body aside like discarded refuse.

"Now you know that I am not joking! That's how I silence squealing piglets! Now, I want the rest of the ringleaders unless you want me to continue slaughtering piglets!"

"We'll have to give ourselves up! We can't let him kill more of the kids," said Shane, stepping forward to look like a hero. He was followed by the three Bridlane brothers and Lorna, all handing themselves over to save the infants. All of them were handcuffed, taken to Woodwill and forced to kneel in front of him, beside Josh and Stuart. They were all handcuffed, that is, except for Shane.

"Well done, Shane," said Woodwill, stepping forward to shake the boy's hand. "You have done well. I'm proud of you!"

Josh desperately wanted to feel his fingers around Shane's throat, squeezing the last breath out of him. How could he have done this? How could he betray his friends and cause infants to be killed?

"Now I have your leaders! They don't look such heroes now do they. These are the people who led you into this trouble! You have two minutes to disperse and go home! If you remain here after that, I will shoot one of your leaders every thirty seconds until you DO disperse! If you still remain here after that, we will start firing at the rest of you and we WILL shoot to kill! Now, I think we will start with this girl!" Woodwill pulled Lorna close to him and put his gun to her temple. Lorna began to tremble as he continued. "You have about fifteen seconds left!"

"We'll have no more killing!" yelled Adam Mollison. "We're not going to kill any more innocent civilians, especially children!"

"Arrest that traitor!" ordered Woodwill.

There was no response from the Brownshirts. A few Blackshirts tried to move forward towards the Commanding Officer but were stopped by Mollison's men. A shot rang out and Hugo Woodwill fell to the ground, dead.

A fire fight broke out between the Blackshirts on one side and the Brownshirts backed by the PDM on the other. A small group of PDM quickly rescued Lorna, Josh and the others from the clutches of the ATS and tried to usher the rest of the children to safety. The Blackshirts, having suffered heavy losses, being leaderless, outflanked, outnumbered and outfought, fled in disarray. Shane fled with them. A cheer went up from the children. The demonstration was over! The battle was over! THE REVOLUTION HAD BEGUN!

When the dust had settled, it was time for Jock Munroe and Adam Mollison to have a serious and important discussion.

First of all, they both commended Josh, Stuart, Lorna and the Bridlane brothers for their bravery. Without them the events of that day would never have taken place. Josh and his friends were relieved that none of the children had been hurt except for the one infant killed by Woodwill.

Commanding Officer Mollison told Jock Munroe that there had been a lot of unrest in the PEO. The Brownshirts had had more than enough of the ATS, The Party and their oppressive actions. The vast majority of the Brownshirts were ready to throw their weight behind the PDM in a bid to overthrow the Valentine regime. The two decided to try to arrange a meeting between George Richmond and the supreme commander of the PEO, Commander-In-Chief Hadrian Lubeck.

A meeting took place two days later, on neutral territory just outside Barnsley. Commander-In-Chief Lubeck did not take part.

He had resigned and gone on the run, in fear of retribution for his part in supporting The Party. His place was taken by Deputy Commander-In-Chief Ed Gilfedder. Richmond and Gilfedder agreed to officially combine forces to overthrow The Party and Nigel Valentine. It was agreed that, if successful, a new government would be formed under the leadership of George Richmond. A cabinet would be formed including Gilfedder, other senior PDM and PEO members, along with some chosen civilians. The ultimate aim would be to re-establish the United Kingdom as a democracy and to restore the freedom of the people.

The PDM had also filmed the events on the day of the demonstration and the film was broadcast nationwide the following day. This triggered more demonstrations in other parts of the country, no longer led by children but by adults who were finally throwing off their fear. The demonstrators were backed and protected by the PDM and the PEO. The demonstrators even began to arm themselves and form a civilian militia. Their shackles had finally been thrown off. Now only the ATS supported Nigel Valentine and they were definitely on the retreat.

Chapter 21.
DRONE ATTACK

Following the agreement between George Richmond and Ed Gilfedder a combined force was formed, the United Revolutionary Army (URA), consisting of the PDM, the PEO, most of the DDPU and civilian militia, all under the ultimate command of George Richmond. The ATS were initially overpowered and the URA rapidly took complete control of most of Scotland, Cumberland, Durham, Northumberland, Yorkshire, Lancashire, Cornwall, Devon and Dorset, creating a pincer movement pushing south and north towards the central government areas. Due to being outnumbered, out-thought and outfought, the only time that the ATS held their own in skirmishes was when they were supported by the Drone Air Force (DAF).

The DAF consisted of two squadrons of drones. Number One Squadron was based at Kings Langton Air Base, near to Salisbury, in Wiltshire. Number Two Squadron was based at Grescott Air Base, near to Mansfield, in Nottinghamshire. Both squadrons consisted of U.A.C.P. (Unmanned Air Combat Planes) Cougar FXs and U.R.P. (Unmanned Reconnaissance Planes) Vulture OXs. Number One Squadron consisted of twenty-five Cougars and fifteen Vultures. Number Two Squadron consisted of twenty-seven Cougars and sixteen Vultures.

The URP Vultures carried no weapons and were used purely for reconnaissance. The UACP Cougars were routinely armed with Rapier laser cannon. They could also carry four Hades missiles for air-to-ground or air-to-air attack and up to four high impact incendiary bombs for attack on ground targets. All of the drones could be preprogrammed to automatically fly a preset course and carry out a preset action before flying back to base and automatically landing themselves.

Alternatively, a ground crew of three men per plane could control the flight and any action from the base. The crew would have full vision of events, full control of the plane and full control of its weapons. All drone controls were equipped with an Automatic Recall button. When the ground crew had finished carrying out their actions, they could simply hit the Automatic Recall button and the plane would fly itself back to base and land itself safely.

Now that the revolution was in full swing, nearly all of the PDM agents had left Brookslade Airfield. Not only the fighting men but even the technicians and most of their equipment had been moved out. The women and children still remained, along with a protective garrison of eight combat agents. Part of the camp had rapidly been converted into a hospital for the seriously injured rebels. Nick was now the hospital's senior doctor, backed by four medical officers from the PEO and one volunteer civilian doctor, Freddie Carlysle. The roof of the main building had been painted white with a large red cross which would easily be seen from the air. Other signs, red cross flags and white flags, placed strategically around the camp, left no doubt that this was a hospital and a home for women and children, not a military base. It was hoped that the ATS and particularly the DAF would respect the red cross and leave the base alone. Unfortunately, on two occasions, Cougars flying over the base had randomly opened fire on people seen in the open, killing one of the PEO medics. Trust in the protection of the red cross had gone. The base did have an old, World War Two, air-raid shelter. It consisted of a large underground bunker which had not been used in just over a hundred years. After checking that it was still structurally sound, it was decided that the women, children and mobile wounded would take shelter in the bunker if drones were anywhere in the vicinity. An anti-drone station was set up for the use of two agents with M.P.A.D.S. (Man-Portable Air Defence Systems) armed with Hornet shoulder launched S.A.M.s (Surface-to-Air Missiles) if the drones attacked.

★★★★

OWEEEOWEEOWEEOWEEOWEEOWEEOWEEOWEE-OWEE ...

The peace of Brookslade Airfield was suddenly shattered by the howling alarm warning of a possible imminent air attack by two approaching drones spotted on the radar. The base became a scene of pandemonium and panic. The mothers, organised by Charley, were desperately trying to get terrified, screaming, uncooperative children into the safety of the shelter at the same time as the medics were trying to get the walking wounded to safety. Agents Jordan Lorder and Fred Whitlow headed for the missile launchers.

The leading drone opened fire, sending both agents scuttling for cover as they were narrowly missed by the laser cannon. The drone quickly dropped two incendiary bombs on the hangars and outbuildings. Clearly the DAF must have believed that there might be munitions and equipment still stored at the base.

Suddenly Charley screamed, "MADDY!"

"What's wrong Charley?" shouted Nick.

"It's Maddy! She's run off! She must have sensed the panic and the explosions but she wouldn't know what was happening. She slipped her hand out of mine and just ran. Nick, I don't know where she's gone!" cried her distraught mother.

"I think I saw her running into one of the hangars, the middle one I think!" yelled Jonathan. "I'll go and look for her!"

"I'm coming too!" shouted Nick. "You look after the other kids Charley! Don't worry, we'll find her! Just make sure everybody else is safe! We'll get her!"

Jon and Nick both took off, heading for the hangar which, fortunately, had so far not been hit by a bomb. As they approached the hangar two more incendiary bombs exploded, one close by and the other scoring a direct hit on the hangar which erupted in a ball of flame.

Jon got to the door first and, spotting Maddy, yelled, "She's in here Nick!"

Maddy was cowering in the corner, freaking out and petrified, surrounded and trapped by collapsed burning beams which completely blocked any escape route. She was frozen with terror, unable to move as she felt the scorching heat of the flames whichever way she tried to move. The unstable appearance of the burning roof showed that she could be enveloped at any moment. It would be impossible to get her out without moving the beams. Nick wasted no time in wrapping his jacket around both hands, for protection, grasping a beam and pulling it back to try to clear an opening. The heat from the burning wood seared his flesh, causing him agony, but he persevered until he had cleared a space just wide enough for Jon to get through. Jon immediately ran into the burning cell. As he attempted to pick Maddy up, she recoiled from his touch, afraid of anything inside that flaming hell. Jon was afraid that, if she pulled away from him, she would back into the very flames from which he was trying to save her. She might even bring the burning roof down on them both. He grasped her wrists very firmly and quickly placed her hands on his face. She immediately recognised his features and relaxed, just a little, when she realized it was Jon. He quickly scooped her up in his arms and ran out through the gap that Nick had created; only just in time as the roof collapsed behind them leaving a raging inferno where they had just been standing.

They got outside, into the fresh air, to find that more incendiaries had been dropped. The hangars and outbuildings had been almost completely destroyed. Jordan Lorder was dead, taken out by a Hades missile which destroyed his defence post. Another missile had hit and demolished part of the hospital block. Fortunately, no patients had been seriously hurt but one of the PEO doctors had been killed by the explosion. Fred Whitlow had managed to get a direct hit on one of the Cougars, with one of the Hornets. The drone exploded in a ball of fire, somewhere over Brookslade Wood. The other drone headed back to base.

As the smoke began to settle, the full extent of the carnage and devastation became apparent. Charley was so relieved when she saw that Maddy was safe. Maddy was still shocked and distraught but was beginning to calm down thanks to the attention of Jonathan who was busy signing into her hands, trying to explain what had happened and trying to convince her that she was safe.

Charley was shocked when she saw the state of Nick's hands.

"It's OK!" said Nick. "It looks worse than it really is. They'll be healed in no time at all."

" You'd better let me be the judge of that Nick," said Freddie Carlysle, stepping forward to examine the burnt hands.

The pain was excruciating but Nick didn't want Charley or Jonathan to know how bad it really was."You've been so lucky that the burns haven't gone deeper," said Freddie. "Let's get your hands dressed and I'll get you some pain relief."

"Thanks Freddie. I could certainly do with something for the pain right now," said Nick, beginning to be overcome by pain and exhaustion now that the adrenaline was settling.

"Well, if you will go playing the hero, what do you expect? Seriously Nick, you and Jonathan did a brilliant job saving young Maddy today," said Doctor Carlysle, as he busily dressed the seared and scorched hands. Soon the dressings were complete. "Right! You're all finished! I would guess your hands will take about a month to heal completely. You won't be much use around here in the meantime so just take it easy for a bit and spend some time with Charley, Maddy and Jon. That's doctor's orders."

"Thanks Freddie," said Nick, smiling as best he could despite the pain.

There was still enough left of the Brookslade base for it to continue as a hospital and as a home for the wives and children, despite the loss of medical staff. Freddie Carlysle stepped up brilliantly, taking on a phenomenal work load. George Richmond decided that they couldn't risk any similar attacks in the future. Obviously, the DAF could not be trusted to respect the Red

Cross in the future. The time was right to organize attacks on the Grescott and Kings Langton DAF bases.

****

The URA wasted no time in responding to the attack on Brookslade Airfield. The very next day, large scale attacks were carried out on both drone bases.

The attack on the DAF base at Grescott was carried out by the PDM under the command of Deputy Commander Mark Grigson. It involved three waves of attack. First a small group of agents, led by Jock Munroe, advanced on the north perimeter of the base. Armed with MPADS they carried out a surprise action, firing Hornet missiles at the UACP Cougars, scoring several direct hits. This, as well as putting several Cougars out of action, caused pandemonium and attracted all the attention to that side of the base. At the same time a demolition team, led by explosives expert Dennis Wheatington, proceeded with stealth to enter the airfield from the south side and plant explosive devices on as many Cougars as possible before rapidly withdrawing. The resulting explosions lit up the sky with a brilliant, scintillating firework display which destroyed at least half of the squadron of Cougars. With the base and its garrison in disarray, Mark Grigson and the main force carried out a frontal attack on the garrison and the control room. Drone pilots were desperately trying to scramble the remaining functional Cougars, to get them airborne and in attack mode when the PDM forced their way in. The following short but fierce firefight resulted in the ATS and DAF officers being quickly overpowered. The recall buttons were activated and all remaining scrambled Cougars were brought back to land safely. Victory was complete! Most of the Cougars had been destroyed. Those which survived were now under the control of the URA, as were the URP Vultures and Grescott Air Base itself.

At the same time, an attack on Kings Langton Air Base was carried out by the PEO. This followed a similar plan and achieved the same result.

George Richmond was both relieved and delighted when he heard the news. Both actions had been a total success. The DAF had been completely destroyed. Any remaining drones, combat or reconnaissance, were now in the hands of the URA. The two captured bases now gave the URA a foothold in Nottinghamshire and Wiltshire.

★★★★

Back at the Brookslade base it was a huge relief to hear that the DAF had been destroyed and there was no chance of further attacks from the air. Thanks to the care of Charley and the medical attention of Freddie Carlysle, Nick's hands were soon on the mend. Despite the discomfort, Nick was actually quite pleased to be out of action for a few weeks, as it allowed him to spend more time with Charley. Charley and Jonathan seemed to take everything in their stride but Maddy struggled, for a while, to get over the air raid. Although she had not been hurt physically, she frequently had nightmares, occasional bed wetting and became quite withdrawn. Fortunately, with a lot of attention and gentle reassurance, from Charley and particularly from Jonathan, she gradually got over it and returned to being the happy child that she had been before. The almost catastrophic events of that day only served to bring all four people even closer, if that was possible. Theirs was a bond that nothing could break, or so it seemed.

Chapter 22.
SPECIAL RELATIONSHIP

Having prevented any threat from the DAF, the URA rapidly moved on. The northern army quickly took control of Nottinghamshire, Lincolnshire, Derbyshire, Cheshire, Shropshire and much of North Wales, as well as tidying up any minor resistance in Scotland. The southern army rapidly took control of Wiltshire, Somerset, Gloucestershire, Herefordshire, much of South Wales, The Home Counties and most of the South East. Government forces had been forced back by the URA juggernaut until they only controlled Staffordshire, Warwickshire, Worcestershire and Northamptonshire. Being cut off, surrounded and demoralized, defeat for the Blackshirts and The Party now seemed imminent and inevitable. Nigel Valentine's only chance of survival now was to reach out to an old ally for help, an ally who had always boasted of having a "Special Relationship" with the United Kingdom. The only possible saviour now was Dallas Donaldson, the unpredictable and erratic President of the United States of America. President Valentine had to try to get help from the United States in any way possible, whatever the consequences.

★★★★

For several decades, a large white telephone had stood on the desk of the United Kingdom premier. It provided a direct link to the Oval Office in the White House. Nigel Valentine was dithering, unsure whether to ring the President of the United States or not. In recent years, the so called "Special Relationship" had withered a little, as Britain's importance on the world stage had also withered. The connection between the USA and the UK was not as strong as it once had been. President Valentine could see no other way out of the current predicament but he was afraid that he might not get a positive response from President Donaldson. Finally conquering his nerves, he lifted the receiver and dialled one.

"Hello, you're through to the office of the President of the United States, Executive Secretary Henry Sigmeyer speaking."

"Hello! This is the President of the United Kingdom, Nigel Valentine. I wonder if it's possible to speak to the President."

"I'm afraid I don't know if he's available but, if you can give me some idea of what you wish to speak to him about, I will find out."

"I really need to speak to him directly," said Valentine, trying to be a little more assertive. "It's a very confidential and very urgent matter!"

"Hold the line please and I'll see what I can do for you."

The Secretary went off to speak to Donaldson who was sitting in his private study, relaxing with a coffee. "The President of The United Kingdom is on the phone, sir. He has asked to speak to you confidentially. I am afraid he won't tell me what it's about, Mr President," said the Secretary.

"That slippery little weasel, he probably wants help to save his country. I hear it's in a pretty disastrous situation. I can't be bothered to speak to him now. He's bad news. Bad, bad news. Just tell him that I'm in an important meeting. Tell him that I'll try to find time to ring him back later," said the President, smugly, with no intention of returning the call.

"President Valentine," said the Secretary, resuming the call, "I'm afraid President Donaldson is unable to speak to you right now. He is in a very important meeting! He did say that he will try to find time to ring you back later."

"Alright," said Valentine. "I guess I'll just have to wait for his call."

Nigel Valentine cursed loudly as he slammed down the receiver, not believing for one moment that the P.O.T.U.S. had any intention of ringing back.

★★★★

Nigel Valentine was in his office, constantly pacing back and forth, his nerves jangling as he waited for a reply from Dallas Donaldson. It had been forty-eight hours since he was promised a return call. He knew that the P.O.T.U.S. was playing games, Donaldson was renowned for it. Despite common sense telling him to just let it go, he lifted the receiver of the white phone to try again.

"Hello, you're through to the office of the President of the United States, Executive Secretary Henry Sigmeyer speaking," came the now familiar greeting.

"Hello! This is the President of the United Kingdom, Nigel Valentine. I spoke to you two days ago and you promised me that Mr Donaldson would call me back when he had the time. I still need to speak to him and it is very urgent!"

"I'm sure you can appreciate that the President is a very busy man. If you would like to tell me what the call is about, I can see if someone else can deal with your call. President Donaldson is away on a golfing trip at the moment."

In reality, Dallas Donaldson was taking a gentle morning stroll in the Rose Garden, but Sigmeyer had already been warned that the P.O.T.U.S. did not want to speak to Nigel Valentine.

"I can't do that," said Valentine, his irritation growing. "I need to speak directly to the President in person and only the President! I must stress just how important and urgent this matter is!"

"All I can do is to let the President know that you have called again and see what he wants to do!" replied Sigmeyer.

"Alright! Thank you! You will make sure that he understands how urgent the matter is, won't you?" asked Valentine, feeling very alone and distraught.

"I certainly will. sir! Have a nice day!" said the Secretary as he put the phone down.

"Have a nice day!" Valentine repeated to himself as he slammed the receiver down. "I'm on the brink of losing control of the country and that fucking jumped-up little prick tells me to Have a Nice Day!"

****

Having finished his stroll in the Rose Garden, President Donaldson returned to the Oval Office.

"You know, Hank, this guy is not going to just go away. He's like an irritating little fucking mosquito! He'll keep buzzing around until he either gets what he wants or somebody swats the motherfucker! The next time he rings, Hank, I'll speak to him unless I really am busy," said the President, laughing at the irony.

"Very well Mr President," said Sigmeyer. "Whatever you say, sir!"

Dallas Donaldson had been President of the United States for the past seven years and was not a politician to be trusted. In his younger days he had been a top professional golfer, winning numerous national and international trophies. When he retired from golf, he invested his already significant wealth in hotels, casinos and entertainment. He was already in his sixties and a multibillionaire when he decided to go into politics. Now, at the age of seventy-five, he was probably the most powerful man in the world and power was the one thing that gave him a buzz these days. He knew only too well the perilous position that Nigel Valentine was now in. Whether he decided to help Valentine or not, it gave Donaldson immense pleasure to know that he had the power to save or destroy his opposite number from the UK.

The President was a very big, powerful man and not just politically. He stood six feet six inches and weighed in at a still very muscular two hundred and forty pounds. His hair, which was almost black when he was younger, was now grey but still immaculate. He sported a neat, almost white moustache. His face looked somewhat weather-beaten from years on the golf course. His appearance and manner showed that, even if he couldn't be trusted, he was a man that you crossed at your peril. He was ruthless and it showed, even more than his innate arrogance and narcissism.

His trophy wife, Naomi, was barely half the President's age. She was a former film star. At public events Naomi was always there at his side, expensively dressed and beautiful, always doing what Dallas told her to do and looking like she hated every minute of it.

In the oval office, where once hung tasteful paintings of former presidents and important politicians of the world, now hung photographs of hotels, golf courses and celebrities from the world of sport and entertainment. Statuettes of George Washington and Abraham Lincoln had been replaced with Dallas Donaldson's golf trophies.

This was the man who wanted to make Nigel Valentine squirm and he was enjoying every minute of it.

★★★★

The URA pressed on. The area still held by the ATS was getting smaller day by day. Defeat of the Valentine regime seemed both inevitable and imminent.

Still having heard nothing from the POTUS, Nigel Valentine swallowed his pride and decided to try to call Dallas Donaldson again. It was an action born out of desperation rather than any real hope of help.

"Hello! You're through to the office of the President of the United States, Executive Secretary Henry Sigmeyer speaking," came the irritating and now all too familiar reply.

"Hello Mr Sigmeyer. This is the President of the United Kingdom, Nigel Valentine, again. Look, I'm sorry to keep pestering but it really is vitally important that I speak to the President as soon as possible."

"That's fine, sir! You're in luck! The President is free and would like to speak to you! If you could just hold the line for a moment, I'll put you through to him," said Sigmeyer.

"Nigel, my old friend!" came the apparently enthusiastic greeting from Dallas Donaldson. "I'm sorry I couldn't speak to you before but I have been so busy, incredibly busy! You would not believe how busy! Not a minute to spare! Anyway, I have a little time for you now. I hear you're having quite a tough time right now. I guess that is probably what you want to talk about. So, tell me Nige, what can I do for you, my friend?"

"I'm not going to beat around the bush, Mr President. The rebel army has taken over most of the country! We're only holding on to a small area and even that could be lost at any time. My boys will fight to the death! They're loyal but they're badly outnumbered and surrounded. My combat drones have all been destroyed or taken over by the rebels. I badly need your help if we are to have any chance of saving the country!"

"That sounds like you're in a tough situation Nige, very tough! It's really a tough one to get out of and I'd like to help you, I really would, but I don't see what I can do," said Donaldson.

"Dallas we've always had that special relationship, haven't we? That special link between the UK and the US?" asked Nigel Valentine.

"Yes! That's true! We have always been very close allies. The US and the UK have been through a lot together in the past. We've always been good together. I would really like to help you Nige, I really would."

"I was hoping, Mr President, that maybe you could send some troops, call it a peacekeeping force, to boost our forces and protect my government. Maybe even some combat planes. Our ATS with your marines or paratroopers and the US Air Force, we'd have this revolution beaten in a few weeks. I know we would! What do you think, Dallas?" asked Valentine. "Can you help me?"

"Now Nige I really want to help, I really do, but you can't really expect me to commit American military to defending your government. The world would see us as aggressors if we acted against your rebels. It's not like the US has anything to gain by such an action. You get your country back but we get nothing! We would get nothing out of it, absolutely nothing! Years ago, Britain was an important world power, but now you are a little insignificant island with nothing to offer! Nobody really cares what happens to little Britain, not on the world stage! The UK is not important any longer! Why should I send my boys over there, to maybe come back in a pine box, risking the reputation of this beautiful country of ours just to support a failed regime which can give us nothing in return? I'm sorry Nige, I really am, but this is a bad situation that you've got yourself into! A bad, bad situation! It's so bad, it's awful really but I can't help you, Nige! Not in that way anyway! Not by using US military!"

"Please Dallas!" begged Valentine, sobbing as he began to lose any remaining composure. "Please! You're my only hope now! I don't know what else I can do!"

"Pull yourself together pal! Are you really the leader of a country? Get some backbone! Grow some balls! Look Nige, I'm not going to send American soldiers over there to die for your country but I will tell you something that you can do, if you've got the guts to try it."

Nigel Valentine regained a little of his composure with the thought that he might be thrown a lifeline, no matter how tenuous.

"Nigel," continued the POTUS, "you have short range nuclear missiles, don't you? I know we have Intercontinental Ballistic Missiles (ICBMs) based in your country but under our control. They wouldn't be any use anyway as they work at long range. I'm talking about your own short range nuclear missiles. I believe they are Golden Arrow Missiles. Do you still have control of those? They have not fallen into the hands of the rebels, have they?"

"No Dallas! We still have control of them," replied Valentine.

"OK, in that case you need to pick two UK cities and nuke both of them with a Golden Arrow. Then you give your rebels an ultimatum. They surrender or you continue to nuke more cities. There's no point in them governing a country that's been totally destroyed by nuclear missiles."

"Perhaps, if I give them the ultimatum first, they might back down without us having to nuke anybody," reasoned Valentine.

"No! That won't work Nige! They'll never believe that you'll really go through with it!" said an irate Donaldson. "They'll think you're bluffing! You have to nuke a couple of cities first! Sacrifice them! Let the rebels know that you're not bluffing! Then they will know that you mean business! It looks to me that it's your only chance Nige! Anyway, I'm gonna have to love you and leave you

Nige. I'm very busy right now. Good luck Nige, you can do it! Go get 'em buddy!" With that, Dallas Donaldson ended the call.

A nuclear attack on his own country felt like a step too far even for Nigel Valentine but maybe, just maybe, it might give him a chance to hold on to power. He would have to act quickly. If the URA got control of the missile base it really would be all over.

★★★★

President Nigel Valentine had called for a meeting of the War Cabinet, consisting of himself, Vice-President Edwina Sykes and Commander of the Security Forces, Glyn Quinlan. The President told them how they had been thrown under the bus by Dallas Donaldson who had refused to provide any military aid. He explained that they had been thrown a possible lifeline in the form of the POTUS' suggestion.

"You can't seriously expect us to consider a nuclear attack on our own cities Nigel," said Edwina Sykes."On the contrary Edwina," said Quinlan. "We've run out of options and it might just work. What do we have to lose? If we don't try it, we're finished anyway."

"We can't just nuke our own people," the Vice-President protested. "Killing rebels is one thing, but a nuclear attack will kill thousands of innocent, unsuspecting people, including women and children."

"They've done it to themselves," argued Quinlan. "We wouldn't have needed to do this if they had stayed loyal to The Party."

"Nuclear missiles will even kill loyalists," said Edwina.

"That's unfortunate," conceded Quinlan, "but it's just collateral damage and a small price to pay if it saves the country from the URA."

"Edwina, can't you see that there is just no other alternative?" asked Nigel Valentine.

"I suppose so," said the Vice-President, reluctantly. "I just don't feel that it's right."

"Have you had any thoughts about which cities to hit?" asked Quinlan.

"Not yet," replied the President. "It would be best if they were deep within rebel territory."

"Can I make a suggestion?" asked Quinlan. "I would suggest Carlisle in the north and Truro in the south. They're at opposite ends of the country, they're small enough to be completely destroyed by one Golden Arrow and, if we do manage to retain the rest of the country, they are no great loss."

"Yes, I can see the sense in that," agreed the President. "Truro and Carlisle are both pretty expendable. So, we agree on the targets. I think we need to go ahead with it tomorrow. We can't afford to delay and risk the URA capturing the nuclear base."

"Definitely!" affirmed Quinlan. "It's our only chance."

"I still don't really like the idea, "said Edwina Sykes, "but I can see that it makes sense. If you two are both in favour, I guess I'll go along with it."

"Right, Carlisle and Truro tomorrow it is then," said Nigel Valentine, smiling for the first time in days. "Shall we go for two p.m.?"

"That sounds good to me," said Glyn Quinlan. "If we start the process to set everything up around noon, we should be good to go with a two p.m. firing. The URA won't know what's hit them. We need to go on TV just after the attack, to inform the public about what's happened and to deliver the ultimatum. Even if the URA don't back down at that point, it will destroy any popular support for them. Hit more cities if we need to and they'll be forced to surrender eventually."

"Edwina, I sense that you're still not really buying into the idea," said Nigel Valentine.

"No Nigel, I don't really like it. We're going to kill around a hundred thousand innocent people."

"If they were innocent, they wouldn't have sided with the URA. So, we kill a hundred thousand people. How many would be killed if the revolution continued and how many have already been killed?" asked Quinlan.

"It's the only chance we have, Edwina! I hope you wouldn't suggest that we should surrender, because that would probably be the only other alternative and that wouldn't go well for any of us," said the President.

"No of course I'm not," said Edwina, "but there has to be some other way."

"You know there's not," replied the President. "I know we don't entirely have your approval, but can we at least count on your loyalty?"

"Of course you can! I've never let you or The Party down in the past and I won't now!" replied an irate Edwina.

"In that case we start to win the country back tomorrow," said President Valentine.

"Well, whatever is left of it," said Glyn Quinlan.

Chapter 23.

AN OLD FLAME

Vice-President Edwina Sykes was beside herself with frustration and desperation. She had tried her best to persuade Nigel Valentine to drop his idea of nuclear attacks on Carlisle and Truro but he was determined to go ahead. He was emboldened even more by the support and encouragement of Glyn Quinlan. Quinlan had even appeared to be almost excited by the thought of nuking his own citizens. She had hated Quinlan from the first time she set eyes on him. She saw him for what he was, a cruel man with no morals and no conscience. Unfortunately, in the current situation, the President was only prepared to listen to Glyn Quinlan and Dallas Donaldson. She could see that it was probably The Party's only chance of survival, but was it really worth the cost, a hundred thousand lives of innocent, unsuspecting people and total devastation of both cities.

The cost in lives and destruction could even be vastly greater than that if the URA refused to surrender, leading to more cities being nuked. Hardnosed politician that she was, she found it impossible to justify such destruction and slaughter. She had no doubt that the overthrow of The Party would probably mean a long prison sentence, even possibly the death penalty, for her personally and for other top government officials. Despite that, she still could not get past the idea of a hundred thousand people being slaughtered.

How could she stop the attack? She did not have the power to call it off. Only Nigel Valentine had the power to do that and he, encouraged by Glyn Quinlan, had absolutely no intention of changing his mind. If she was going to try to stop it, she had to have outside help, help that could only be given by the URA. Somehow, she had to find a way to let the rebels know what had been planned, but how? She couldn't just find a number in the telephone directory, under REBEL LEADER. There was one possible link but it was a long shot.

Many years before, when she was just starting out on her political career, she had a relationship with Ed Gilfedder, the same Ed Gilfedder who now commanded the PEO section of the URA. They had been together for three years before her ambition and her career started to get in the way. She still had a phone number for Ed, although she had not spoken to him in more than five years. Maybe he no longer had that number. Even if it was still the right number, he might not be prepared to speak to her. They were on opposite sides now after all. If she did speak to him, would he believe her? Even if he did believe her, would he be able to do anything to stop it? So many questions were whirling around and around in her head. Finally, she decided to make the call. She was greeted by the familiar voice of a frail, elderly woman.

"Hello, Joyce Gilfedder speaking." It was Ed's mother.

"Hello Mrs Gilfedder. I'm trying to contact Ed," said Edwina. "I don't suppose he's there, is he? I really need to speak to him urgently."

"I'm afraid Ed doesn't live here anymore. He hasn't lived here for over two years now. Can I ask who's calling?" asked the old lady.

"It's Edwina Sykes. I don't know if you can remember me."

"Of course I remember you, Edwina. How are you doing dear?" asked Joyce.

"I'm fine," lied Edwina. "Look Joyce, I really need to speak to Ed! Can you give me a number where I can contact him."

"I'm sorry dear, I can't do that. Obviously, I'm aware that you're on opposite sides now. I can't just give you his number," said Joyce.

"I have to speak to him somehow," persisted Edwina. "I can't stress too much just how important it is, not just for me but for the whole of the country. Listen, if I give you a number where Ed can contact me, would you ring Ed and ask him to call me? I'm really desperate. Do you have a pen and paper to take the number down?"

"Yes, I've got a pen and paper dear."

"Could you ask him to ring me on nine, nine, one, one, one, zero, zero, four, two, zero, three as soon as he possibly can."

"Let me make sure I have the number correct," said Joyce. "Nine, nine, one, one, one, zero, zero, two, four, zero, three."

"No! It's four, two, zero, three Joyce! Nine, nine, one, one, one, zero, zero, FOUR, TWO, ZERO, THREE!" stressed a very nervous Edwina.

"That's right dear. Nine, nine, one, one, one, zero, zero, four, two, zero, three," repeated Joyce.

"Yes! That's right Joyce! Will you give him that number and ask him to ring me as soon as possible, please?"

"Very well dear. I'll pass the number on but I don't know if he'll ring you back."

"Please!" begged Edwina. "I'd be really grateful if you'll try but it MUST be tonight! Tomorrow will be too late! MUCH TOO LATE!"

Putting down the phone, she poured herself a drink to calm her nerves, a tumbler of neat vodka. She didn't really like the stuff without a mixer, but she wasn't drinking it for the taste. She gulped it straight down and refilled her glass. The first glass burned her throat. The second hit the spot and eased the unbearable wait just a little.

After about half an hour and a third tumbler of vodka, the phone rang. She grabbed it immediately.

"Edwina Sykes."

"It's Ed," came the reply.

"Oh! Thank God!" exclaimed Edwina.

"Edwina are you okay? What's wrong?"

"Ed, this sounds crazy I know but there's going to be nuclear attacks tomorrow with an ultimatum of more to come unless the URA surrender! They are going to nuke Carlisle and Truro. Ed, you've got to stop them! I've done my best to change the President's mind but he won't listen! I can't just sit back and allow that carnage. I can't stop it so my only hope is that you can.

The plan is to start getting everything set up from noon with the intention of launching the missiles at two p.m."

"This isn't some kind of trap, is it? You're not setting me up, are you?" asked a very cautious Ed.

"No, Ed! I swear! You've got to believe me! I would never do that to you of all people. We were good together while it lasted. I still miss you! Somehow this has to be stopped and I don't know how else it can be done. I know I've sometimes been a ruthless bitch. I know I've sometimes run roughshod over people to get where I am, but this is something else. I can't condone this. I can't just let it happen," said Edwina, desperate to convince Ed that it was all genuine.

"Calm down Edwina, I believe you. Where exactly is the missile base?" asked Ed.

"It's next to a village called Knappers End, near to Stafford." She gave him the map coordinates to make sure there was no mistake. "There are forty Golden Arrow short range missiles. The missile base was set up in case they ever had to be used against Europe. There's also an American ICBM base in Hop Bridge, about twenty miles from Knappers End. The Hop Bridge base has a small US garrison and can only be fired by the US. They are long range missiles anyway, so they can't be used against the UK. The ICBM base is no threat. The threat is from the Golden Arrows at the Knappers End Missile Base."

"How many men are we likely to encounter on the base, Edwina?" asked Ed.

"There's a garrison of around thirty ATS," replied Edwina, "plus about a dozen engineers and technicians."

"Thanks Edwina! I'll speak to George Richmond. The first thing is to convince him that we're not being led into a trap."

"It's honestly not a trap, Ed. I wouldn't do that to you. I just can't let this happen."

"I believe you Edwina! I'll do my best to sort it out. How about you? When Valentine's plan fails, will he know that you're to blame? Perhaps you should get out of there, for your own safety?"

"He'll assume it was me! He knows that I was against the idea but don't worry about me. I can take care of myself," said Edwina, trying unsuccessfully to reassure Ed.

"I am worried about you," said Ed. "I still care about you, you know."

"I'll be OK Ed. Don't worry. Just make sure that you stop the bastard!"

"Stay safe Edwina and, if you can, get out of there before the shit hits the fan." Ed put the phone down, still hoping that somehow Edwina could avoid any backlash.

Having ended the call, with tears rolling down her face, Edwina quickly poured another glass of vodka. However this ended up, it would go badly for her. Whether she was caught by the URA or suffered the wrath of Nigel Valentine made no real difference. It was bound to end in disaster now, whatever happened. There was no point in running. There was no way out.

****

Ed immediately got on the phone to George Richmond. Richmond's initial reaction was to believe that it was a trap. It took a lot of persuasion from Ed to convince the Commander that it could be genuine. Still unsure but feeling that he could not risk taking no action, George Richmond sanctioned an attack on the Knappers End Missile Base. The attack was to be commanded by Ed Gilfedder himself.

Three hundred men were moved into the area overnight, ready for an assault on the nuclear facility at nine a.m. The attack was swift and clinical. The garrison was quickly overpowered, offering little resistance against such overwhelming odds. The URA took complete control of the missile base. The danger of a missile attack on Carlisle and Truro had successfully been prevented.

A smaller force of around fifty men, under the command of Idris Llewellyn, put a protective cordon around the US ICBM base at Hop Bridge. The Commander of the US base was advised that his men were free to come and go as they pleased. No URA went onto the base. The cordon was purely to make sure that the ATS could not try to take over the base.

When Nigel Valentine heard the news of the successful URA attack on the Knappers End Missile Base, he was apoplectic with rage. His final chance of survival had been destroyed. Assuming that Edwina Sykes was responsible, he rushed to her office, accompanied by two ATS officers, intending to do who knows what. When they burst through the door, they found the body of the Vice-President slumped over her desk. Beside her was a lipstick-stained tumbler, an empty vodka bottle and an empty pill bottle.

Chapter 24.

ASSAULT ON THATCHER SQUARE

As the revolution rolled on to its inevitable conclusion, there was concern amongst the URA leaders regarding how the end would be played out. George Richmond held several discussions with Mark Grigson and Ed Gilfedder. They shared a common consensus that it was necessary to capture senior government officials and put them on trial for their actions against the people. They had to be held accountable and justice had to be seen to be done, to prevent any possible danger of a counter-revolution. Their greatest worry was that Nigel Valentine and his confederates might try to escape and flee the country before all resistance was completely crushed. It was decided that an attack on key government buildings had to be carried out as soon as possible.

The government buildings were situated just outside Birmingham, around Thatcher Square. They had been built in the twenty thirties, when the seat of government was moved from London to Birmingham due to flooding of the Thames Valley.

Access to Thatcher Square was from the south side. The entrance to the square was guarded by a statue of Margaret Thatcher, Britain's first female Prime Minister.

Along the west side of the square stood the Britannic Empire Building, a fifteen storey, shiny, stainless steel and glass structure, housing the offices of the former Bank of England as well as a host of vast offices for numerous major trade and financial organizations. In front of the main entrance to the Britannic Empire Building stood a statue of empire builder Robert Clive.

Along the north side of the square stood the George Jeffreys Citadel and Law Courts, named after the famous "hanging judge" from the "bloody assizes" of the seventeenth century. The Citadel once housed the headquarters of all security forces, but now only the ATS. It also housed two law courts which were used for only the most important trials and an incarceration block. The incarceration block included holding cells for those awaiting trial, rooms for carrying out Age Acceleration, cells for those undergoing Civil Correction and cells used for those undergoing interrogation. The walls and floors of the latter were left permanently spattered and stained with blood and excrement to increase the fear and anxious anticipation of the poor souls being interrogated. The Citadel looked like a huge concrete bunker, with no windows and only one front entrance. There was also one door at the rear of the building to enable the removal of bodies. The size and the dour starkness of the building made its appearance both imposing and intimidating. Its architecture left much to be desired and yet it seemed to dominate Thatcher Square. Its front entrance was graced by statues of Judge George Jeffreys himself and Councillor William Hulton, the man responsible for the Peterloo Massacre in eighteen nineteen.

Along the east side and part of the south side of Thatcher Square was a large L-shaped building which had much more elaborate architecture and decoration. This was The House of the Nation. This was the building from which the government ran the country. There were no great debating chambers or vast lobbies as in the old House of Commons and House of Lords. Instead, there were offices and smaller meeting rooms where the cabinet and smaller committees could meet. There were reception rooms where meetings could be held with visiting foreign dignitaries. The largest and most ornate of the official rooms was the President's Office with its unique telephone connections directly to the President of the United States, the George Jeffreys Citadel, the Britannic Empire Building and the Knappers End Missile Base which, of course, was already in the hands of the URA. The southern end of The House of the Nation consisted of accommodation and catering facilities. This part of the building rose to five stories, the rest of the building only having three floors. The top floor was a vast penthouse suite which was home to the Valentine family, President Nigel, his wife Elizabeth, their eight year old son Oliver and six year old daughter Esme.

Elizabeth Valentine was a very neat and precise woman with a very strong sense of duty. While she did not agree with everything that her husband had done, she believed that it was her duty to stand by him. As the years went by, she found it more and more difficult to justify that duty and loyalty to her husband. She was totally devoted to Esme and Oliver. She had always struggled to protect her children from the stress of political life, particularly during the revolution.

The fourth floor provided a home for some of the senior government officials. Glyn Quinlan had an apartment there, as had the late Vice-President Edwina Sykes, neither of which had any family. The new Vice-President, Harry Harefield, also had an apartment, where he lived with his wife Sandra and their one year old baby, Jacob. As well as the apartments, there were rooms available for ministers who needed to stay overnight due to working late.

The ground floor contained a large dining room and bar for the use of ministers. There was an even larger and far more impressive dining room and bar for entertaining visiting dignitaries and several large suites for their accommodation.

The floors in between housed catering facilities, accommodation for live-in catering and house-keeping staff as well as rooms for live-in security guards.

In front of The House of the Nation stood an enormous floodlit fountain, flanked by statues of Britannia with a lion and Boadicea in her war chariot. At the rear of The House was Wellesley Gardens, a large area of formally laid out flower beds, lawns, trees and shrubs with a large area of open park land. Wellesley Gardens also contained a helipad, sometimes used to receive visitors, watched over by a large statue of the Duke of Wellington, Arthur Wellesley, mounted on his horse Copenhagen.

The complexity of the buildings would make an attack very difficult. The House of the Nation and the George Jeffreys Citadel would have to be attacked simultaneously and severe resistance had to be expected at the Citadel. It was important to avoid too much bloodshed, particularly at The House of the Nation. Stealth would be required to capture Nigel Valentine and the other ministers without the attack developing into a shoot-out. How much resistance would be encountered from the security guards was unknown. It was important to avoid any injury or killing of families and civilian staff at all costs. Most crucial of all, they had to make sure that Nigel Valentine could not escape or be rescued by helicopter.

The Britannic Empire Building would also have to be secured but it was not expected to show much resistance or pose any threat, despite its size. It could be taken over after the Citadel and The House of the Nation had been secured.

The assault was going to be under the overall command and coordination of George Richmond himself. Ed Gilfedder would lead the frontal attack on the Citadel, while Jock Munroe would lead the attack on the rear. Around one hundred and fifty men would be involved, assisted by explosives expert Dennis Wheatington to blow open the external doors. Around fifty men would be involved in a frontal attack on The House of the Nation, under the command of Mark Grigson. Another one hundred men, under the command of Idris Llewellyn, would secure the helipad and attack the building from several rear entrances. The men moved into position in the early hours of the morning with the assault timed to start at four a.m., a time when it was hoped most people would be safely tucked up in bed except for a small number of ATS and security men on guard duty.

The essence of the assault on The House of the Nation was that there would be attacks at several points all coordinated to happen simultaneously. Four men were detailed to guard the helipad. Twenty men were detailed to get to the penthouse and the fourth floor using the fire escapes for access. They could not move in too early in case they triggered alarms or were seen on CCTV but they had to gain access within seconds of the attacks beginning at the other entrances. They had to secure those floors, arresting the leaders, immobilizing the lifts and defending the stair wells against any rescue attempt. At the same time, the attacks via the other entrances would quickly neutralize any opposition.

At the Citadel, the attack would be simpler but potentially more dangerous. Explosives would be used to blow open the front and rear doors. The attackers would then pile in fast and return any fire. Unfortunately, with only two small entrances, they would be sitting ducks until they could gain access and spread out. It was hoped that the initial use of stun grenades would allow a few seconds for sufficient men to access the building safely.

Everyone was prepared and knew their roles. At precisely four a.m. the trap was sprung. Alarms began to go off and pandemonium broke out as men approached and broke in through the doors of The House of the Nation. There was gunfire as they met resistance, combined with the sound of explosions and distant gunfire from the Citadel. Idris immediately led his group up the fire escapes, amazingly ascending at such speed that they gained access before anyone had been able to escape from the top floors. Lifts were immediately immobilized and men detailed to the stairwells, opening fire as guards attempted to reach the upper floors. Idris accompanied by two men entered the President's apartment. Nigel and Elizabeth Valentine were both still in the bedroom, not knowing what to do except wait in the hope of being rescued.

"Mr Valentine, I have to place you under arrest. If you don't resist, you have my word that neither you nor your family will be hurt," said Idris.

"Can I go to my children?" asked Elizabeth, looking smart and immaculate in a long white nightdress, even at this hour of the morning. "They must be terrified."

"Yes of course," replied Idris. "I'm afraid one of my men will have to accompany you."

She quickly went to collect Esme and Oliver. She cuddled them both to reassure them that everything was okay and that they were safe. Nigel Valentine sat on the bed looking a broken man, in his purple silk pyjamas, with his head bowed and buried in his hands.

Fred Whitlow and three other men had entered the suites of Glyn Quinlan and Harry Harefield. Vice-President Harefield had surrendered without resistance, being most concerned for his family's welfare. In contrast, Glyn Quinlan had immediately reached for his gun before the fist of Fred Whitlow knocked him to the floor and sent the gun spinning from his hand.

There was a brief outbreak of gunfire on the stairs as the security guards attempted a rescue but it stopped almost immediately as they were outflanked by Mark Grigson's men coming up from the lower floors. The battle for The House of the Nation was over in little more than ten minutes with only two URA casualties. Two security guards and three ATS had been killed in the fight. The mission had been a complete success. Nigel Valentine, Harry Harefield and Glyn Quinlan had all been arrested and would be incarcerated in the Citadel to await trial at a later date. The two families were unharmed and allowed to stay in their accommodation, as were the civilian staff.

The battle for the Citadel had been a much fiercer and bloodier affair with significant losses on both sides, fifteen of Ed Gilfedder's men and twenty-two ATS. With nowhere to go, the remaining ATS had surrendered and were temporarily incarcerated in the Citadel's cells.

With The House of the Nation and the Citadel secured, Ed Gilfedder's men turned their attention to the Britannic Empire Building which was secured quickly and easily with absolutely zero resistance.

When news spread of the capture of their leaders, any remaining hostile ATS surrendered immediately and unconditionally. The revolution was successfully over. The freedom of the country had been won. George Richmond was installed as the new President and head of an interim government. The country was finally at peace.

"We've done it! We've finally won! It's all over!" said Mark Grigson with a big self-satisfied smile on his face, when things finally calmed down.

"We've won nothing!" exclaimed a very serious George Richmond, bringing everybody back down to earth. "This is where it all begins! We've gained the right to run the country. If we don't put things right now it'll all have been for nothing. There's so much that needs to be done. This is only the start! I just hope we're up to the job."

Ed Gilfedder was concerned that there had been no sign of Edwina Sykes during the assault. He went to the Citadel to visit Nigel Valentine.

"What are you here for?" snapped a still defiant ex-President.

"I was surprised that there was no sign of the Vice-President when we attacked this morning," said Gilfedder.

"The Vice-President was there, Harry Harefield, you arrested him."

"I'm referring to Edwina Sykes," said Ed Gilfedder. "I wondered where she was. Did she escape somehow before we arrived?"

"Edwina Sykes is hopefully rotting in hell," said Valentine. "She was not only a traitor but she was also a coward and I hope the bitch rots in hell."

"I don't understand," said Gilfedder. "Have you done something to her?"

"Have I done something to her?" laughed Valentine. "She kills off the one chance, the only chance that we had by informing the URA of our intention. Then the bitch can't even face the fucking music, can't face up to what she's done! She fucking kills herself! Tablets and booze. The fucking coward's way out! When we found out what she'd done, I'd have gladly killed the fucking bitch myself but she even took revenge away from me."

Incensed, Ed grasped Valentine by the throat. He was stopped by the guard who had accompanied him into the cell.

"Why the hell are you so fucking bothered about her anyway?" asked the ex-President, rubbing his throat. "Anybody would think that you and she had some kind of relationship. Wait a minute… I seem to remember something about the two of you being a couple years ago. Is that why she informed on us?

Was it you that she gave the fucking information to? Did you still have feelings for each other? Were you hoping to carry on where you left off? Were you the cause of the bitch signing our death warrants? Well, she won't be any fucking use to you now!"

Every fibre of Ed Gilfedder's body wanted to seriously hurt Nigel Valentine, wanted to kill Nigel Valentine as painfully as possible. Fortunately, he managed to keep control of himself until he had left the cell and heard the door slam shut behind him. Then, only then, tears began to trickle down his cheeks.

Chapter 25.

PROMISE TO THE NATION

Despite the exhaustion from the events of the night, the country had to be informed of the defeat of The Party as soon as possible. The technicians worked feverishly in the following hours to set up the broadcasting equipment at The House of the Nation. At ten a.m. George Richmond went live on air to speak to the country.

"You probably all know me by now," George began, "but in case any of you don't, I am George Richmond, Commander-In-Chief of the United Revolutionary Army. At four a.m. today the URA carried out attacks on The House of the Nation and the George Jeffreys Citadel. Both of these attacks were completely successful. The ATS have surrendered and the government have resigned. Former President Valentine and other government officials have been placed under arrest and will stand trial for crimes against the nation. The ATS have been disarmed and disbanded. Some individual members of the ATS may be prosecuted for criminal acts. An interim government has been formed, consisting of PDM and PEO officers along with some civilians, with myself as President. We intend to bring about a return to a democratic government. Unfortunately, as so much needs to be done in as short a time as possible, this cannot be done just yet but I give you my word that the United Kingdom will become a democracy again within two years. In the meantime, the UK will become a free country once more and your personal freedom will be restored.

With immediate effect you will be able to talk freely and express your own opinions openly, provided those views are not intended to provoke violence. You will be allowed to criticise the government. Independent news agencies will be allowed to broadcast news on TV, via newspapers or online.

People will be allowed to gather in unlimited numbers, as they once were, providing it is for a peaceful purpose. You will be able to hold weddings and parties without numbers being restricted. You will be free to hold funerals and to bury or cremate your loved ones without government interference.

From now on it will be legal to form and to join political parties, providing their aims are non-violent. In fact, it will be essential to have opposition political parties if democracy is to function properly.

The legal system will be completely overhauled. There will be a return to trial by jury and every man will have the right to defend himself in court. Punishment by Civil Correction will be completely abolished. The penal colonies will be closed down and replaced by new prisons on the mainland. Custodial sentences will be adjusted according to the severity of the crime committed and will not be life sentences except in the most serious of cases. Those survivors currently incarcerated in the penal colonies will be brought home, pardoned and released as soon as possible. The death penalty will be retained but only for extreme crimes such as murder. It will not be used on the grounds of age, illness or for convenience. Homelessness will no longer be treated as a crime.

The charity hospitals will, from now on, be funded by the government. We will provide better equipment, better supplies of drugs and paid full time doctors and nurses. We will create a National Health Service, as good as it was in the past, where everyone is entitled to free and adequate health care. Of course, this is a huge undertaking and will take some time to carry out completely. In order to enable the change to take place as quickly as possible, I have already spoken to the International Red Cross and the World Health Organization. They have both promised to provide immediate assistance.

We will immediately cease trading in disposal of waste from other countries. The waste which we have already accumulated will be disposed of in a fit and proper manor. Waste will no longer be dumped on open tips or dumped in the sea. We will also be taking other steps to take our rightful place in the worldwide battle to reduce the effects of climate change. To help with this we intend to promote the use of renewable energy and I promise that all UK energy will be from renewable sources within two years.

We intend to make massive improvements to public transport now that larger gatherings of people are allowed. The train service will be restored. Bus and coach services will be greatly improved.

A new government support agency will be set up to provide assistance with natural disasters such as earthquakes, storms and flooding. In the future, you will not be left to cope with these on your own.

While we will continue to trade in armaments, strict new ethical controls will be introduced regarding who we supply and their purpose. We will not produce or supply any nuclear weapons, chemical weapons or any other weapons of mass destruction.

The changes will leave quite a large hole in our trade and in our economy. I can assure you that we will do everything that we can to develop new trade deals and find new trading partners. That work will begin today.

We intend to make the United Kingdom a free country again! We intend to make the United Kingdom a great country again! We can only do that with your help, support and cooperation! If we work together, we can achieve our goals! I trust that we have your support."

As the broadcast came to a close, everyone in the room congratulated President Richmond for giving a great speech. George was not fooled by the compliments or the euphoria. He realized what a tough job lay ahead and he had no intention of getting carried away by his own rhetoric. The road ahead would be hard but even George did not realize just how hard it would become within the next seventy-two hours.

Chapter 26.

DALLAS DONALDSON'S DEMANDS

For the rest of the day new President George Richmond and the rest of his cabinet were busy contacting heads of state of countries around the world by telephone or e-mail. The cabinet consisted of George Richmond himself plus Mark Grigson, Pip Holgrave and Dominic Welland from the PDM, Ed Gilfedder from the PEO, Doctor Freddie Carlysle and two civilians from the world of business and finance, Arthur Forswick and James Radburn. More would be added to the government later but these eight men were the ones given the responsibility of beginning to rebuild the country.

The response from world leaders was generally good, with all apparently accepting the new regime warmly and many wanting to initiate new trade agreements. One country was conspicuous by the absence of a reply despite being the very first country to receive an e-mail. No reply had been received from Dallas Donaldson or any other government official of the United States of America. The following day George Richmond was shocked to find out why.

****

The white phone rang in George Richmond's office. The phone with a direct link to the Oval Office in The White House and the President of the United States. George answered it immediately.

"Hello, this is President Richmond." It still seemed strange and a little overwhelming for George to hear his new title.

"Hello President Richmond! This is the office of the President of the United States, Executive Secretary Henry Sigmeyer speaking.

President Donaldson would like to speak to you if that is possible, sir!" said Hank Sigmeyer.

"That is fine, Mr Sigmeyer. I'm happy to speak to the President," said George, pleased to finally be making contact with the POTUS.

"Thank you, sir," said Sigmeyer. "I'll just put him through."

"Hello, Mr Richmond," said Dallas Donaldson. "I received your e-mail yesterday."

George thought it strange that Donaldson had not used his title. He had said Mr Richmond rather than President Richmond. Neither had he gone for friendly informality by calling him George.

"Hello President Donaldson. I'm glad that we have a chance to talk at last. I was a little concerned that we had received no reply to the e-mail that I sent yesterday."

"I didn't reply because I was considering our options," said Donaldson. "You've left us with quite a problem my friend. Quite a problem. I know that you have been trying to set up new trade deals with several countries and that includes several major communist countries, in particular Russia, China and North Korea."

"Any potential trade deals are strictly confidential between the United Kingdom and the other country but we have spoken to those countries," replied George Richmond, beginning to feel a little angry and very suspicious.

"The United States would be very unhappy to have a vulnerable country such as yours aligning itself with such powerful communist countries. Very unhappy indeed!"

"We are not aligning ourselves with anyone, Mr President. Any contact has been to obtain acceptance of our new government and to sound out the possibility of new trade deals. We have no intention of forming any kind of alliance with any other country, neither a political nor a military alliance. Our only interest is in trade and for that purpose we have contacted the countries that you mentioned as well as most of Europe, former British Commonwealth countries and Japan." George was trying to stay cool but finding it increasingly difficult.

"I wish I could believe that, I really do. The fact is that I don't trust your government. I don't trust you at all! Not at all!" repeated

Dallas Donaldson. "As far as the United States is concerned, you have an unstable government which stole power by a revolution led by terrorists! My country does not accept you as the legal, legitimate government of the United Kingdom. Furthermore, the United States demands that President Valentine and the legal government are restored to power immediately!"

"I'm afraid that is not going to happen Mr President. We are the new and legal government of the United Kingdom. We have already been recognised as such by ninety-seven countries worldwide. No other country has challenged our right to govern." George felt as if he was being pushed to his limit.

"You've created a bad situation, a bad... bad situation. A situation so bad that the United States cannot accept it. You've left me with no alternative other than to insist that your government stands down and reinstates the rightful government under President Valentine," repeated the POTUS.

"I can't do that Mr President," said George Richmond, still showing amazing patience and self-control.

"You don't have any choice my friend, not if you care about the safety of your people! I regret that you are forcing the United States to give you an ultimatum," continued Donaldson. "If we have not heard that the Valentine government has been reinstated by three p.m. G.M.T. tomorrow we will immediately launch a nuclear attack on the United Kingdom."

"You can't do that Mr President. We are the legal government and you are threatening a nuclear attack? I can't believe that!" said George. "You have no right to do that! The world will see that as a needless act of unnecessary aggression."

"The U.S. does not recognise your government! If you have not reinstated President Valentine and his government by three p.m. G.M.T. tomorrow then an immediate nuclear attack will take place and you will have brought it on yourselves," said Dallas Donaldson as he put down the receiver.

George looked at his watch. It was two p.m. He had just twenty-five hours to try to avoid disaster. What could he do? There was no way that they would just hand the country back to Nigel Valentine. He immediately called an emergency cabinet meeting. It was agreed unanimously that they would not even consider reinstating Nigel Valentine and his regime. They decided that the only option was to contact as many of the most powerful and influential countries as possible to request that they help by putting diplomatic pressure on the US or even possibly applying sanctions against the US. They spent many hours asking for assistance. The response from most countries was very favourable, wanting to do all that they could to help, but would it be enough? No other countries wanted the UK to submit to Dallas Donaldson's bully boy behaviour but how much protection could they give? How much notice would the POTUS take of their support?

The cabinet also discussed what action should be taken to warn and protect the people. There had been no indication of where the missile attack would be directed so evacuation was impossible. Broadcasting the threat to the populace would only cause panic and chaos. Who knows what the result of that might be. Although in principal George believed in being honest and open with the people, it was agreed that nothing would be gained by going public, not for the time being anyway. All they could do for now was to follow the diplomatic process, stay calm, hope and pray.

★★★★

POTUS Dallas Donaldson and Vice-President Ethan Summervale were in the Oval Office discussing the nuclear threat against the United Kingdom when Secretary of State, John Flitnell, burst into the room. Large beads of cold sweat had broken out on his forehead and were already rolling down his face.

"John, for heaven's sake what's wrong?" asked the President.

"Mr President, Dallas, we're on the brink of a nuclear war!" exclaimed the Secretary of State.

"What the hell are you talking about, John?" asked the President.

"I've just received official notifications from Russia and China! They have both said that, if we go ahead with a pre-emptive nuclear strike against the UK, there will be retaliatory nuclear attacks against the US. Dallas we can't take on both Russia and China. Not in a nuclear war," said John Flitnell, beginning to shake just a little and finding it difficult to catch his breath as a panic attack set in.

"Those bastard British!" said the President, slamming his fist down on the table. "I knew they'd jump into bed with the fucking commies first chance they got! That's why I wanted to get the bastards out of power!"

"Dallas we can't risk causing a nuclear war!" said Vice-President Summervale. "It looks like we have to back down!"

"Ethan, if we back down now they'll think they've got the better of us!" said the POTUS. "That new President of theirs, that George Richmond, he's a cool, tricky customer. Give them an inch now and who knows what they might try to take next time! These guys have to be put in their place!"

"But Dallas," said Ethan Summervale, "think how much damage a strike from Russia AND China will do! How many Americans will die? And what about the escalation? We strike back. They hit us again even harder. We're into World War Three! Armageddon! America is destroyed and for what? To get rid of a President that you don't like in a little country that's irrelevant!"

"Ethan's right, sir!" said Flitnell. "It's just not worth it, not worth the number of American lives that will be lost!"

"If we back down now, we'll appear weak! We'll be showing weakness to the rest of the world!" said Donaldson.

"Look Dallas, there's still three hours to go to the deadline," said Vice-President Summervale. "I suggest we say nothing to the UK. We let them sweat and panic. They'll be shitting themselves right now. If they go public there'll be panic and pandemonium all over the country, maybe demonstrations, maybe looting, maybe… who knows what. After the deadline has passed, we go on TV worldwide. We tell the public that the UK has been putting out fake news, trying to cause international unrest by making false claims about a nuclear attack. Maybe we can discredit them in the eyes of the world. Okay, so it won't get rid of them, but we can sure as hell make life more difficult for them."

"I guess you might be right Ethan," said the President, reluctantly. "It just sticks in my craw to let those upstart bastards get away with anything. As you say, we can still make life difficult for 'em and let 'em know that they haven't bested the USA."

Ethan Summervale and John Flitnell both agreed. Both men were extremely relieved that they had managed to talk the President down from his potentially disastrous plan.

****

Two forty-five p.m. G.M.T. The cabinet were together in George Richmond's office, ready to face and deal with the impending nuclear attack. They had decided not to inform the public to avoid probable blind panic. They had done all that they could on the diplomatic front. The forces were all on alert, ready to deal with a possible national emergency but without being informed what that emergency might be. Now all the cabinet could do was to wait, worry, sweat and pray.

Messages had been received from Russia and China to say that they had threatened retaliatory strikes on the US. That added an extra dimension to the problem. Sure, it put pressure on Dallas Donaldson not to attack the UK but, if he still went ahead, the chance of a worldwide nuclear war was now a strong possibility. For the next fifteen minutes they just had to hold their nerve, listen to the clock ticking towards possible annihilation and try to hide the total panic which they were all feeling.

****

Three fifteen p.m. G.M.T. The deadline had passed and no nuclear attack had materialized. Eight very relieved men began to breathe again, began to relax again and even began to smile again. Their huge communal sigh of relief was echoed in Washington, Moscow and Beijing. Hopefully, the world would never know how close it came to nuclear annihilation.

Four p.m. G.M.T. United States President, Dallas Donaldson, made a live broadcast on US TV which was also broadcast worldwide.

"I have come here today to inform the world that a country with ideas above its station and a new revolutionary government has been trying to cause trouble for the United States by telling blatant lies," began the President. "A rumour has been spread by the new President of the United Kingdom, George Richmond. He has stated, in certain quarters, that I had threatened a nuclear strike against the United Kingdom unless his regime resigned and reinstated the old government under Nigel Valentine. This is Fake News! It is total fiction, total fantasy! Furthermore, I am supposed to have set a deadline of three p.m. G.M.T. today for the attack. That deadline has passed and the nuclear strike has not happened. You all know that I am a man of my word, a man who always follows through with threats. Had I given such a threat and deadline, with no response from the United Kingdom, that threat would have been carried out by now. The fact that no such attack has taken place can be taken as proof that the whole thing has been prevaricated by President Richmond to cause trouble for the United States.

It is true that I and the United States do not accept this regime as a legitimate government, having been formed from terrorists who gained power by revolution. It is also true that I gave my opinion that the best thing for the United Kingdom would be for Richmond's government to stand down and reinstate the Valentine regime. However, it is pure fantasy to say that the United Kingdom was threatened at all.

The United States still has a missile base in the United Kingdom. I will not have US missiles in a country whose government I do not trust. We will therefore ensure that those missiles are decommissioned and removed from the UK within the next three months.

The United States will never form any kind of alliance with nor contemplate trade deals with such a government who clearly have set a course to cause international mayhem. We also advise all other countries to turn their back on such alliances."

The broadcast ended with the playing of the "Star Spangled Banner".

So, a nuclear catastrophe had been avoided. How much Dallas Donaldson's lies had influenced other countries was yet to be seen, but for the time being the United Kingdom was safe.

Chapter 27.
RETURN FROM SAINT KILDA

It was essential to bring the convicts back from the Saint Kilda archipelago at the earliest opportunity. Conditions in the colonies on Hirta, Soay and Dun were expected to be unbelievably bad but nobody was prepared for just how bad the reality was.

When the colonies were first set up, almost thirty years earlier, twenty-five thousand men and women were deposited on the islands. They were provided with only a supply of HCR, some timber, canvas, tarpaulin and a few very basic tools. Twenty-five thousand people on an archipelago which, in its heyday, had provided a living for barely more than three hundred people. The convicts were crammed in like bees in a beehive, like flies on a cow pat. Inevitably overcrowding caused fierce fighting between rival groups with many killed. Those who did not meet a violent end frequently died of starvation, exposure or disease. People were literally fighting for survival. Within the first year, twenty thousand of the original twenty-five thousand had died. Despite an extra two thousand people being sentenced to the penal colonies each year, the population continued to dwindle. As time went by and the population was reduced, most of the convicts learned to cooperate and to help each other. Even so, very few people survived for more than eighteen months.

While a small amount of farming, hunting and fishing went on, people relied almost completely on the Human Carcass Reconstitution (HCR) food supplied by The Party which contained GDN93, the carcinogenic and hepatotoxic preservative. Those who survived the conditions were poisoned by the government. By the time the convicts were released and repatriated only around eight hundred had survived and most of those would soon be dead from cancer or liver failure.

There was a dearth of large vessels capable of transporting the convicts back to the mainland, so an armada of fishing boats, pleasure boats and other small craft were commandeered to bring them home. They had arranged to dock in Oban, on the Scottish mainland. Nick Kaydon had been given the responsibility of receiving and repatriating the liberated convicts. Buildings, including the former ferry terminal and other dockland facilities, had been quickly converted to provide a hospital, offices and hostels. The ex-convicts, now pardoned and freed, were given a thorough medical examination upon docking in Oban and were taken either to hospital or to a hostel, depending on their state of health. Their condition was such that the majority found themselves in hospital.

★★★★

Nick was standing by the jetty of the ferry terminal watching the ex-cons coming from a boat which had just docked. The sight was absolutely pitiful. Moving skeletons, some walking, some barely shuffling, covered by loose, hanging skin and little else, dressed in only the minimum of basic rags. Unkempt and unwashed, they looked more like zombies than humans. Expressionless, blank faces with soulless eyes showed that all hope had long since deserted them. Heads bowed, shoulders dropped, totally disconnected from their surroundings, lacking even the slightest enthusiasm about their release, the sight of them was almost bringing tears to Nick's eyes. How could The Party have treated people in such an inhuman and inhumane way? How could they have inflicted the suffering which was so painfully on display?

All would be registered, thoroughly examined, treated as appropriate, fed, given decent clothing and, if possible, eventually transported back to their families. Those who were dying would be given the best possible care and made as comfortable as possible.

As Nick watched he noticed a woman, every bit as pitiful as the rest, who seemed to stand out. Her blond hair was down to her waist, filthy and matted. Her complexion was bluish white, with a hint of jaundice. Her cheeks were sallow and sunken. Her breathing was deep and laboured with an occasional cough. She struggled to keep putting one foot in front of the other. She was barely recognisable as a woman and yet there was something that seemed familiar. Despite her eyes having sunk deep into their sockets, with no hint of sparkle or interest, there was something familiar about those eyes. Suddenly the realization of reality hit Nick like a sledgehammer to the brain.

"Jenny?" he asked in complete shock.

She looked up. "Nick?" Her words ended suddenly as she collapsed on the ground in a limp heap.

★★★★

When Nick saw Jenny, the following morning, she had been cleaned up and put in a side ward on her own. When Nick walked in, she was sitting up, connected to an intravenous drip and a heart monitor.

"That's better," said Nick. "You gave me a real fright last night. You look almost human this morning."

"Thanks for the compliment. You certainly know how to make a girl feel good about herself. Actually, I feel a lot better. It's amazing how much some fluid and some rest can do!" said Jenny.

"What a shock you gave me! I thought you were dead! Then it turns out that you're alive but you do your best to die on me after all!"

"I'm sorry for putting you through all that babe."

"Well, that's nothing compared to what you must have been through," said Nick, smiling for the first time since he saw Jenny.

Jenny began to cough. She had done that a lot since being admitted.

Nick looked uneasy again as he continued in a soft, gentle voice. "Look Jen, I was going to wait for you to get a bit stronger before we talked about your health, but maybe I'd better tell you now."

"Don't worry babe! Don't try to cover anything up or soften the blow," said Jenny. "I know I'm dying!"

"How?" asked Nick, in surprise.

"Don't forget I was a trained nurse and I'm not stupid. I've seen a lot of this on the island. I used to call it Hirta Syndrome. Almost everyone died from it! I reckoned it was a combination of cancer and liver failure. So, Nick, just tell it how it is. I can handle it. If I can cope with being on Hirta I can handle anything." She forced a smile in an attempt to reassure him.

"When you collapsed last night, we took some radiographs and did some blood tests. The radiographs showed patches on both lungs which look like cancer. There were also signs of tumours in your liver and colon. The bloods showed severe hepatopathy. Renal function is not great either. I'm sorry Jen!" Nick struggled to hold back the tears, but he had to. The last thing that would help Jenny now was to see him fall apart.

"Well, that's not great is it babe, but it's pretty much what I expected." She too was putting on a brave face but, unlike Nick, the diagnosis held no real fear for her. She had faced death and suffering for most of her days on Saint Kilda. "How long do you reckon I've got?"

"Hard to say. Not long. Maybe a few weeks if you're lucky. Possibly only days." Nick choked on the words as he tried to get them out. "The intravenous fluid has helped temporarily and medication will help, but all we can really do is to keep you as comfortable as possible for as long as possible."

"Don't be too sad babe. After the hell of Hirta, it's almost a relief," said Jenny and then, changing the subject, "So you've finally got rid of The Party!"

"Yes," replied Nick, trying to perk up just a little. "George Richmond's the new President."

"That's great news! I'm sure he'll do a great job. It's a pity I won't be around to see too much of it. How's Jonathan?"

"Jon's been fine. He's really missed you a lot but he's been OK. He doesn't know anything about this yet. I've not had chance to tell him. He's living at PDMs headquarters at the moment. He still thinks you're dead, like I did.

A few days after you ran away, I tried to find you. I went to your flat and it had obviously been ransacked by the ATS, so I went to Saint Jude's to see if Sister Mary-Beth knew anything. She said that you had been arrested at the hospital and Quinlan had said that you'd be going for Age Acceleration. I believed that you would already have been dead by then."

"Yes," said Jenny. "Quinlan was ranting about Age Acceleration but, when they took me to court the next morning, another ATS officer had taken over the case. Somebody said something about Quinlan being promoted or something."

"Yeah. He was made Commander-In-Chief of all security forces. He's in prison now, awaiting trial," said Nick.

"I'm glad to hear that. They need to throw the book at that bastard! Anyway, the replacement officer asked the judge to send me to the Penal Colony instead. I'm not sure which was the worst sentence to be honest, the way the cons were left to suffer!"

"If I'd realized you were still alive, I would have tried to find you somehow," said Nick.

"You weren't to know Nick and, if you had, you couldn't have rescued me on Hirta," said Jenny, putting a reassuring hand on his arm.

"Have you managed to eat anything this morning?" asked Nick.

"The nurse gave me some of that concentrated liquid stuff that's a bit like a milk shake. I didn't really want it but she's quite persistent. I drank it in the end just to keep her quiet."

"Which nurse was that?" asked Nick.

"I think her name is Sally."

"Oh, that must be Sally Pallette. She's a good nurse. Not as good as you used to be of course, but she'll look after you and she is stubborn so you had better do as you're told.

I don't want to tire you out too much," continued Nick, "so I'd better go and see some other patients. I'll be back to see you later."

"I'll look forward to it," said Jenny. "It doesn't look like I'll be going anywhere soon."

Nick gave her a little kiss on the forehead before he left.

****

Nick needed to speak to Charley and explain about Jenny as soon as he could. Charley was currently still staying at the Brookslade base along with Maddy, Jonathan and many other families. Nick rang her at the first possible opportunity.

"Hi Charley. It's good to hear your voice again," said Nick. "How are Maddy and Jon?"

"We're all fine. Is something wrong Nick?" she asked, sensing something slightly unusual in his tone.

"Not exactly, but there is something big that I need to tell you about. It's Jenny! It turns out that she wasn't dead after all. She'd been sent to Hirta instead. She's here in Oban now. She's one of the convicts who have just been brought back home."

"That's amazing!" Charley found herself saying. While she was pleased for Jenny, she was already beginning to struggle with wondering what it would do to her own relationship with Nick.

"The trouble is that she's got cancer and liver failure like a lot of the convicts and she's not got long to live. She's in a bad way Charley. I was not supposed to be here in Oban for more than another couple of days but I can't just leave her while she's like this. I'm going to stay here for a while. Can you look after Jonathan for a bit longer?"

"Of course I will, Nick. Have you got any idea how long you'll be there?" asked Charley.

"For as long as she needs me, I guess," was Nick's reply.

"Do you want me to tell Jonathan? I'm sure he'll want to know why you're not coming back."

"I guess you'd better tell him, if you're okay with that," said Nick. "We can't really lie about it. If he wants to come and see Jenny, try to put him off. I don't think it's a good idea for him to see her like this."

"Okay Nick, I'll try to handle Jonathan the best I can. Don't worry. I'll make sure he's alright."

"Thanks Charley. I knew I could count on you. I'd better get back to work. Bye!"

"Bye Nick! Don't worry, I'll look after Jon. I love you!"

Did she really say that? I love you was a phrase that she never said to Nick, although she did. Surely this was a totally inappropriate time to say such a thing. After all, where exactly did Charley stand now? Jenny was dying but, with no other complications, would Nick have chosen to be with Jenny or Charley? How could she compete with a dead woman, or in this case a dying woman? She found herself wishing that Jenny had been dead and had not come back. How could she do that? Charley never had any feelings of ill will towards anyone. How could she find herself wishing that Nick had never found Jenny, dying or not?

★★★★

"Hi Jen! How are you feeling this morning?" asked Nick as he entered Jenny's room.

"I'm feeling OK at the moment Babe," said Jenny with a smile. "Listen Nick, there's something I want to ask you. While I was on Hirta and you thought I was dead, did you find anybody else?"

"What?"

"Did you find another girlfriend when you thought I was dead?" Jenny persisted.

"Are you warm enough? It sometimes gets a bit draughty in here," said Nick, being far from subtle in changing the subject.

"I'm fine Nick but…"

"There's something I wanted to ask you about if you're up to talking about the island," interrupted Nick. "Do you remember the night we made an air drop over Saint Kilda? We dropped food and a load of leaflets warning people about HCR."

"Yes, I remember it as clearly as if it was yesterday," said Jenny, giving up on her previous question for the time being.

"We believed that the plane was shot down but we always hoped that the two pilots had ejected and landed safely. We thought we had heard one man, Max Nedwell, jump. It sounded like the other man, Declan Dunleavy, was preparing to jump but then there was an explosion. Did you see anything that night?"

"I saw it all," said Jenny, her face suddenly showing extreme sadness. "The plane exploded after being hit by a drone. There was only one man who jumped."

"Are you sure?" asked Nick.

"Absolutely certain!" said Jenny. "I was watching from the shore, like many others. One man jumped and then the plane exploded. If there were two men in the plane, one of them must have still been in the plane when it blew up."

"So, Max must have jumped and Declan must have been killed by the explosion. Do you have any idea what happened to Max after he jumped? Did he land safely?" enquired Nick.

"He landed safely but he was killed by The Collectors," said Jenny, clearly looking upset by recalling the events of that night.

"The Collectors?" queried Nick.

Jenny began to explain the gory details. "In my time on Hirta, people had learned to cooperate with each other and to help each other. The one exception to that was a gang called The Collectors. They called themselves that because they collected things. They always made sure that they got more than half of everything; HCR, any birds, animals or fish that were caught, any timber, any canvas, anything that could be useful or people might need. If anyone argued they took it by force and they were brutal. When people were desperate for supplies The Collectors would provide what they needed, at a price. Often the men would have to labour for them, particularly those who had a skill or trade of some kind. The older women had to do their washing, repair their clothes, even make new clothes if cloth was available. The younger women and even teenage girls had to be available for sex. Most consented because they were too scared to refuse. Any who didn't consent were raped anyway. They called it MAKING USE of them. If anybody objected or failed to cooperate, they were beaten, sometimes to death or until they were crippled. They showed no mercy.

Their leader was an evil guy called Dante and the second in command was called Grainger."

"Did they ever hurt you?" asked Nick, clearly very worried. "No!" said Jenny. "Somehow, I always managed to avoid them!

Anyway, the guy from the plane landed in the sea. He managed to get free from his parachute and swim to the beach. The Collectors were waiting for him. Dante was angry about the warning leaflets. He reckoned it would spoil his trade in HCR. He ordered his men to kill your guy, slowly, as a warning to the cons not to cross him. There was about eight of them. They beat him with clubs, on his body only. They didn't want to hit him on the head and knock him unconscious. They wanted him to suffer as much as possible. By the time he died I doubt if there would have been a bone in his body that was not broken. Then they just tossed his shattered body back into the sea, like a child throwing away an unwanted rag doll.

Nick, they need to be punished for the things they have done. They can't be allowed to get away with it!"

"If we find them, would you be able to identify them?" asked Nick.

"You catch them and I'll identify them for certain. Dante has a tattoo on his right arm, a skull with a snake coming out of the eye socket. He also has a large scorpion tattooed on the right side of his neck. Grainger is exceptionally tall. I'd guess maybe six foot eight and he has a shaved head."

"I'll get the lads on to finding them right away," said Nick as he left the room. A man on a mission.

★★★★

Nick walked into Jenny's room just as nurse, Sally Pallette, was about to leave after checking her drip. "How's the patient this morning nurse?" asked Nick. "She's not doing too badly at all," said Sally. "Everything is stable at the moment."

"You know I can answer for myself Nick," chided Jenny. "Sally's doing a great job of looking after me."

"Actually, Jen we've got two men who we think are Dante and Grainger. If we bring them in here, is there any chance that you can ID them?" asked Nick. Jenny looked terrified. "If it's too much," continued Nick, "you don't have to do it. They'll be handcuffed and accompanied by guards so there will be no danger to you. I do understand if you don't want to do it."

"Of course I'll do it. They're the last people that I ever want to see again but I'll do it. Whatever it takes to put those two psycho bastards away for a long time!" said Jenny."Don't you go stressing her out or getting her too tired," said Sally. "She's not well enough for that!"

"It's OK Sally. I'll be all right and I do want to do it," said Jenny reassuringly.

"We've got them waiting just down the corridor, Jen. Can I bring them in now?" asked Nick.

"Might as well get it over as soon as possible," said Jenny, trying to sound brave despite feeling as if she wanted to run away to avoid any contact with them.

"I'll leave you to it, but you look after her," said nurse Sally as she left the room.

Nick called to the guards to bring the two men in, two guards to each man and both men handcuffed. Both men appeared cocky and arrogant despite their arrest. Dante was staring at Jenny, trying to intimidate her with his gaze. His glare was returned by Jenny's look of utter hatred and contempt.

"They're the ones!" said Jenny. "The one with the tattoos is Dante and the other one is Grainger."

"We could have told you that and saved you all this trouble," said Dante. "We've never denied who we are. I'm Dante Pigden and my friend is Bartholemew Grainger. Why have we been arrested anyway? We were told that all the convicts had been pardoned."

"Pardoned for the crimes that sent them to the colonies, NOT for crimes committed ON Hirta," replied Nick.

"We've done nothing," said Dante, "only what we had to do in order to survive, just like anybody else. What are we supposed to have done?"

"Murder, extortion, rape!" said Jenny, spitting the words at them. "Battering a pilot to death. Making people's lives intolerable!"

"Have we ever done anything to you?" asked Dante.

"No!" replied Jenny, "but only because I managed to keep out of your way, you bastard!"

"My, my, you are a feisty one. No-one would really know it by your appearance now but I reckon you would have been a looker when you first came to Hirta. We should have MADE USE of you when we had the chance. I would have enjoyed that!" said Dante with a grin.

Nick had struggled to hold his temper throughout at the thought of what had occurred on Hirta. Dante's final comment went too far. Nick felt the satisfying crunch of nasal bone and cartilage under the full force of his fist. He saw Dante's nostrils explode, spitting forth blood as he fell to the floor. In a second, Nick had hold of Dante's collar, ramming his head into the wall, again and again until he was stopped by the guards.

With the guards preoccupied, Grainger, who had been conspicuously silent throughout, grabbed his chance to try to escape. He shot out through the door and off down the corridor, despite still being handcuffed.

Idris Llewellyn had heard about Jenny's plight and was just on his way to visit her. As he turned the corner, he saw a handcuffed man push a nurse out of his way and into the wall as he ran down the corridor towards him. He could hear the pandemonium of the chasing guards close behind. As Grainger attempted to run past him, Idris kicked Grainger's legs out from under him, causing him to crash face first into the floor. In a flash Idris was on him, his knee in Grainger's back forcing him down. He had him in a headlock forcing Grainger's head back and twisting his neck.

"You… break… ing… my… neck!" spluttered Grainger, struggling to get his words out.

"No, I'm not! Not yet, but I can if you continue to struggle," said Taff, applying even more pressure to prove his point.

"It's OK Taff, we can take him from here," said one of the guards who had now caught up with the escapee.

"Well, I hope you take better care of him this time," said Idris. "What were you thinking of, letting a scrote like this get away from you?"

"We took our eye off the ball because we thought Nick was going to kill the other one."

Just then the other two guards frogmarched Dante, now back on his feet, down the corridor. Dante, face covered in blood with a shattered nose and a large gash on his forehead, had finally lost his swagger and was looking worried.

Back in Jenny's room, prisoners removed, Nick was beginning to calm down.

"You didn't have to go that far Nick," said Jenny. "I thought you were going to kill him."

"I know. I just saw red when I thought what he could have done to you, what he did to the others, what he did to Max Nedwell," said Nick.

"Listen Nick, I'll make a written statement obviously, but I think it might be a good idea to make a film of me telling the story of what those two did on Hirta," said Jenny. "By the time they go on trial I may be too ill to give evidence, or I might not be here at all. If we've got it on disc, the court will have the evidence whether I'm around or not."

"Don't talk like that," said a shocked Nick.

"Face it babe. I might not be here and I don't want those bastards getting away with it because I can't give evidence."

"Okay, I'll see to it," said Nick with a smile, knowing when to give in gracefully to Jenny's determination.

Just then there was a tap on the door and Idris popped his head round. "Is it all right if I come in?" he asked.

"Idris! I didn't expect to see you!" said Jenny with surprise and excitement. "Come in!"

"I didn't expect to see you either, girl," said Idris. "We all thought you were dead."

"No! I'm still around," said Jenny, "although I may not be here for much longer."

"I heard about that, Jen. I'm so sorry, but how are you feeling at the moment?" asked Idris.

"Oh, I'm not too bad Idris, at least I wouldn't be if Nick didn't provide too much drama," said Jenny.

"Yes, I heard about your little fracas, Nick," said Idris. "What was going on?"

"It's just two scrotes from Hirta who need to be put away for a long time," said Nick "and one of them just pushed too many buttons."

"Now that Idris is here, Nick, why don't you go and get yourself cleaned up a bit? You've still got Dante's blood on your hands." Looking a little more closely, Jenny was surprised. "Actually Nick that's not just Dante's blood. It looks like your hand is bleeding."

"Oh, it's alright. I got my hand burned a little while ago and the punch just opened up one of the scars a little. It's nothing."

"Well go and get it cleaned up and dressed!" ordered Jenny. "Idris and I can have a catch up in private for a few minutes while you're gone. I'll still be here when you come back."

"I hope that doesn't mean that you want to talk about me while I'm not here," joked Nick.

"Why would we want to talk about you, boy?" asked Idris. "We've got far more interesting things to catch up on."

"I don't know! Anyway, I won't be long," said Nick as he walked out of the door.

As the door closed behind Nick, Idris pulled a chair up beside Jenny and sat down.

"Now then Jenny, girl, how are you coping?" enquired Idris quietly.

"Oh, I'm as good as can be expected," said Jenny with a brave smile. "Being here is almost like heaven compared to Hirta."

"I know you're trying to put a brave face on, Jen, particularly for Nick. You don't need to do that with me. You can say whatever you want," said Taff in a manner so gentle that it seemed almost strange from such a big, powerful, confident character.

"The truth is Taffy I'm terrified," confided Jenny, finally letting her feelings out, tears running down her cheeks. "Nick's been brilliant. He's hardly left my side since I came back but, in a way, that puts me under more pressure. Sometimes I'm struggling to hold it together, but I feel like I've got to, for Nick even more than for me. I'm scared of what's coming but I'm even more scared of what it might do to Nick."

"Nick's a big boy," said Taff, taking hold of Jenny's hand to comfort her. "He'll get through this. Don't you worry about that. I'll do everything I can to make sure of it and there are others who will help."

"That brings me to what I really wanted to talk to you about," said Jenny, sniffing back her tears and reaching for a tissue. "I want you to tell me about Nick's girlfriend."

"Shouldn't you talk to Nick about that?" asked Taff, trying to avoid getting drawn into a conversation about Nick's personal life.

"I tried," said Jenny. "I asked him if he'd found anyone else."

"And? What did he say?" asked Idris, hoping to find a way to avoid answering the question.

"He changed the subject, so it's obvious that he has. Tell me about her."

"I'm not sure I should say anything," said Taff.

"Please!" implored Jenny. "I just need to know that he'll be okay. Who is she? Do I know her? Are they good together?"

"I don't think you've ever met her," said Idris. "Her name is Charley McCarthy. Do you remember Derek McCarthy from the safe house?"

"Yes, I remember Del. How could I forget after what happened?"

"Well Charley is Del's widow. Nick got to know her when they were both grieving. They helped each other a lot and things just gradually developed from there," said Taff.

"Are they good together?" Jenny asked.

"They seemed like a very good couple. Charley is a teacher with a disabled daughter called Maddy and of course Nick had Jon to look after, so their friendship helped both of them to cope with the kids as well."

For a while Idris found it impossible to read the expression on Jenny's face.

"I don't want Nick to destroy his relationship because of me," said Jenny. "He deserves to have a good life with a woman that he loves and a family. It looks like he had that until I came back. I don't know what impact me coming back will have. I'm so grateful that Nick's been here for me, I really am. He's been my rock, but I don't want him to risk losing Charley just because he's looking after me. I'll be gone soon enough, and I need to know that Nick will be okay." Jenny thought for a few seconds before continuing. "I'd really like to meet Charley. Do you think you could get her to come and see me Idris? I'd really like to see Jonathan as well. I can't bear to think what Jon must be going through right now."

"I can't make any promises Jen, but I'll see what I can do," said Idris.

Just then Nick returned.

"It's all right boy, you can come in. We've finished talking about you!" teased Idris with a wink.

Nick went to give Jenny the gentlest of hugs and was horrified when he felt her recoil from him, not wanting to be touched and beginning to cough. He said nothing but her reaction made it obvious just how much pain she was in and how hard she had been trying to conceal it.

★★★★

Back at PDM headquarters, Idris called to see Charley, having driven back from Oban. She was with Maddy and Jonathan.

"Hi Idris! I thought you were going to be in Oban for a few more days yet. How come you're back already?" asked Charley, surprised but pleased to see the big guy.

"Actually Charley, I've come back to collect you and Jonathan and drive you up to Oban, if you're willing," said Idris.

"What do you mean?" asked Charley, with a puzzled look on her face.

"Actually girl, I was talking to Jenny about you, only because she asked point blank. Jenny said she'd like to see you and Jon. She asked me if I would take you," said Idris.

"Why would she want to see me?" asked Charley. "Until you just mentioned it, I didn't think she knew I even existed."

"I think she wants to discuss what happens between you and Nick when she dies."

"There probably won't be any me and Nick any more, when she dies!" snapped Charley.

"What do you mean?" asked the Welshman.

"It's obvious Nick still has feelings for her. I don't mind him still wanting to be there for her. If he didn't, he wouldn't be the man that I fell in love with. But when she's gone, he'll be grieving for her and quite rightly. Where would I fit in? How can I compete for his love with a dead woman?"

"Nick hasn't stopped loving you because Jenny is back. He's spending so much time with her because she needs him right now. His feelings are going to be pretty messed up at the moment but that doesn't mean that he's giving up on you. Just come with me and talk to Jenny. I'm sure you'll feel better after you've talked to her. She's desperate to see Jon as well," said Idris.

"Nick told me before that he didn't want Jon to see her in hospital," argued Charley.

"Well, I want to go and see her!" interrupted Jonathan. "Don't my feelings count?"

"Of course they do Jon. Nick's just trying to protect you in case you can't handle it," said Charley, trying to convince Jon that Nick was only trying to do the best for him.

"You worry more about what you don't see," argued Jonathan. "I want to see her before she dies. I owe her that at least."

"Looks like there's your answer," said Idris. "If Nick's annoyed about Jon being there you can just blame me for carrying out Jon and Jenny's wishes. I've got broad shoulders."

"I'm not convinced it will do any good," said Charley with a resigned smile, "but we'll go. When were you planning on driving back?"

"We might as well go this afternoon if you can do that," said Idris.

"Give me an hour to find someone to look after Maddy and I'm all yours," said Charley. "Thanks Idris. You're a good friend.

I don't have any idea how things will work out but thank you for caring."

****

"Hi Idris," said Nick, looking over his shoulder as he heard the door to Jenny's room open. "Charley? Jon? What are you doing here?"

"I wanted to see them," said Jenny. "I asked Taff to bring them."

Jonathan rushed over to the bed to give Jenny a big hug, which made her squirm and started a fit of coughing. Jon recoiled in horror, wondering what he had done.

"It's alright Jon," Jenny reassured him. "I'm just a bit fragile, that's all. No harm done."

"Come on boy," Idris said to Nick. "Why don't you and I go and get a cup of tea and leave everybody to get acquainted."

Nick looked enquiringly towards Jenny.

"It's alright Nick," said Jenny. "You go with Idris and relax for a bit. I need some time with Charley and Jon."

"Okay then, we'll see you later," said Nick as he and Idris left the room.

Jonathan, now realizing that more contact was impossible, stood holding Jenny's hand.

"Pull up a couple of chairs and take a seat," said Jenny, beginning to cough again.

The coughing fits were beginning to get more frequent and a little more prolonged. Jenny had also vomited a couple of times earlier that day, although for the time being her stomach was settled. Jon looked shocked and horrified. Despite knowing how ill Jenny was, Charley was surprised to see just how frail Jenny appeared to be.

"All the way here I've been planning what I was going to say to you," said Charley, sitting down "and now I'm here I haven't got a clue what to say."

"You know, you should hate me for what I've done. It was my fault that Derek got killed and now I'm making things complicated for you and Nick," said Jenny.

"I don't hate you. I never have. What happened to Del was a mistake. I know you never intended for anyone to get killed. As for the situation now, you deserve anything that will make that easier. You've already suffered more than anyone should have to," reassured Charley.

"I'm not sure I'd be so forgiving if things were the other way round," said Jenny. "I need to make sure this doesn't split you and Nick up. You're obviously good together. He's only here with me, at the moment, because I'm dying. I have no doubt about that. Oh, he's still got some feelings for me, of course he has. We went through too much together for that to be any different, but you're the one that he really loves and wants to be with. Don't ever doubt that."

"I wish I could believe that, I really do," said Charley. "I'm just so afraid of losing him."

"You have to believe that!" said Jenny. "I know it's true! Look, right now his feelings are all mixed up and they will be even more when I die. He'll feel like he's being disloyal to me if he's with you. He'll feel like he's being disloyal to you if he's grieving for me. I'll bet you went through something similar when you first met Nick and you were grieving for Derek. All that I ask is that you hang in there, give him some time, patience and understanding. You won't lose him! Trust me!"

A tear trickled down Charley's cheek. "I don't understand why you're so concerned about my relationship with Nick."

"Believe me," said Jenny, "if I thought there was any chance of Nick and I having a future I would be fighting you for him, but that can't happen. When I'm gone, I want the happiest possible future for Nick and I know that's with you."

Neither woman had noticed that Jonathan had his face buried deep in his hands, tears streaming down his face.

"Jon don't be upset babe," said Jenny when she saw his heartbreak. "I know it's a lot to deal with right now, but everything will be alright in time."

Charley threw her arms around him and hugged him as close and as tight as she could. She hugged him all the more to make up for the hug which Jenny was unable to give him.

By the time Nick and Idris returned, emotions had settled and a more normal conversation was taking place. When they parted, Jenny and Charley appeared to be the best of friends, having laid bare their souls and come together with a common cause.

****

The following morning Jenny's health was clearly deteriorating, and she was struggling badly. Although she was sitting up in bed, she looked very tired. The cough was continuing to become more frequent and she had vomited quite a lot during the night. Her breathing was clearly becoming more of an effort, with her chest heaving and nostrils slightly flaring at times. Oxygen had been made available for her in case she needed it and sometimes she would breathe from the mask, although most of the time she tried to manage without it.

Despite her struggle she still brightened up when Nick walked into the room.

"Hi Nick! How are you this morning, babe?" she enquired with a smile which left him in no doubt of how pleased she was to see him.

Idris, Charley and Jon had returned home the previous night. Charley had warned Nick just how upset Jonathan had been and they had both agreed that it would be too distressing for him to see Jenny when her condition deteriorated.

"It was nice to see…" Jenny sounded as though it was hard to concentrate on her words and almost fell asleep in mid-sentence. She tried again. "It was nice to see Jon and Charley, yesterday." Her eyes closed for a few moments as she rested, exhausted by speaking.

"You seem really tired today, Jen. Do you want me to go and let you get some rest?" asked Nick.

She took quite a few seconds before she found the energy to answer. "No babe, I like you being here even if I don't say much."

"That's OK then," said Nick. "I'm going to be here just as long as you want me to be."

"I like Charley. It's obvious she thinks…" Jenny went back to her momentary sleep again before suddenly recovering her thoughts. "She thinks a lot of you and Jonathan. She's a good woman." Again, Jenny slumped back into her resting place.

"She's one of the best," said Nick.

Nick left Jenny briefly to speak to Bill Kempson, the doctor who had been overseeing Jenny's treatment. He explained how she had been drifting off in mid-sentence.

"I'm sorry Nick but I'm afraid everything in her body is starting to shut down. It's taken such a toll on her that she's totally exhausted and all of her organs are starting to fail," said Doctor Kempson.

Nick knew what was going on already but somehow it helped to get things in perspective by talking about it.

"How long do you think she's got left?" asked Nick, already knowing the answer.

"It could just be a few hours. I'd guess twenty-four hours at most. The medication should keep her comfortable and stop the vomiting, but if you feel the pain is building up come and get me right away."

Nick returned to sit with Jenny, still only having a very limited conversation as she drifted in and out of consciousness. Around mid-afternoon he told Jenny that he was just going to get something to eat and he would be back in half an hour.

When Nick returned, he was stopped in the corridor by Sally.

"I'm afraid Jenny seems completely comatose now," she warned. "She's not responding any longer. We can't tell how much she's aware of her surroundings so still talk to her if you want to, but don't expect any response."

Nick took a chair as close to the bed as possible and sat holding Jenny's hand, under the blanket so that her arm did not get cold. She seemed to respond to his touch, although not to his voice when he spoke. He was convinced that she knew he was there and reassured by his presence. She lay comfortable and relaxed, looking as though she was just in a deep sleep. Occasionally she seemed to become distressed and move as though she was uncomfortable or frightened. When that happened, Nick's soothing voice seemed to help her to settle down again.

Nick sat holding Jenny's hand and speaking occasionally for four or five hours with no real change. It seemed as if she was trying to hang on to what life remained for as long as possible.

At one point Nick said, "Jen, if you're hanging on because you're worried about me and Jon, there's no need to. We'll both miss you like crazy, but we'll be OK. We'll look after each other and we'll be OK, so you just go when you're ready."

Jenny slept on for about ten minutes, at which time she began to jerk and react as though shocked or surprised by something. She suddenly turned her head towards Nick, opening both eyes and looking him straight in the face. She smiled and her eyes had a sparkle which Nick had not seen for a very long time. Then her expression relaxed and the sparkle faded away. Her body relaxed and her breathing faded away.

Nick collapsed with his head on Jenny's breast, unable to control the tsunami of tears that poured in torrents down his face.

Jenny's suffering was over.

Chapter 28.

TRIAL AND RETRIBUTION

Arrest of leading members of the government and the ATS was followed by weeks of painstakingly collecting evidence, of which there was certainly no shortage. People came forward in droves to provide statements and to offer their services as witnesses. The whole country waited with bated breath, hoping and praying that the new government would make certain that The Party could never rear its ugly head or harm people again. Only knowing that adequate retribution had been carried out would allow people to breathe easy and move on once more.

The decision had been taken to return to the old-fashioned trial by jury system, with prosecution and defence lawyers. Witnesses would be cross-examined to ensure that the trials were not only fair but seen to be indisputably fair. To assist that outcome the trials would be broadcast live on TV, not only to the nation but to the world. Justice had to be seen to be done for the peace of mind of the populace and to begin to establish a new international reputation.

The trials were to be held at the George Jeffreys Citadel. Most courtrooms were far too small to accommodate trial by jury, let alone TV coverage. The Citadel was large enough to be easily adapted to accommodate such a trial. Carpenters worked frantically for long hours to increase the security of the dock by incorporating firearm resistant glass, creating seating for the jury, adding desks to accommodate the defence and prosecution lawyers, building a witness box, creating a working space for TV broadcasting crews and adding a public viewing gallery.

As the trials would continue for several weeks, three judges were chosen from the existing judiciary. Only those judges who still believed in trial by jury or at least had an open mind were considered. Those, such as Justice George Grisedale, who had championed The Party's legal system were excluded. George Grisedale was in fact to play a major part in the trials as a defence lawyer. Due to The Party's legal system, there were no experienced prosecuting or defence councils. Each side was given the right to choose whoever they wanted to represent them, legally qualified or not.

Despite not being government officials, the trials began with the case against Dante Pigden and Bartholemew Grainger. Both men were to be tried together.

The judge, Justice Ernest Oakdean, began the proceedings. "Dante Pigden and Bartholemew Grainger! You are charged with assault, causing grievous bodily harm, rape, extorsion and murder on the island of Hirta, on numerous occasions, over many years! How do you both plead?"

"Not guilty sir!" said Dante, no longer showing his usual swagger.

"Not guilty sir," muttered Grainger, staring at the ground and visibly shaking.

The prosecution began their case by reading Jenny's statement out loud to the court. Unfortunately, Jenny had died before she was able to make the video which she had suggested. Nick Kaydon was called to confirm that the statement was an accurate record of what he had been told by Jenny. He also confirmed that Jenny had positively identified Dante and Grainger at the hospital. Other witnesses from Hirta had come forward, each with their own story to tell about the actions of The Collectors but one stood out from the rest. He was a small, wiry man in his mid-sixties with grey hair and a white beard but looking in surprisingly good health for a survivor from Hirta. John Trenchard was one of the very first convicts to be sent to Hirta and he had seen what The Collectors had done throughout all of that time.

"Mr Trenchard," said the prosecuting council, "would you tell the court about your time on Hirta?"

"When I first arrived, it was like stepping into a war zone. Everyone was fighting for their own existence. Rival gangs fought for food and supplies. There just wasn't enough of anything to go around. It was survival of the strongest but, pretty soon, people began to realise that we really only had a chance to survive if we cooperated with each other and worked together. The gangs all gradually dispersed, that is all of the gangs except The Collectors. They continued to take whatever they wanted by force, by coercion, by creating fear, whatever it took. They stopped at nothing! They took the lion's share of everything and then, when people had nothing, they provided them with supplies at a price, a very harsh price! Usually, the men and older women had to provide labour of some kind. The younger women usually had to provide sex. They even sometimes turned people out of their homes and took over the dwellings themselves."

"If people refused their demands, what happened then?" asked the prosecutor.

"If a woman refused sex they raped her, often more than one of them and more than once. If someone withheld their labour, they were beaten so badly that they were no longer able to work. If someone refused to get out of their home, they burned it down and hurt them so much that they couldn't rebuild it. If they protested too much they were killed. Punishments were always handed out in the nastiest, most painful way possible as a warning to others not to cross The Collectors. Many years ago, the islanders suffered from an illness which we called the coughing sickness. I heard from convicts who had newly arrived that the disease had also occurred on the mainland. It was some sort of virus. I think it was called a Coronavirus or something like that. We had no treatment for it. It wiped out three quarters of the population on Hirta. If anyone coughed near one of The Collectors, regardless of whether it was the sickness or for some other reason, they were killed. If any of the gang developed a cough themselves, they were killed by the other gang members."

"You've done remarkably well to survive so long on Hirta," said the prosecutor. "My understanding is that most people only last a few years at most. How do you explain your survival?"

"I only ate what I could catch or forage for myself. I never touched that shit that the government provided. I also kept on the move so that I could stay away from The Collectors and I made sure that my supply of food was a secret and safely hidden. It was a bit like being a fugitive and it meant that sometimes I went hungry, but it kept me safe."

"You have talked about The Collectors," continued the prosecutor. "What is the relationship between the accused and The Collectors? What part did the accused play?"

"Dante was the leader. He didn't get his hands dirty when it came to the beatings and killings, but it was all done on his instructions and he took great pleasure in watching people suffer. Grainger was second in command, Dante's puppet. He would sometimes take part in the violence."

"Did you witness these events first hand?" asked the prosecutor.

"Many, many times!" replied Trenchard.

"Do you remember a plane being shot down over Hirta?" asked the prosecutor.

"Yes. As clear as day. I was heading to the beach to fish. I didn't get to the beach because The Collectors were there. The guys in the plane had dropped some leaflets warning people not to eat the HCR. I saw the plane explode but one of the guys had parachuted down into the sea. He really struggled to make it to the beach but, when he got there, Dante ordered his men to beat the guy to death, slowly, as a warning to others. Dante didn't want anything to interfere with his trade in HCR."

The defending council declined to question John Trenchard. In fact, he had declined to question most of the prosecution witnesses.

In their defence, all Dante and Grainger had to offer was that people had lied and massively exaggerated any actions taken by The Collectors. Dante also tried to make himself sound like some kind of benefactor who was just helping people to survive.

It took only a very short time for the jury to return a guilty verdict. As the judge passed sentence of death by hanging, Dante stood with a defiant smirk on his face and a look of hatred burning in his eyes.

Grainger broke down and fell to his knees, sobbing. "It wasn't my fault! It was Dante! He made me do it! We were all afraid to cross him! Please don't hang me! It wasn't my fault! It was all Dante!"

"Get up you snivelling fucking coward!" growled Dante as both men were taken away. "Show some fucking balls. Get up and act like a fucking man!"

Nine senior ATS officers were tried for offences against the people. All nine were convicted and given prison sentences ranging from ten to twenty years.

Twelve members of the government were tried for crimes against the nation. All stated in their defence that almost everything was controlled by the highest powers in the government, notably the President, the Vice-President and the Commander-In-Chief of the security forces. Nevertheless, all twelve were convicted and given prison sentences ranging from seven years to twenty years. Recently appointed Vice-President, Harry Harefield, only received a ten year prison sentence as he had only been in such a high-profile position for a short time after taking over from the late Edwina Sykes. His previous roles in the government had been relatively unimportant.

Only two key people remained to stand trial: former Commander-In-Chief of the security forces, Glyn Quinlan and former President, Nigel Valentine, the two most hated men in the country. The previous trials had been followed with great interest by the populace but now the whole nation held its breath in anticipation.

The judge appointed for both trials was Justice Selwyn Tyneward, a very experienced member of the judiciary and a staunch supporter of trial by jury, who had not been afraid to express strong doubts about The Party's legal system. He was very tall, clean shaven and wearing spectacles. He stood very erect, despite his advancing years, which emphasized his towering height. His imposing appearance indicated that this was a man of strength, honesty, wisdom and integrity.

The prosecuting council, also for both trials, was senior PDM investigator Dominic Welland. In recent times he had grown a fairly unkempt beard and lost much of his hair as well as gaining some weight. Time had not been a friend to Dom Welland but, despite his somewhat scruffy appearance, he remained what he always had been, a very shrewd, dogged, relentless investigator. Despite a lack of legal training, he was not a man to be taken lightly.

The man entrusted with defending Nigel Valentine was the former Justice George Grisedale, now in forced retirement but nevertheless a very experienced lawyer who was a strong supporter of The Party's legal system and was not to be underestimated.

Glyn Quinlan, in a typical gesture of defiance and arrogance, had chosen to defend himself despite it being made very clear to him that the government would be asking for the death penalty if a guilty verdict was returned.

The trials began in the middle of a heatwave. Every day, for the previous two weeks, temperatures had soared past thirty-five degrees and on one occasion had reached a sweltering forty degrees. The courtroom was equipped with air conditioning but even at nine a.m., when the court first sat, the heat was so intense that the air con was already struggling to cope. The oppressive heat was making people tetchy and irritable before the trial even began.

As the courtroom clock ticked to nine o'clock, Justice Tyneward's voice boomed out.

"The Government versus Glyn Quinlan. Please all be seated." Then, turning to face the dock, he continued. "Glyn Quinlan you are charged with crimes against the people while carrying out your duties as Commander-In-Chief of the security forces. These crimes include murder, rape, torture, conspiring with your subordinates for them to commit these same crimes and conspiring with former President, Nigel Valentine, to commit genocide against the people of Carlisle and Truro. How do you plead? Guilty or not guilty?"

"Not guilty sir!" replied Quinlan confidently, proudly and defiantly. "All I ever did was to carry out my duty to The Party to the best of my ability."

"Who is representing your defence?" asked the Justice.

"I have chosen to represent myself sir," replied the defendant, remaining the coolest person in that pressure cooker of a courtroom.

"I have already strongly advised you to take council and I still maintain that recommendation. However, if it is still your wish to represent yourself, the court will grant and respect that wish."

"It is still my wish sir!" replied Quinlan.

"So be it, although I feel you are making a huge mistake. Who is prosecuting on behalf of the Government?"

"I am sir! Government investigator Dominic Welland!" said Dom, looking no less scruffy than usual despite the public scrutiny of the occasion.

The jury having been chosen and agreed upon by all parties, Dom Welland began the case for the prosecution. A vast number of witnesses were called and questioned, witnesses who had suffered at the personal hands of Glyn Quinlan and those who had suffered at his command. The stories of several of the witnesses will already be known to you. When Quinlan was offered the chance to cross-examine witnesses he declined on every occasion. He accepted their evidence without question. In fact, he appeared almost proud of what he had done.

As his final prosecution witness, Dom Welland called Quinlan himself.

"Mr Quinlan, is it true that you, together with former President Valentine and the late Vice-President, Edwina Sykes, planned to carry out nuclear attacks on the cities of Truro and Carlisle?"

"Yes, that is true!" replied Quinlan without even a flicker of fear or remorse.

"Let me be absolutely clear!" continued Welland. "You were complicit in a plan to totally destroy two cities in your own country?"

"Yes! Absolutely!"

"Please explain to the court how such a heinous plan came about."

In a purely matter of fact manor, without even a pause, Quinlan continued. "We were clearly losing the fight against the URA. The Party's days were numbered. President of the United States, Dallas Donaldson, had suggested to President Valentine that a nuclear attack on our own people, followed by an ultimatum, would be a possible way of stopping the revolution. I was totally in favour of that action. It was The Party's only chance of survival."

"Fortunately, that nuclear attack never took place. What prevented it?" asked Welland.

Quinlan looked angry as he answered, letting his emotions show for the first time. "That treacherous bitch Edwina Sykes! She stopped it! She sold us out to the URA and gave them the opportunity to capture the nuclear base before we could nuke anybody. That bitch finished The Party and then took her own life. If she hadn't committed suicide, I would have killed her myself for such treachery."

"So let me be absolutely clear Mr Quinlan. You had no qualms at all about killing so many of your own people?"

"None at all!" replied Quinlan, as defiant as ever. "It was necessary!"

The case for the prosecution drew to a close and Quinlan's chance to defend himself had come. He called no defence witnesses and challenged no prosecution witnesses. He accepted all of the testimony which had been given and requested only a chance to put forward his point of view. He declared that everything he had done was to protect the state and The Party. Far from being put on trial, he believed that he should have been commended for his attempts to prevent the disruption caused by immigrants, dissidents, non-conformists and revolutionaries. He believed that he was the one true patriot who stood against the destruction of The Party. Throughout his closing speech he appeared to burn with a fierce pride and belief in his actions.

It did not take long for the jury to return a guilty verdict. As Justice Tyneward passed sentence, both men faced each other in a stand-off of defiant confrontation. Each hated what the other represented. Two strong men, one very powerful, the other once powerful and now powerless yet still very intransigent. It was ordered that Quinlan was to be hanged, two days after the final trial was completed. There was no reaction from Quinlan as sentence was passed. Even as he was taken back to his cell, his demeanour showed a mixture of arrogance and self-satisfaction. He appeared proud of what he had done, as heinous as it was in reality, but he remained angry at the failings of others who had supported him.

In stark contrast to Glyn Quinlan, when Nigel Valentine entered the dock, he had the appearance of a broken man. Staring constantly at the floor or at his hands he was dishevelled and unkempt. He had certainly not shaved for several days and looked like he probably hadn't washed. The immaculately dressed and groomed President was no longer there. The "man of the people" now looked more like the man of the gutter. The swagger had disappeared. His face was expressionless. He made eye contact with no-one. In fact, he never raised his head from its downward gaze. The continuing heatwave made the courtroom unbearable and yet Valentine appeared cold and on occasions appeared to be shivering. He appeared to be oblivious of what was going on around him as though he was trying to block it all out.

"Nigel Valentine!" boomed out the voice of Justice Tyneward, leaving no doubt as to who was in charge of the trial. "You are charged with genocide and conspiring to commit genocide! How do you plead?"

Valentine spluttered faintly, "Not guilty." so quietly that only those closest to him could hear the words on which he choked.

"Speak up!" boomed out the Justice. "How do you plead?"

Valentine cleared his throat before speaking more audibly. "Not guilty sir."

"Who is representing you?" asked the Justice.

"I am sir," came the reply, "former Justice George Grisedale."

"And who is representing the prosecution?" asked Tyneward.

"I am again sir! Government Investigator Dominic Welland," replied Dom Welland.

"You seem to be very busy at the moment Mr Welland," commented Justice Tyneward.

The case for the prosecution was based primarily on the deaths caused by Age Acceleration of the elderly and the sick, the removal of all medical care in the 2029 pandemic, the use of HCR to feed the cons on Saint Kilda and the planned nuclear strikes against Carlisle and Truro.

Numerous witnesses were called to describe the lack of medical care, particularly during the 2029 pandemic when all medical care was withdrawn from everyone except for the elite. None of the witnesses were questioned by George Grisedale.

Witnesses were called from the justice service and from the PEO to testify about punishments handed out by the legal system, particularly Age Acceleration. Again, they went unchallenged by Grisedale.

Nick Kaydon was called as a prosecution witness to give evidence about HCR.

"Doctor Kaydon," began Dom Welland, "I believe that the PDM carried out a raid on the premises of the Williamson Meat Corporation and that you played a major part in that raid. Is that correct?"

"Yes, that is correct," replied Nick.

"Would you tell the court about that raid and why it took place?" continued Welland.

"Williamson Meat Corporation were the producers of HCR. They were the only producers. HCR was the food supplied primarily to the prisoners on Saint Kilda. Occasionally it was sold to the general public, when other meat products were scarce, but it was the staple food for the convicts. We had reason to suspect that HCR might have been produced from human bodies. We had to find out for sure. The raid was carried out under the command of Idris Llewellyn and our aim was that, if our suspicions were proved correct, we would destroy the factory and any stock of HCR."

"And were your suspicions proved correct?" asked Welland.

"It was even worse than we feared," continued Nick. "Because of my medical knowledge it was my job to break into the office and gather information about the contents of the food. It was indeed made from human carcasses, its full name being Human Carcass Reconstitution. As if that wasn't bad enough, it also contained very high quantities of a banned preservative, GDN93. GDN93 had previously been banned from use in food as even very small quantities were found to be carcinogenic and hepatotoxic. It was added to HCR in such quantity that it would be certain to kill anyone who ate it regularly over a sustained period."

"Why was this added to the food?" asked Welland.

"Primarily because it enabled the food to be stored for months without need of refrigeration."

"You say primarily to preserve the food," continued Welland. "Does that mean that there might have been another reason for adding it to the food?"

"It was a certain death sentence for anyone eating it for any length of time. The number of prisoners sent to Saint Kilda could not possibly have been accommodated, with the overcrowding. Vast numbers died on Saint Kilda and I believe that GDN93 was used to cull the population," said Nick.

"I object!" interjected George Grisedale. "The witness is guessing at the purpose of the additive being included. He could not possibly know the reason."

"Objection overruled!" replied Justice Tyneward. "The witness is more than qualified to be able to pass an educated medical opinion. Please proceed."

"As my learned friend appears to doubt your suspicion, perhaps you could tell the court about the condition of the survivors who returned from Saint Kilda. I believe you were in charge of their return," continued Dom Welland.

"I was," replied Nick. "We carried out full medical examinations on all survivors. We found that almost all of them were dying and that most would not survive for more than a few weeks, some for only days."

"Thank you, Doctor Kaydon. I have no more questions."

"Mr Grisedale," asked the Justice, "do you have any questions for this witness?"

"No sir," replied Grisedale, sheepishly.

"Thank you, Doctor Kaydon. You may return to your seat," said Justice Tyneward.

Dom Welland proceeded with his case. "Sir, I would like to call cabinet member Ed Gilfedder."

Ed Gilfedder was called to the witness stand and Welland continued. "Mr Gilfedder, just before the culmination of the revolution, were you contacted by Edwina Sykes who was Vice-President at that time?"

"Yes, I was!" replied Gilfedder. "She rang me."

"What was the reason for her call?" asked Welland.

"She wanted to warn me that there were going to be nuclear attacks on Carlisle and Truro the following day. She was against the attacks but had been overruled by the President and the Commander-In-Chief of the security forces. She estimated that the attacks would kill around a hundred thousand people; at which point an ultimatum would be issued demanding an end to the revolution and surrender of the URA or the destruction of more cities would follow. She hoped that the URA could prevent the nuclear attacks. She also gave me the coordinates for the position of the missile base."

"Were you able to prevent the missile attack?" asked Welland.

"We attacked and captured the missile base before the missile attacks could be launched. Thanks to her, Carlisle and Truro were saved. Unfortunately, after enlisting my help, she took her own life. She left a suicide note explaining everything in more detail."

Once more, George Grisedale declined the chance to cross-examine the witness.

At last Dom Welland called his final prosecution witness, none other than former Chief Commanding Officer, Glyn Quinlan. Quinlan confirmed everything that had been stated by previous witnesses. He also confirmed that, although he himself had a lot of power, the ultimate final decision was always made by President Valentine. Quinlan tried to make certain that, if he was going down, he took Nigel Valentine down with him.

None of the prosecution witnesses had been cross-examined by defence council, George Grisedale. He now called his one and only witness for the defence, Nigel Valentine himself.

Nigel Valentine did not deny anything that had happened. He merely tried to deflect blame onto other people and in some cases insisted that he had had no alternative. Indeed, at times he made it sound like he was not the man running the country at all.

Regarding Age Acceleration for the elderly and the sick, he insisted that the system had been set up by his predecessor, President Grosvenor. He personally hated the system but was unable to do anything about it due to intense pressure from fellow cabinet members who were strongly opposed to change.

Supplying HCR to Saint Kilda had also been authorised by President Grosvenor, before Nigel Valentine held any real power. Valentine stated that he personally had no knowledge of the contents of HCR and therefore had no reason to change it.

He told the court that the planned nuclear attacks on Carlisle and Truro had been strongly advised by the President of the United States, Dallas Donaldson, when Valentine asked the POTUS for help. Valentine was totally against the idea himself but his wishes were overruled by Glyn Quinlan and initially by Edwina Sykes. He had reluctantly given in to their pressure but he felt very uneasy about it. He may have changed his decision overnight, particularly if he had known that Edwina Sykes had changed her mind.

He defended withdrawal of all medical aid in the Covid pandemic of 2029 by stating that it was only that action which kept the number of deaths in the UK due to Covid 29 RS down to just under one point five million. If he had allowed the charity hospitals to continue, there may have been more than four million

Covid deaths. The deaths from non-Covid illnesses, he believed, were just necessary unavoidable collateral damage.

Throughout his trial Nigel Valentine looked like a man on the edge, occasionally briefly looking like his usual confident self but mostly appearing uncertain and afraid, sometimes appearing completely crushed and broken. He had even had fits of shaking and times when tears visibly welled up in his eyes. He exhibited the whole gamut of emotions except for remorse. Just like Quinlan, he was not apologetic for any of his actions at any time.

The jury took almost no time at all in considering the case and returning a guilty verdict. As Justice Tyneward passed sentence of death by hanging, Nigel Valentine stumbled as his legs started to buckle and almost fainted. He was a gibbering, simpering wreck as he was led back to his cell. The trial was finally over and in two days the two most hated men in the country would be executed.

****

In the days following his trial, while awaiting his execution, Glyn Quinlan was like a caged tiger constantly pacing back and forth in his cell, hardly settling for more than a few minutes at a time. He appeared to be a man on a mission, a coiled spring which was ready to unleash its power at any time. What bothered him was not that he was going to die. He had known that would happen since the day that he was arrested. What bothered him was that he would die by another man's hand. The man who had always thought that he could control everything bitterly resented someone else having that final control over him. He accepted that his life had to be terminated but he didn't want anyone to have the satisfaction of being his executioner. The only solution was for him to take back control and take his own life, thereby cheating the hangman.

Every waking minute he was busy, trying to think of a way of committing suicide. He even dreamed about it when he slept. Security measures had ruled out every possibility and time was running out fast. There had to be a way. Finally, he decided that he could only think of one possibility…

An air vent high up in the wall had a metal handle to enable opening and closing of the vent. If he stood on his bed and reached out, he could just about reach the handle at full stretch. He also found a very sharp corner on the metal frame of his bed, which he might be able to use to tear a bed sheet.

On the night before his execution, while guards were nowhere near his door and unable to see or hear him, he frantically set to work. He quickly pulled a sheet from his bed and, using the sharp corner of the bed, ripped it in half lengthways. He feverishly knotted the two halves together to make a rope. He prayed that the guards would not hear anything. He stood on the bed and just about managed to attach one end of the makeshift rope to the handle of the air vent. He tied the other end of it into a noose and put it tightly around his neck as he perched on the edge of the bed. With everything firmly tied, he leapt off the bed, hopefully into oblivion. As the weight of his body crashed downwards the handle of the air vent broke, as he always believed it most likely would. He crashed onto the floor with an almighty noise which alerted the duty guards. Two guards ran into the cell, a third guard stayed in the doorway. One of them ran to Quinlan, seeing him lying on the floor looking apparently unconscious, to check if he was seriously hurt. In a flash, Quinlan stopped faking unconsciousness and grabbed the surprised guard in a headlock while snatching his firearm from its holster. Quinlan then released the guard, flinging him well out of the way, put the barrel of the weapon to his own temple and pulled the trigger. Death was instantaneous as his skull shattered and his brain exploded. Glyn Quinlan had succeeded in cheating the hangman and defying the new justice system for one last time.

****

Only the execution of Nigel Valentine remained. Broken and without hope he was mentally destroyed, incapable of looking after himself and losing his grasp on reality. His execution was due at nine a.m. At eight-thirty a.m. the gibbering, tearful wreck of a man was visited by George Richmond and Selwyn Tyneward. The former President was told that the death penalty had been revoked. He fell to his knees in a simpering display of gratitude and relief. This shattered shell of a human being would be no future threat to the security of the country. Instead of execution he was to be deported and exiled, under permanent house arrest, providing a country could be found which would accept him. Nearly all countries refused to offer him any form of sanctuary. Only one premier agreed to accept him, amazingly President Je Dong Woo of North Korea, a most unlikely bedfellow. President Je just accepted him as another way of cocking a snook at the West. No way was Nigel Valentine suited to the North Korean way of life, nor a life under constant house arrest, but at least he had found a safe haven.

Elizabeth Valentine had requested to be allowed not to accompany her husband. She was allowed to stay in the UK, with her children, Oliver and Esme. In the years that followed, she built a career of writing and public speaking to educate the new generation about the true events of the previous thirty years.

The country could now breathe a sigh of relief and focus on building a new and prosperous future. The past had been well and truly, once and for all, laid to rest.

Chapter 29.
A FAMILY DESTROYED

"How are you today grandma?" asked little, five year old Bryn Llewellyn. He had a smile from ear to ear as he walked into his grandmother's bedroom with his mother Megan. As always, he was bouncing with excitement to see his gran.

"I'm all the better for seeing you dear," she replied, somehow summoning the strength to smile at him, for the first time that day, putting on the mask of wellness.

Agnes had been lying in bed exhausted and much too ill to get up. For the last six months she had been dying of cancer, cancer which had eaten away at her and had sapped every last bit of strength and energy from her decaying body. She knew that she did not have long to live, days at most and she was relieved that her suffering would soon be over. Nevertheless she was sad that she would be leaving her family behind: her son Aled, her daughter-in-law Megan and the pride of her life, her grandson Bryn. She always tried to hide her pain and suffering from her family although, at this stage, it was impossible to hide it except from little Bryn. She wanted them to have the strength to get through this, but most of all she didn't want Bryn to be upset.

Aled was already sitting on a chair beside his mother's bed. "Now you take it easy young man. Don't you wear your gran out too much. She's feeling very tired, so you be a good boy."

"He's always a good boy for his gran," said Agnes, still smiling at the boy.

When Agnes' cancer was first diagnosed, the local charity hospital had done what they could; but In truth they could do very little. When Agnes knew that she was terminally ill she had decided that she wanted to spend her remaining time at home. There was no point in staying in hospital when there was nothing they could do. She wanted to spend her remaining weeks, remaining days with her family. Aled and Megan could not have done more. They did everything they possibly could to make her remaining time as pleasant and comfortable as possible.

Agnes' bedroom was simply furnished but clean, fresh, comfortable and welcoming. There was a TV on one wall which was switched on almost continually throughout the day. Not that she always watched it, but the background noise helped to blot out the silence when no-one else was around and helped to stop her thinking too much about the future or, in her case, the lack of a future.

"What rubbish are you watching today mum?" asked Aled. "Do you want me to turn it off for a bit, while we are all here?"

"I suppose so," said Agnes. "I'm not really watching it. They're showing the trial of the old government, but I don't really know what's going on anyway. I don't seem to be able to concentrate on things these days."

Aled picked up the remote control and turned to point it at the set.

"Aled! Wait a minute! Don't turn it off!" Agnes suddenly sounded very agitated.

"What's wrong mum?" asked Aled, very much taken by surprise.

"Look at the screen!" said Agnes. "Aled! The very tall man at the back! You probably won't recognize him. You were too young when we left to remember what he looked like! That man at the back Aled, I'm sure that's your father! That's Idris! Of course he looks a lot older now but I'm certain that's Idris!" Tears began to well up in her eyes at the same time as her lips began to crack into a smile.

"Steady on mum, calm down," said Aled, concerned that her excitement would take its toll on her well-being. "You've not seen him for over twenty-five years and the TV's not giving you a close-up view of him. It's probably just someone with similar features. What chance is there really of that being dad."

"Aled, it is him! I know it! I know it's been a long time, but I'd still recognize him anywhere! That's your dad!" Agnes was not going to let the matter drop. "Where is the trial being held?"

"In Birmingham, I think. In Thatcher Square, where the government buildings are."

"Could you take me there son, maybe tomorrow? I really want to see him before I die. I want to tell him I'm sorry. I want him to see you and your family. He may not want to know us now, but I have to try. We won't have any amount of time together but maybe you could get to know him again and I'm sure he'd want to see Megan and Aled. We can't deprive him of a relationship with his grandson if he wants it. We have to give him that chance."

"I can't take you to Birmingham mum! Not just like that. You'd never survive the journey! You're just not well enough! In any case, it might not even be him and even if it is he might not want to know us."

"Aled, if I can see your father before I die and we can patch things up, then I can die a happy woman," said Agnes, definitely not in the mood to give up.

"Listen mum, you're not well enough to go to Birmingham but, if you really want me to, I can drive to Birmingham tomorrow, see if I can find him and see if I can persuade him to come here to see you."

"Oh, thank you Aled! That would be wonderful," said Agnes, still very excited.

"Don't thank me yet," said Aled. "I can't guarantee that I can get him here."

"Well, thank you for trying anyway son. That's all you can do. It's all any of us can do." Agnes settled back onto the bed, resting her head on her pillow, completely exhausted by the events of the day.

Later, she could see that Aled was brooding about something. When she had recovered a little and no-one else was around, she asked him what was wrong.

"I'm not really happy about looking for dad," was his reply. "He wasn't around when we needed him before. He deserted us. For years I prayed every night that he would come back and save us from Clive and he never did."

"That wasn't your father's fault Aled. Your father was a sweet, kind man and he would never have left us in that situation if he could have done anything to help us. When we left our old home, I was the one who had been having an affair with Clive. Your dad was a member of the PDM and that scared me."

"You mean he was a terrorist," Aled butted in.

"No! Some people called them that in the old days, but the PDM only did the things that they did for the good of the country. Your dad never harmed anyone unnecessarily. Don't forget that it was mainly the PDM who were responsible for finally getting rid of The Party. Anyway I begged your dad to leave the PDM but he wouldn't. He cared too much and his principles wouldn't let him. I could have stayed with him, but I was terrified that the ATS would find us, your dad would end up dead and we would end up in a penal colony. I couldn't face that. Because I was so scared, it was easy to find solace by turning to Clive Carter. When Clive decided to move to Cardiff, I decided that we'd go with him and make a fresh start somewhere that I thought we would be safe. It broke your dad's heart, particularly because I made sure that he didn't know where we had gone and had no way of finding us. I was afraid that, if he came to visit you, the ATS might find us. I'm sure your dad would have kept in touch with you if he'd had any idea where we were. If he'd known, he would never have let Clive treat us the way he did. It was all my fault son and I'm so sorry for it." Agnes began to weep as she thought how different things could have been.

"Don't get upset mum," Aled said as he gently rested a reassuring hand on her forearm. "I'll go and look for dad tomorrow and I'll do my very best to bring him back to see you."

Unfortunately, time took its toll and decided that a reunion between Agnes and Idris would never be. Later that night Agnes deteriorated rapidly, so rapidly that everyone was shocked. After just an hour of struggling to breathe, relying on oxygen and strong pain medication to ease her distress, she sank into a coma. Her final release was quick and painless as the breath simply and quietly left her body.

Chapter 30.
FAMILIES REBUILT

As life began to settle down after the trials, Nick began to think about the future. He worked in the government building now, having been given a major role in developing the new, reborn and rebuilt National Health Service which once more provided free quality health care for all. He and Jonathan had moved into a nearby house which they shared with Charley and Maddy. Idris also lived close by, having been given an important role in the newly formed Department of Social Justice. Consequently Idris had become a frequent and very welcome visitor.

One morning when Nick and Charley were all alone, which very rarely happened, Nick started to become very fidgety and unsettled. It seemed as if there was something on his mind which was making him very nervous. He was constantly on the move, never sitting for more than a few moments before he was up again. At one point he even began to nibble at his fingernails, something which Nick never normally did. He cleared his throat a couple of times as though he was about to say something, but the words never came.

"Are you alright babe?" asked Charley, who could clearly see that something was wrong.

"Of course! I'm fine. Why wouldn't I be?" he replied, sounding very unconvincing while visibly squirming and looking very sheepish.

"You seem a bit on edge and distracted as though you've got something on your mind. If there is something, you know you can always talk to me about it. I might even be able to help."

"Charley I'm fine! Honestly, everything is fine! There's nothing to worry about. You know I'd tell you if there was."

Despite his words Nick was fiddling and fidgeting even more. Several more uncomfortable minutes went by. Finally Nick cleared his throat in preparation as he obviously had something to get off his chest.

"Charley, you're right. Something is bothering me and I need to talk to you about it now, before I lose my nerve completely," said Nick, the words finally gushing and tumbling rapidly from his mouth like a cascading waterfall.

"I knew there was something," said Charley, smiling knowingly and reassuringly. "Well it can't be that bad, can it? Come on, tell me all about it. You know I'll help if I can. I don't think there's anything that we can't sort out together."

"Well we've been together for quite a long time now and we've come through a lot together. I think we make a pretty awesome team. As you say, there's nothing that we can't sort out together."

"We can cope with anything as long as we have each other," interrupted Charley.

"That's what I thought. That's why I wanted to ask you, Charlotte Coventina McCarthy," he said, sinking down on one knee and flourishing a ring, "will you marry me?"

"How the fuck did you find out my middle name was Coventina?" demanded Charley. "I've tried to keep that hidden all my life! It's so embarrassing!"

"I have ways of finding things out," replied Nick with a chuckle, finding Charley's reaction to her name hilarious. "Well? Will you?"

"Of course I will," replied Charley, throwing her arms around his neck and drawing him close, "providing you promise to never say anything to anyone about my middle name being Coventina and you never ever call me by it again."

"Why? I think it's a lovely name," said Nick, still grinning.

"Do you? Do you really? I hate it. It's Anglo-Saxon. I think I must have done something to really piss my parents off the day they gave me that name."

"Coventina," laughed Nick. "No it's not really the best, is it? Anyway, was that a yes – about getting married?"

"Yes! Of course it was Nick! I can't wait to become Mrs Charley Kaydon." Charley's face was alight and she was positively bouncing with excitement.

"Say it again," teased Nick.

"Yes! Yes! Yes! I'll marry you! I'll marry you tomorrow if you like."

"Well perhaps not quite that fast. We have got a wedding to arrange first."

"We need to tell Maddy and Jonathan," said Charley, briefly sounding quite serious. "I think they'll be really pleased. I know Maddy will be. She loves you and Jon so much."

"Actually we need to talk about the future for Maddy and Jon," said Nick, also coming back down to earth for a moment.

****

When Jonathan came home, he was greeted by Charley and Nick who had still not come down from cloud nine. Maddy was seated at the table, playing quietly.

"Hi Jon," said Nick. "Come and sit down. We've got some big news. When I say big, it's massive!" Nick held his arms out wide to demonstrate just how massive it was. He was babbling as he still struggled to get his excitement under control. He continued. "We've already told Maddy. We couldn't wait for you to come home. We had to tell somebody! The thing is, Jon, Charley and I are getting married!"

"Is that all? It's about time! You had me worried that something was seriously wrong," said Jon dismissively.

"What do you mean, is that all?" asked Nick, feeling a little bit snubbed.

"Obviously, I'm really pleased but it's been so obvious to everyone else for a long time that you two belong together. You're made for each other. We've all been waiting for an announcement for ages. I was beginning to think you'd never get round to it." The expression on Jon's face showed just how thrilled he really was as he hugged Nick and Charley.

"There is a bit more to tell you," said Nick, looking a little more serious again. "We've decided that I'm going to adopt Maddy."

Just for a moment Jonathan had mixed feelings. He was pleased for Maddy, he really was, but so far Nick had said nothing about him. Could Nick really be adopting Maddy and not adopting him? Looking at it logically, Jon thought that he would soon be old enough to make his own way in the world so did it really matter? He didn't have long to ponder.

"There is something else," interjected Charley. "We both want to adopt you Jon, if you'll have us as parents."

Jonathan's face exploded with pleasure. "Of course I'll have you! I couldn't wish for anything better. You'll be the best parents ever! You already are the best parents ever!"

Jon was choking back the tears as he hugged Charley and Nick again. He then rushed over to Maddy who was still sitting quietly and oblivious to the conversation.

Jonathan signed into her hands, "I'm going to be your new big brother."

Maddy looked blank and confused. Did she understand? Jon wondered if he had made a mistake when signing. He repeated it. "I'm going to be your new big brother!" Still there was no reaction from Maddy. Perhaps she wasn't happy about the idea, although Jonathan found that hard to believe.

He tried signing a third time. "I'm going to be your new big brother." Maddy's face split from ear to ear in the widest smile imaginable and she flung her arms as wide as possible to invite the huge hug that she received from Jon. She understood alright and she made sure that her approval was obvious.

Now, finally, they could all be a real family.

★★★★

Hearing a knock on the front door, Nick opened it to find Idris on the doorstep.

"Hi Idris, come on in," said Nick.

"I was just passing, boyo and I thought I'd call in for a chat and see how you all are. I hope it's not inconvenient."

Working and living so close, Idris frequently called in for a chat and a cup of tea. Living on his own with no family, Charley sometimes wondered if he was a bit lonely. In any case, Charley and Nick were always pleased to see the big guy.

"Actually I'm really glad you're here Taff," said Nick. "We wanted to see you. We've got something to tell you."

"We're getting married!" said Charley with a big smile still permanently fixed on her face.

"That's great news!" said Idris, giving Charley a hug and shaking Nick's hand.

"And I'm adopting Maddy and we're both adopting Jonathan," said Nick.

"I'm so pleased for you all. We've been waiting for ages for you to make it official."

"Not you as well Taff," said Nick. "That's exactly what Jon said."

"You're obviously so right for each other. It was only a matter of when, not if," said the big Welshman. "When is the wedding?"

"We thought next month, on the sixteenth," said Charley. "So put it in your diary and make sure you're there."

"I wouldn't miss it for the world!" said Taff. "I'm free that weekend but even if I had something else on, I would cancel it. Nothing will keep me away from the wedding of my two favourite people. Have you decided on a best man yet?" Idris was hoping that Nick would want his best friend to be his best man.

"I've asked Jon to do it," said Nick.

Despite finding it very hard to hide his disappointment, Idris said, "That's a great choice boy. I can't think of anyone better that you could have picked."

"We did think about asking you," said Nick, "but then we decided that Jon was the better option. I hope you're not disappointed Taff."

"No, of course not boy. Jonathan's the perfect choice."

"You won't be available to do it anyway," interrupted Charley. "You'll be too busy."

"No I won't!" said Idris, feeling somewhat irritated and a little confused. "I think Jon's a great choice, but I wouldn't have been too busy. I've already told you I'll be there, come hell or high water!"

"You will be too busy," insisted Charley, "because I want you to give me away. I've got no father to do it and I can't think of anyone that I would rather have to walk me down the aisle. Will you do it for me Taffy? Will you stand up with me in church? Please!"

Taffy's face was a picture of confused happiness.

"I'll be proud and honoured to girl!" said the big man, with an even bigger smile but with a little tear of happiness just beginning to escape from his eye.

★★★★

As Idris sat in his office in the Department of Social Justice, there was a knock on the door.

"Come in!" shouted the big Welshman.

One of the security staff entered. "I'm sorry to bother you Mr. Llewellyn but there's a man in reception wanting to see you. I've told him he needs to make an appointment, but he asked me to tell you that his name is Aled. He seemed to think that would make a difference and you would agree to see him."

"Did he tell you his last name?"

"No. He just said Aled. He said you'd know who he was."

Taff wondered if this could really be his son. No, surely not after so many years. It was too much to hope for, but he was unable to think of any other Aled that he knew.

"You'd better show him in."

The security officer disappeared and returned a few moments later with the mystery man. Despite not having seen him since he was a child, more than twenty-five years ago, Idris immediately recognized the likeness.

"Aled? Is it really you boy? It's been so long."

"Dad? I can't believe we're finally both here," said Aled, awkwardly holding out his hand for a handshake but then, throwing caution to the wind, grabbing his father and giving him a big hug. Two big strong men embracing with tears rolling down their cheeks.

"How did you find me?" asked Idris.

"Mum saw you on TV, when the trials were being televised. You were just standing in the background, but she recognized you. Once I knew that you were working for the government it wasn't too hard to track you down."

"How is your mum, boy?"

"I'm afraid she passed away a couple of weeks ago," replied Aled. "When she saw you on TV, she wanted me to come and find you. She wanted to see you again before she died. Unfortunately, she passed away that night."

"I'm so sorry to hear that son!" The big guy had a tear starting to trickle down his face again. "What was it?"

"Cancer!" replied Aled.

"I'm sorry boy! How are you holding up?"

"I'm alright dad. We knew it was coming for some time so we were prepared for it, well as prepared as you ever can be. The end came a bit faster than we were expecting!"

"You know I never stopped loving her in all those years. I always hoped that, somehow, we'd get back together, the three of us. The trouble is I had no way of finding you. When you left, your mum did a good job of hiding where you'd gone. She was frightened of me leading the ATS to you. Sometimes I think I should have just finished with the PDM when she asked me to."

"Dad, you couldn't just turn your back on the PDM any more than you could walk on water and mum realized that."

"It was sheer arrogance to think that the PDM needed me so much that I let it become more important than my own family. I couldn't blame you if you hated me Aled."

"There was a time when I did, but mum explained everything before she died. She believed she should have stuck by you, even if you were with the PDM. Plenty of other wives had done it, but she just became too afraid and Clive Carter was an easy way out. Mum never really loved him. She was fond of him, but she didn't love him the way she loved you. After we moved, things were okay for a while. We both missed you, but mum was relieved to feel safe. After a while, Clive started drinking way, way too much and he couldn't control it. The trouble is that, when he was drinking, he got nasty. I think he hated me, maybe because I wasn't his son. I don't know. Anyway he used to fly into a rage and hit me if he could find the least, most pathetic excuse. If mum thought he was building up to having a go at me, she'd do or say something to annoy him so that he'd turn on her instead. She took so many beatings to protect me. He put her in hospital twice."

"God I'm so sorry son!"

"Every night for years I prayed that you would come and save us. Every night I prayed that you'd come but you never came!"

"Why did she stay with him? If he was treating you both like that? Why didn't she just take you and go?"

"Fear of the authorities. Clive said that, if she ever tried to leave, he would report her to the ATS for being married to a PDM member. She knew how they would have treated us. Even if he hadn't reported us, where would we have gone? You know how the party treated homeless people. We could have been tortured and ended up in the penal colony, or worse. So we stayed and just put up with it. Years later it was such a relief when the alcohol finally got the better of Clive and he died. We were fine on our own."

"Oh Aled! I really am so sorry son! It was all my fault. I should have been there for you! How could I have let all that happen? Sorry sounds empty and pathetic now, but I really am." Idris was clearly fighting hard to avoid breaking down in tears again

"Dad it wasn't your fault! Mum wanted you to know that. She knew that you'd blame yourself, but you couldn't have done anything." Aled put a comforting hand on his dad's shoulder. "Anyway dad, I've got two people that I want you to meet. They've been waiting outside in the corridor."

"Who are they?" asked Idris, trying to pull himself together before meeting them.

Without speaking, Aled opened the office door and ushered them in. "Dad, I want you to meet my wife, Megan and this little chap is your grandson, Bryn."

The big man finally cracked completely, crying like a baby, while hugging his new found family.

"Don't cry grandad," said Bryn. "I'm really glad that I've got a grandad now! I hope that we can spend lots of time together."

"That goes for me and Aled too," said Megan.

"I'll make sure of that!" said Idris. "Now I've got my family back I'm never going to let any of you go again. Never!"

Chapter 31.
The Day After Tomorrow

When George Richmond first became president and formed a government, with the support of the United Revolutionary Army, a new governing political party was formed, the Liberty Party. As promised, other new political parties were allowed to form.

George had promised a return to democratic elections within two years. In fact, he did better than promised as the country held its first democratic election just one year after the Liberty Party had taken control. It was a landslide victory for the Liberty Party who won eighty-five per cent of the popular vote. They were riding high on the vast wave of popularity and gratitude for regaining the country's freedom. There was also another contributing factor. The newly-formed opposition parties had been in existence for such a short time that none were yet strong enough to pose a serious threat.

By the time a second general election was held, four years later, there was a new, much stronger, kid on the block. The Reform Party was getting stronger by the day. The Liberty Party still won the election but with a very reduced majority. They gained fifty-five per cent of the votes with the Reform Party picking up most of the remaining forty-five per cent. The Reform Party provided powerful and valuable opposition. They were never afraid to criticise the government when it was thought necessary, not that the Liberty Party did much wrong. Under George's leadership and guidance, they had kept their promises and the United Kingdom was a thriving, happy country once more.

Unfortunately, gratitude only lasts for so long. New ideas are always required and usually welcomed. By the election of 2066, the popularity of the Reform Party had grown even more and they won, polling fifty-three per cent of the vote. After nine hard years in power, the Liberty Party took on a new but still very important role of being the main opposition party.

When George heard the result, he smiled, a smile of deep satisfaction. It wasn't that he wanted to lose the election, certainly not. It was the proud smile of a parent who carefully nurtures a child and watches it grow up only to find that the child has become an adult, able to stand on its own two feet and capable of achieving more than the parent ever could. It felt good. He had no doubts about the ability of the Reform Party to lead the country forward. They were not extremists in any way, not by any stretch of the imagination and they would be balanced by facing a strong opposition party in the form of the Liberty Party.

When it was clear that the election was lost, George stepped down from the leadership of the Liberty Party. The new party leader would be none other than Dominic Welland, the man who had been the prosecuting council at the trials of Glyn Quinlan and Nigel Valentine. George was happy that he was leaving the Liberty Party in good hands, under Dom's leadership.

Come tomorrow, George could finally retire, as he had wanted to do many years earlier. Come tomorrow, George could relax with memories of the great achievements of the past. Come tomorrow, George could spend as much time as he liked fishing, his favourite pastime. Come tomorrow, George could landscape his garden in the way that he had planned for years, with a huge pond full of koi carp. Come tomorrow, George could sit with others of his generation exchanging stories from the past and what stories he would be able to tell.

novum PUBLISHER FOR NEW AUTHORS

Rate
this book
on our
website!

www.novum-publishing.co.uk

The author

Anthony R. Johnson was born in Stoke-On-Trent in the UK. He then attended Wolstanton Grammar School and went on to study to become a veterinary surgeon at the Royal Veterinary College in London. Anthony comes from a working-class family. He spent forty-two years as a Veterinary Surgeon; initially in Derby and Shrewsbury, followed by forty years in Crewe. He was married for twenty-eight years before his wife died in 2004. He has one daughter and one adult granddaughter. He is an ardent supporter of Port Vale Football Club, is a Samaritans volunteer and is a member of the Green Party. Anthony began writing in 2018 and 'There's Always a Tomorrow 'will be his first published work. He has also written numerous poems, short stories and a children's book; as yet unpublished.

novum PUBLISHER FOR NEW AUTHORS

The publisher

He who stops getting better stops being good.

This is the motto of novum publishing, and our focus is on finding new manuscripts, publishing them and offering long-term support to the authors.
Our publishing house was founded in 1997, and since then it has become THE expert for new authors and has won numerous awards.

Our editorial team will peruse each manuscript within a few weeks free of charge and without obligation.

You will find more information about
novum publishing and our books on the internet:

www.novum-publishing.co.uk